D0324052

The European Renaissance

THE MAKING OF EUROPE

Series Editor: Jacques Le Goff

The *Making of Europe* series is the result of a unique collaboration between five European publishers – Beck in Germany, Blackwell in Great Britain and the United States, Critica in Spain, Laterza in Italy and le Seuil in France. Each book will be published in all five languages. The scope of the series is broad, encompassing the history of ideas as well as of societies, nations, and states to produce informative, readable, and provocative treatments of central themes in the history of the European peoples and their cultures.

The European Renaissance

Centres and Peripheries

Peter Burke

Copyright © Peter Burke 1998

The right of Peter Burke to be identified as author of this work has been asserted in accordance with the Copyright, Designs and Patents Act 1988.

First published in 1998 by Blackwell Publishers Limited and by four other publishers: © 1998 Beck (Munich) German; © 1996 Critica, Barcelona (Spanish); © Editions du Seuil, Paris (French); © Laterza, Rome and Bari (Italian).

2 4 6 8 10 9 7 5 3 1

Blackwell Publishers Ltd
108 Cowley Road
Oxford OX4 1JF
UK

Blackwell Publishers Inc.
350 Main Street
Malden, Massachusetts 02148
USA

All rights reserved. Except for the quotation of short passages for the purposes of criticism and review, no part of this publication may be reproduced, stored in a retrieval system, or transmitted, in any form or by any means, electronic, mechanical, photocopying, recording or otherwise, without the prior permission of the publisher.

Except in the United States of America, this book is sold subject to the condition that it shall not, by way of trade or otherwise, be lent, resold, hired out, or otherwise circulated without the publisher's prior consent in any form of binding or cover other than that in which it is published and without a similar condition including this condition being imposed on the subsequent purchaser.

British Library Cataloguing in Publication Data

A CIP catalogue record for this book is available from the British Library.

Library of Congress Cataloging-in-Publication Data

Burke, Peter.
The European Renaissance : centres and peripheries / Peter Burke.
p.   cm. — (Making of Europe)
Includes bibliographical references and index.
ISBN 0–631–19845–8 (hb : alk. paper)
1. Renaissance.   I. Title.   II. Series.
CB361.B79 1998
940.2'1—dc21   98-5901
                                                CIP

Typeset in 11.5 on 13pt Sabon by G&G Editorial, Brighton
Printed in Great Britain by MPG Books Ltd, Bodmin, Cornwall

This book is printed on acid-free paper

Contents

Illustrations

For Maria Lúcia

On n'a pas encore écrit, ni même tenté d'écrire, pas à pas, l'histoire complète de la diffusion des biens culturels à partir de l'Italie qui éclairerait dons et transferts d'une part, acceptations, adoptions, adaptations et refus d'autre.

Fernand Braudel

Series Editor's Preface

Europe is in the making. This is both a great challenge and one that can be met only by taking the past into account – a Europe without history would be orphaned and unhappy. Yesterday conditions today; today's actions will be felt tomorrow. The memory of the past should not paralyse the present: when based on understanding it can help us to forge new friendships and guide us towards progress.

Europe is bordered by the Atlantic, Asia and Africa, its history and geography inextricably entwined, and its past comprehensible only within the context of the world at large. The territory retains the name given it by the ancient Greeks, and the roots of its heritage may be traced far into prehistory. It is on this foundation – rich and creative, united yet diverse – that Europe's future will be built.

The Making of Europe is the joint initiative of five publishers of different languages and nationalities: Beck in Munich; Blackwell in Oxford; Critica in Barcelona; Laterza in Rome; and Le Seuil in Paris. Its aim is to describe the evolution of Europe, presenting the triumphs but not concealing the difficulties. In their efforts to achieve accord and unity the nations of Europe have faced discord, division and conflict. It is no purpose of this series to conceal these problems: those committed to the European enterprise will not succeed if their view of the future is unencumbered by an understanding of the past.

The title of the series is thus an active one: the time is yet to

come when a synthetic history of Europe will be possible. The
books we shall publish will be the work of leading historians,
by no means all European. They will address crucial aspects of
European history in every field – political, economic, social,
religious and cultural. They will draw on that long historio-
graphical tradition which stretches back to Herodotus, as well
as on those conceptions and ideas which have transformed
historical enquiry in the recent decades of the twentieth century.
They will write readably for a wide public.

   Our aim is to consider the key questions confronting those
involved in Europe's making, and at the same time to satisfy the
curiosity of the world at large: in short, who are the Europeans?
Where have they come from? Whither are they bound?

                                                Jacques Le Goff

Acknowledgements

I am indebted to Jacques Le Goff for suggesting that I write the book and offering it a place in his series; to the library of the Warburg Institute, designed to assist interdisciplinary research in this area; to Renaissance scholars all over Europe for discussions, references, gifts of books, articles and xeroxes; and to my wife, Maria Lúcia Pallares-Burke, for helping me formulate my ideas.

Peter Burke
March 1998

Introduction:
Framing the Renaissance

Another book on the Renaissance? How can it possibly be justified? The most obvious reason for a new study is the continuing research on the subject. Indeed, there have probably never been so many people writing on different aspects of the Renaissance as there are today. Collectively, all this work adds up or should add up to a new interpretation. Ironically enough, however, the very proliferation of research, published in scores of specialized journals, makes a general synthesis more and more difficult. If they could return to earth, the artists, writers and scholars of the period would surely be astonished to discover the movement in which they once participated cut and sliced into monographs on different regions and different disciplines such as the history of architecture, the history of philosophy, the history of French literature and so on. Writing about the importance of the 'Renaissance Man', many specialists avoid universality like the plague.

In conscious contrast – although its author is all too well aware of the limitations of his knowledge – this book will attempt to present the movement as a whole. The emphasis will fall on the Renaissance as a movement rather than as an event or a period. This is not a general history of Europe between 1330 and 1630. It is not even a cultural history of Europe at a time when the Reformations, Protestant and Catholic, probably affected the lives of more people more deeply than the Renaissance did. It is a history of a cultural movement which – simplifying brutally – we may describe as beginning with Petrarch and ending with Descartes.

Although this movement involved innovation as well as 'renovation', the central theme of the book, the guide through the labyrinth of detail, will be the enthusiasm for antiquity and the revival, reception and transformation of the classical tradition. Where contemporary culture prizes novelty above almost all else, even the major innovators of the Renaissance presented – and often perceived – their inventions and discoveries as a return to ancient traditions after the long parenthesis of what they were the first to call the 'Middle' Ages.

This emphasis on the recovery of antiquity is traditional. Jacob Burckhardt, the great Swiss historian whose view of the Italian Renaissance remains influential, argued that it was not the revival of antiquity alone but its combination with the Italian 'spirit', as he called it, which underlay the Renaissance.[1] All the same, many later scholars have preferred to concentrate attention on the classical revival, which is easier to define or even to recognize than the Italian spirit, and I shall follow their example. In other respects, two in particular, I shall diverge from the tradition.

In the first place, an attempt will be made to dissociate the Renaissance from modernity. According to Burckhardt, writing in the mid-nineteenth century, the importance of this movement in European history was that it was the origin of the modern. In his more colourful nineteenth-century language, the Italian was 'the first-born among the sons of modern Europe'. The signs of this modernity included the idea of the state as a 'work of art', 'the modern sense of fame', 'the discovery of the world and of man', and above all what Burckhardt called 'the development of the individual'.

It is not easy to assent to these ideas today. For one thing, the break with the recent past now seems much less sharp than the scholars and artists of the fifteenth and sixteenth centuries claimed. In any case, even if they were self-consciously 'post-medieval', these scholars and artists were not 'modern' in the sense of resembling their nineteenth- and twentieth-century successors. Burckhardt surely underestimated the cultural distance between his day and that of the Renaissance. Since his day the distance, indeed the divergence between Renaissance culture and contemporary culture has become much more visible, despite continued interest in Leonardo, Montaigne, Cervantes, Shakespeare and other leading figures of that time (see below, p. 236). One purpose of this book is therefore a re-examination of the place of the Renaissance in European or indeed in world history, following the critique of what is sometimes called the 'Grand Narrative' of the rise of Western civilization: a triumphalist account of Western achievement from the Greeks onwards in which the Renaissance is a link in the chain which includes the Reformation, the Scientific Revolution, the Enlightenment, the Industrial Revolution and so on.[2]

In contrast to its traditional position at the centre of the stage, the Renaissance presented here is 'de-centred'.[3] Indeed, my aim is to view the culture of Western Europe as one culture among others, coexisting and interacting with its neighbours, notably Byzantium and Islam, both of which had their own 'renaissances' of Greek and Roman antiquity. Needless to say that Western culture was itself plural rather than singular, including minority cultures like that of the Jews, many of whom participated in the Renaissance in Italy and elsewhere.[4] Historians of the Renaissance have generally given too little attention and too little space to the contribution of both Arabs and Jews to the movement, to Leo the Hebrew (say), otherwise known as Judah Abravanel, or to Leo the African, otherwise known as Hasan al-Wazzân (see below, pp. 206, 212).

Two texts which attracted the interest of Renaissance humanists were the *Picatrix* and the *Zohar*. The *Picatrix* was a twelfth-century Arab manual of magic, and the *Zohar* a thirteenth-century Hebrew treatise on mysticism. The heady mixture of Platonism and magic which so excited Marsilio Ficino and his circle in Florence (see below, p. 37) has a parallel in the ideas of the Arab scholar Suhrawardi, executed in 1191 for deviations from Muslim orthodoxy. Come to that, the Muslim scholarly ideal of *adab*, associating literature with education, is not far from the Renaissance ideal of *humanitas*.[5]

Architects and artists also learned from the Islamic world. The designs of the fifteenth-century hospitals of Florence and Milan borrow directly or indirectly from the hospitals of Damascus and Cairo.[6] The goldsmith Benvenuto Cellini admired and emulated the 'arabesque' decoration on Turkish daggers, a form of decoration which can also be found on both the bindings and the pages of sixteenth-century French and Italian books.[7]

A consequence of this aim of decentring the Western Renaissance is an approach which may be described as 'anthropological'. If we, inhabitants of the world around the year 2000, are to understand the culture in which this movement developed, we would be well advised not to identify ourselves with it too easily. The very idea of a movement to revive the culture of the distant past has become alien to us, since it contradicts ideas of progress or modernity still widely taken for granted despite many recent critiques. At the very least – since there are degrees of otherness – we should view the culture of the Renaissance as a half-alien culture, one which is not only distant but receding, becoming more alien every year; hence the attempt in the following pages to make explicit what used to be implicit, the assumptions common in the period, the dominant modes of thought or 'mentalities'.

In the second place, in this book, as in other works in this series, the emphasis falls on Europe as a whole. It is, of course, easy to find histories of European culture during the period of the Renaissance.[8] It is also easy to find studies of the Renaissance, or of aspects of the Renaissance, in different European countries. What is lacking, despite the need for such a book, is a study of the movement throughout Europe. Even general studies of the Renaissance have often been limited to Western Europe, despite the importance of Renaissance art and humanism in Hungary and Poland.

A recurrent theme in the pages which follow will be the significance not only of the movement of texts and images but also the movement of people. Four diasporas were of particular importance. In the first place, there were the Greeks. One of the best-known myths of the Renaissance attributes the revival of learning to the Greek refugees who came to the West after the fall of Constantinople in 1453.[9] As a story of origins, it is unconvincing. All the same, the Greek scholars who began to come to the West around the beginning of the fifteenth century did make an important contribution to humanist studies, and Greek compositors too were indispensable to the printing of Homer, Plato and other classical texts in their original language. Greek artists did not often move westwards, but one of them was well known in Italy and Spain – El Greco. In the second place, there was the Italian diaspora of artists and humanists, not forgetting the merchants settled in Lyons, Antwerp and other cities whose interest in the art and literature of their native Italy helped draw it to the attention of their neighbours.[10] In the third place were the Germans, especially the printers, though the role of German artists abroad (from England to Poland) should not be forgotten either. Finally there were the Netherlanders, mainly painters and sculptors, and especially active in the Baltic countries (see below, p. 106).[11]

It should be clear that the spread of classical or classicizing style outside Italy was a collective European enterprise of cultural exchange.[12] To take an unusually complex example, French masons introduced italianate motifs into Scottish architecture at Linlithgow. This Scottish example in turn inspired Danish palaces, which were built by craftsmen from the Netherlands.[13] In the case of the ornament of buildings and furniture, as we shall see (below, p. 179), Roman grotesques were combined with Spanish (or Turkish) arabesques and Netherlands strapwork to produce an international style.

A major consequence of the decision to look at the Renaissance at a pan-European level is the emphasis on 'reception' in the sense of an active process of assimilation and transformation, as opposed to a simple spread of classical or Italian ideas. The concern with reception leads in turn to a focus on contexts; on the networks and locales in which the new forms and ideas were discussed and adapted; on the periphery of Europe; on the later Renaissance; and finally on what might be called the 'quotidianization' or 'domestication' of the Renaissance, in other words, its gradual permeation of everyday life.

Reception

The traditional account of the Renaissance outside Italy not only uses certain recurrent metaphors or models but is also shaped by them. There is the impact model, for instance, in which the movement 'penetrates' one region after another. There is the epidemic model, in which different parts of Europe 'catch' the Renaissance by a kind of contagion. There is the commercial model of 'borrowing', debts, exports and imports – some literal, as in the case of paintings and books, others metaphorical, as in the case of ideas. Most common is the hydraulic model, according to which the movement is viewed in terms of 'spread', influence, channels and absorption.

It will be difficult to avoid these metaphors altogether in the pages which follow. The basic model to be employed here, however, is the model of the 'reception' of new forms of Italian culture and of classical antiquity as mediated through Italy. Michelangelo and Machiavelli, for example, both 'received' the messages of antiquity in a creative manner, transforming what they appropriated. Their viewers and readers treated their messages in a similar way. This book is concerned not so much with the intentions of Michelangelo, Machiavelli and other major figures as with the ways in which the works they produced were interpreted at the time, especially outside Italy. Stress will be placed on differences in receptivity in different generations, regions and social groups.

The concept of reception, however, is more ambiguous than it may look. In the nineteenth century, students of law wrote about the reception of Roman law in Germany, and some cultural historians such as Gustav Bauch already discussed the reception of the Renaissance.[14] Reception was the complementary opposite of tradition; the latter a process of handing over, the former of receiving. It was more or less assumed that what was received was the same as what was given, not only in the case of material objects but also in that of immaterial goods such as ideas.

By contrast, contemporary reception theorists believe that whatever is transmitted necessarily changes in the process of transmission. Following the scholastic philosophers (whether consciously or not), they argue that 'whatever is received is received according to the manner of the receiver' (*Quidquid recipitur, ad modum recipientis recipitur*). They adopt the point of view of the receiver, not the original creator or producer, and so say relatively little about what the producer might call 'misunderstandings' or 'misinterpretations' of texts or other artefacts. Instead they present reception or consumption as itself a form of production, noting the creativity of acts of appropriation, assimilation, adaptation, reaction, response and even rejection.[15] Both the classical and the Italian traditions were viewed in an ambivalent manner in this period. Approaches to these traditions were matched by phases of withdrawal, like the withdrawal from 'Italianate classicism' identified by a recent historian of the art of Elizabethan England.[16]

From the point of view of reception theorists, the Renaissance created antiquity as much as antiquity created the Renaissance. What artists and writers practised was not so much imitation as transformation. It was perhaps no accident that two classical writers fascinated by metamorphosis, Ovid and Apuleius, were read with such enthusiasm in this period.

A useful metaphor for understanding the process of reception in this period as in others is that of *bricolage*, in other words, the making of something new out of fragments of earlier constructions. Some writers of the time made a similar point themselves. The Netherlands humanist Justus Lipsius declared in his *Politics* (essentially a selection of passages from classical authors) that 'all is mine', but that at the same time 'nothing is'. Robert Burton offered a similar description of his *Anatomy of Melancholy* (1621): '*Omne meum, nihil meum*, 'tis all mine and none mine.' It is tempting to appropriate this remark as a description of this book.

This idea of creative reception has a longer history than its advocates seem to think. In the case of the Renaissance, the transformations of the classical tradition were already being discussed at the turn of the century by Aby Warburg, an outsider in the academic world but the founder not only of an institute but also of an approach to cultural history.[17] In the 1920s, the French historian Lucien Febvre rejected the concept of borrowing because sixteenth-century artists and writers 'have combined, adapted, transposed', producing 'something at the same time composite and original'.[18] When Fernand Braudel lamented the absence of a full history of the diffusion of what he called Italian 'cultural goods' during the Renaissance, he extended the idea of diffusion to include adaptations and rejections.[19] There is no way in which a study as short as this can respond to Braudel's appeal, but his theme will recur again and again in the pages which follow.

A distinguished Swedish folklorist, Carl von Sydow, appropriated from botany the term 'ecotype' in order to describe the way in which folktales developed stable local variants in different parts of Europe, as if adapted to the local soil. The term is a useful one, particularly in the analysis of architecture, a collective art in which local stone if not local soil helps shape form, and it will be used from time to time in the following pages. So will the phrase 'cultural translation', used – especially by anthropologists – in the sense of rendering one culture intelligible to another.[20]

In the period itself other terms were employed. Writers debated the uses and dangers of 'imitation' (see below, p. 70). The metaphor of Italian 'grafts' and French fruits, used by the French humanist Blaise de Vigenère in the preface to his translation of Tasso, implied the creativity of reception. Missionaries and others spoke of the 'accommodation' of Christianity in new environments, and in similar fashion the sixteenth-century Netherlander Hans Vredeman de Vries, writing on architecture, remarked on the need to 'accommodate art to the situation and the needs of the country'. In his *Architecture française* (1624), the scholar-physician Louis Savot criticized the architects of that country for following the Italian model 'without considering that every region has its own special way of building' (*sans considérer que chaque province a sa façon particulière de bastir*).

One of the central ideas or metaphors in modern studies of reception is the idea of a 'grid' or 'filter', which allows something but not everything to pass. What is selected must be 'congruent' with the culture in which the selection takes place. In the case of the Renaissance, we need to be aware of the ancient Roman filter, since the Romans not only adopted Greek culture but also adapted it to their own needs. In the second place, there were the Byzantine and Arab filters through which ancient Greek culture was received in the Middle Ages. In the third place, there was the medieval filter. A fifteenth-century sketch of the Parthenon, for instance, makes it look somewhat Gothic. In the fourth place, there was the Italian filter, since Italians were pioneers in the revival and reception of antiquity while the rest of Europe often received antiquity via Italy. However, the idea of 'Italy' needs to be dismantled, since a revival of antiquity centred in Florence and Rome was adapted when it reached Milan or Venice, and these adaptations were later exported. In the case of architecture, for instance, following the normal trade-routes, France received the Lombard version of the Italian Renaissance while Germany received the Venetian version.

Contexts

Another central theme in studies of reception is that of 'context', a metaphor taken from weaving. First applied to the parts of the text preceding and following a given quotation, the term gradually widened its meaning to refer to the cultural, social or political surroundings of a text, image, idea, institution or whatever. 'Receiving' ideas creatively means adapting them to a new context. More precisely, this adaptation involves participating in a double movement. The first stage is that of decontextualization, dislocation or appropriation; the second, that of re-contextualisation, relocation or domestication. In the latter case, we need to examine not only the repertoire of items appropriated but also the logic of their selection and their use to construct a distinctive style. Classical or Italian elements were frequently 'reframed', in other words, given a new meaning. Again and again one we find cases of what might be described as *bricolage*, syncretism, or hybridization, in other words the combination of Christian and pagan, Gothic and classical, whether this combination was a conscious aim of a given artist or writer or the result of a misunderstanding of the original text or image.[21] There are no unproblematic or uncontested terms in this intellectual domain, but in the remainder of this study the attempt will be made to reserve the term 'syncretism' for conscious attempts to harmonize elements from different cultures (as Ficino did in the case of Platonism and Christianity), leaving 'hybridization' as a vaguer term for describing a variety of interactions between cultures.

A study of the European reception of the Renaissance must be concerned with the way in which contemporaries perceived and interpreted both antiquity and Italy. Their attitudes were not always enthusiastic, as we shall see (pp. 173–5). Many people hated Italian 'fashions' as they called them, and especially the 'aping' of Italian ways (yet another metaphor for imitation). Others disapproved of ancient Greece and Rome because it was pagan. Even the apparent admirers of Italy and the classics sometimes expressed a certain ambivalence. The relationship between European artists and writers and their classical and Italian models was something of a love-hate relationship, combining admiration with envy. Divergences from the models were sometimes the result of the desire to surpass them, or at least to create something different, congruent with local traditions. Historians of Japan have noted a similar ambivalence in Japanese attitudes to Chinese culture.[22] It will therefore be necessary to discuss resistance to the Renaissance as well as reception, whether it is a case of Christian resistance to paganism, a logician's resistance to rhetoric or northern resistance to Italy. As in the case of receptivity, different groups manifested higher or lower resistance to the new trends. An attempt will be made to make their attitudes intelligible, in other words, to present the Renaissance from a variety of viewpoints, to discuss its cool as well as its warm reception.

Networks and Locales

A study of the Renaissance in context also involves a concern with the channels, networks or groups through which the process of reception took place. Renaissance studies are dominated (to an unfortunate degree, in my opinion) by monographs on individuals. The tradition is as old as the Renaissance itself, in which Giorgio Vasari offered an account of art history dominated by heroes such as Giotto, Leonardo and, above all, Michelangelo. However, a central role in the process of innovation is often played not so much by individuals as by small groups or 'circles', especially if they compete with others and if their members are involved in intense social interaction.[23] It should not be assumed, of course, that every member of the group is equally creative, or that each individual agrees with all the views of the others. It is not easy for historians to reconstruct exchanges which were often informal and oral. All the same, cultural historians surely need to place more emphasis on small groups than they have done in the past. Such an emphasis expresses a double reaction against explaining cultural change either in the romantic mode, by heroic isolated individual geniuses, or, at the other extreme, in the Marxian mode, by Society with a capital S. It is also a valuable corrective to grand phrases like 'the Renaissance in Portugal' or 'humanism in Bohemia'.

Face-to-face contacts were facilitated by sites or locales such as courts, monasteries, chanceries, universities, academies or museums. The importance of these micro-spaces as support systems for the small groups who use them has recently been emphasized by a number of historians, especially in the history of science.[24] The monastery, for example, a traditional site for study, was important in the history of humanism in Italy and elsewhere. In Florence, the monks Luigi Marsili and Ambrogio Traversari belonged to the circle of Leonardo Bruni (see below, p. 27) and their cells in the convents of Santo Spirito and Santa Maria degli Angeli were locales in which humanists met. A number of Italian Benedictine monasteries were also centres of humanism.[25] Monasteries were the main centres of humanism in the Netherlands in the fifteenth century – the Cistercian abbey of Aduard north of Groningen, for example, frequented by Rodolphus Agricola and his friends. In Germany, the Benedictine monastery of Sponheim played an important role in the humanist movement when the scholar Johannes Trithemius was its abbot (see below, p. 89).[26]

However, a network need not depend on a physical meeting-place. It may be united by correspondence, as in the cases of nomadic scholars such as Petrarch, Erasmus and Lipsius. In any case, for its ideas to reach a wider public, the group needs to use other channels of communication. In this period, the invention of printing (including the printing of images, which preceded movable type) allowed new ideas to spread more quickly and to far more people than before. As a consequence of its emphasis on reception, this essay – including its illustrations – will stress graphic art at the expense of painting, sculpture and architecture, and reproduction at the expense of original works. Another consequence of the decision to privilege reception is to focus on those elements and individuals in Italian culture to which other Europeans responded most strongly in the period itself: Raphael, for example, rather than Piero della Francesca, who was viewed as a major painter only in the twentieth century.

Centres and Peripheries

The emphasis on the receiver also implies a concern with the interaction between an international movement and local conditions (whether cultural, social or political). Hence the decision to give more attention than is customary to the peripheries of Europe. Needless to say, the term 'periphery', like 'centre', is problematic. Where is the centre of Europe? In Prague, or elsewhere in 'central' Europe? Or in Florence, at one time the centre of the Renaissance? Or in Rome, whose inhabitants boasted of living in the 'centre of the world'? Italy will necessarily play a central role throughout a book on the Renaissance, but what counts as periphery varies according to the period and also the art or discipline under consideration.

In the visual arts, Hungary, or at any rate Buda and its environs, was central in the late fifteenth century in the sense of receiving the Renaissance earlier than most other parts of Europe (see below, pp. 58–9), even if it was peripheral by virtue of its location on the border between Christendom and Islam. Croatia is not often considered to be central to European culture, but its closeness to Italy meant that trends in Renaissance art, humanism and literature began relatively early there.[27] It is worth considering which regions contemporaries from different parts of Europe considered to be remote from centres of culture. England, for instance, was cited as an example of the periphery by Kochanowski (see below, p. 139). It was especially peripheral in the later sixteenth century, when the religious wars in France and the Netherlands made travel unusually difficult and dangerous.

The point is not to insist that Ivan the Terrible (say) or the Irish chieftain Manus O'Donnell were Renaissance princes, although scholars have made such a case for both of them.[28] It is rather to suggest that creativity was at once more necessary and more visible in the places where the cultural distance from

Italy was greatest at a particular moment or in a particular domain. In the case of Wales, for example, the lack of an urban base for the Renaissance has been emphasized, and so has the predominance of prose in the new style over poetry.[29] The references in this book to Sweden (say) or to Scotland, to Portugal or to Poland, like the references to Asia, Africa and the Americas, are part of a conscious strategy. This emphasis on the peripheries in turn involves a reassessment of local styles in art, literature and learning. From the centre, these local styles have often appeared to be 'corruptions' or 'provincializations' of the original model, the emphasis falling on what was lost. From the periphery itself, on the other hand, what one sees is a creative process of accommodation, assimilation or 'syncretism'.[30] Once again it is necessary to tell the story from multiple points of view.

The Later Renaissance

The organization of the book is chronological. The story begins with the early Renaissance, the 'rediscovery' of antiquity – or more exactly, of fragments of antiquity – in Italy from the early fourteenth to the late fifteenth century (chapter 1), and the repercussions of that discovery on the rest of Europe, whether in the form of 'reception' or 'resistance' (chapter 2). It is followed by the 'high' Renaissance, c.1490–1530, the time that the fragments were tied most closely together. This was the age of 'emulation' in the sense that Italians had come by this time to think of themselves as able to compete with the ancients on equal terms, while the artists, writers and scholars of other countries were beginning to compete with the Italians (chapter 3). However, the book's emphasis on reception necessarily involves a greater emphasis than usual on the later Renaissance, from about 1530 to 1630 (chapter 4).[31] Paradoxically enough, 1530 is the point at which, according to some earlier scholars, the movement came to an end (see below, p. 102). The view taken here, on the other hand, is that although variety signified a return to fragmentation, it was precisely in this period that individuals and groups in many parts of Europe were able to make their most distinctive contributions to the international movement, translating classical and Italian styles into local languages.[32]

It was also in this last period that we find most evidence of what might be called the 'domestication' of the Renaissance (chapter 5), in other words, its social diffusion, its incorporation into everyday practices and its effects on both material culture and mentalities. What had begun as a movement among a tiny group of scholars and artists became a fashion – or gave rise to a number of fashions – and ended by transforming some of the central attitudes and values of European elites and possibly those of other people as well. Some of these attitudes and values outlived the end, or better, the fragmentation of the movement, as the coda on the Renaissance after the Renaissance will attempt to show.

Methods

The following chapters attempt to combine description, analysis and narrative. The description moves back and forth between general surveys and case-studies, long shots and close-ups. The analysis attempts to account for receptivity in particular places, at particular moments and among particular groups, steering between two opposite extremes. One is to assume that classical and Italian cultural 'goods' were accepted because of their inherent attractions. The opposite view takes it for granted that culture was simply an instrument, notably a means for individuals and groups to increase their status and power in the competition with their rivals. The first view is too simple-minded, the second too reductionist. The challenge to the historian is to discuss the 'uses' of Italy and antiquity without falling into a crude utilitarianism.

As for the narrative, it tells the story of the rise, spread, modification and finally the distintegration of a cultural movement. One way of putting this, emphasizing collective rather than individual responses, is to say that the traditional European cultural order was capable of absorbing new elements up to a certain point. In the domain of high culture, the critical threshold was reached in some parts of Europe around 1500. There were so many new elements to domesticate that the traditional order cracked under the strain, and a new order began to emerge.[33]

Another way of describing what happened, leaving aside social and political factors for a moment in order to concentrate on what might be called the 'logic of development', is to identify three stages in the reception of antiquity. The story begins with the rediscovery of classical culture and the first attempts at imitation. Then comes the stage of mastery, the so-called 'high' Renaissance, in which the rules for the combination of different elements have been learned and imitation turns into emulation. The third and last stage is that of deliberate modification, the conscious breaking of the rules.

In some domains at least, we may speak of 'progress' in the sense of increasing ability to achieve certain ends, from writing in Latin in the style of Cicero to mastery of the rules of perspective. A sense of progress is often expressed in the period itself, taking the form of denunciations of the 'Middle Ages', patronizing references to the achievement of earlier generations or, in Vasari's *Lives of the Artists*, an explicit theory of the development of art through various stages or periods. As often happens in the history of culture, however, success in a particular domain was often followed by a change of aim, thus frustrating any simple interpretation of the whole movement in terms of progress or accumulation.

It is also important to emphasize that – like many other movements – this one changed its character as more and more people joined it. Or returning to the distinction between 'movement' and 'period', we might describe the main theme of this book as the transformation of the Renaissance from one into the other. The point is that objects and attitudes which in 1350 or even 1400 interested only a tiny group of people, mainly in Italy, gradually became part of the everyday life of a substantial minority of Europeans.

One danger of a general study like this is to write only 'external history', whether in the form of generalized description of lists of examples, because there is little space for individuals. Another danger is to emphasize similarities at the expense of differences, general trends at the expense of exceptions, conformists at the expense of eccentrics. To avoid these dangers here, two strategies have been employed.

The first is to quote original texts as frequently as possible

in order to allow readers to hear the conversation of contemporaries and not only a historian's monologue. The debates
of the period will be presented through the concepts of the
participants. References to 'rebirth', 'revival', 'restoration' and
so on will be quoted again and again (I hope not ad nauseam),
as a reminder of the importance of this metaphor for the scholars
and artists of the time as a way of organizing their experience.
Recent studies in a number of disciplines have drawn attention
to the importance of metaphors in everyone's thinking and
also to the way in which, whether they are aware of this or not,
people perform or enact these metaphors in everyday life.[34] The
history of the Renaissance may be regarded not only as
the history of an enthusiasm and the history of a movement, but
also as the history of a metaphor which many individuals and
groups tried to enact. However, no assumption will be made
about the cultural unity of the age. On the contrary, the stress
will fall on the multiplicity of contemporary viewpoints, the
conflicting and changing impressions of the events and trends
which were taking place at this time.

The second strategy is to present case-studies, whether of
small groups, individuals, texts or other objects. Particular individuals or objects will be discussed at the expense of others who
were equally important in the Renaissance movement. The same
people and the same works will recur in different contexts, to
show the connections between what are usually studied as
different 'fields'. There is, of course, a danger of assuming that
certain objects or individuals were representative of their age.
The case-studies offered here are therefore intended to subvert
or qualify as well as to illustrate the generalizations they
accompany. For this reason they tend to come in twos and
threes, offering the opportunity for comparative analysis but
also allowing discrepancies between individual examples and
general conclusions to become visible.

It goes without saying that a brief essay of this kind on a vast
subject must be brutally selective. Readers are reminded that –
in contrast to earlier studies of this topic – the peripheries of the
movement will be privileged over the centres, everyday cultural
practices over the peaks of achievement, and the reputations of
outstanding individuals over their original intentions. The point
of this strategy is to focus on a process which might be called

the 'Europeanization' of the Renaissance, or the contribution of the Renaissance to the Europeanization of Europe. As in the case of other cultural movements, the process is a dialectical one. On the one hand we see standardization by borrowing from a common source; on the other, diversification by adaptation to local circumstances, from political and social structures to cultural traditions.

1

The Age of Rediscovery:
Early Renaissance

In his *History of Italian Literature*, the eighteenth-century Italian scholar Girolamo Tiraboschi drew parallels in three consecutive chapters between what he called 'the discovery of books (*Scoprimento di libri*)', 'the discovery of Antiquity (*Scoprimento d'Antichità*)' and the 'discovery of America (*Scoprimento dell'America*)'. This 'Columbus paradigm', as we might call it, had considerable appeal to later generations. In the nineteenth century, Jules Michelet and Jacob Burckhardt extended the idea to include what they both called the 'discovery of the world and of man'.

These larger claims will be left on one side until chapter 5. Here we are concerned with the first phase of the Italian Renaissance, from about 1300 to about 1490. This was the age of the discovery of what would be taken for granted in later phases of the movement, the culture of the ancient Romans and to a lesser extent of the Greeks. It was also an age of reform, following these classical models.

It is impossible for individuals and groups to break completely with the culture in which they have been brought up. The central paradox of all cultural reform is that the reformers come from the culture they want to change. The discoverers remained medieval in most respects. Hence it is useless to draw a sharp line between one period called the 'Middle Ages' and another called the 'Renaissance'. The early Renaissance culture described in this chapter coexisted with that of late medieval Europe.

Among the most distinctive features of that culture were Gothic art, chivalry and scholastic philosophy. All three features could be found in most parts of Europe. The cultural unification of Europe, the 'Europeanization of Europe' as it has been called, had begun long before the Renaissance. The process was already perceptible in the twelfth and thirteenth centuries.[35]

The so-called 'Gothic' style, for instance, was an international language of art.[36] Despite local variations such as the use of brick in Danish churches or the contrast between the French emphasis on height in cathedrals and the English on length, the Gothic style was recognizable from Portugal to Poland. 'Chivalry' – in other words, the values of the late medieval nobility, focused on the art of fighting on horseback – was another international phenomenon. Romances of chivalry, recounting the noble deeds of heroes such as Roland and Lancelot at the courts of the Emperor Charlemagne and King Arthur were avidly read – or heard – in most European countries. What we now call 'scholastic' philosophy and theology, the writings of Thomas Aquinas for example, developed in the lecture-rooms or 'schools' of medieval universities in the twelfth and thirteenth centuries. These studies appealed to a smaller group, but once again an international one. Since Latin was spoken as well as written in the universities, and masters of arts had 'the right of teaching anywhere' (*ius ubique docendi*) from Coimbra to Cracow, academic culture was truly pan-European.

Gothic, chivalry and scholasticism all centred on France. Gothic architecture was invented there in the early twelfth century. The university of Paris was the centre of the teaching of scholastic philosophy. The most famous romances of chivalry were composed in France. Indeed, in other countries, such as England or northern Italy, the romances were often sung or written in French. We might then speak of the high Middle Ages as a time of French cultural hegemony.

All three forms of medieval culture survived into the fifteenth and even the seventeenth century. Scholastic philosophy continued to dominate the arts course in most European universities. Romances of chivalry continued to find enthusiastic readers. Gothic churches continued to be built. What changed in the course of the Renaissance was that Gothic, chivalry and scholasticism no longer monopolized their respective domains but instead competed and interacted with alternative styles and values derived from the ancient world. It was especially in Italy that these 'new' styles and values emerged. Why?

In Italy, the French models of Gothic, chivalry and scholasticism had penetrated less deeply than in some other parts of Europe. Scholasticism came late to Italy, where universities such as Bologna and Padua concentrated on law, arts and medicine, not on theology. The Italian cities, many of them autonomous from the eleventh century onwards, produced an alternative culture, lay rather than clerical and civilian rather than military.

When was the Renaissance?

Historians do not agree when or even where to begin their narratives of the Renaissance. Florence, Rome, Avignon, Padua and Naples have all been presented as the 'cradle' of the movement. Most stories start in Italy, but at different moments and with different individuals. A common choice is the age of the poet-scholar Francesco Petrarcha (anglicized as 'Petrarch') in the 1330s or 1340s. However, some historians of art begin a generation earlier with Giotto. Giotto's fame was based on his creation of a new style of pictorial narrative, and this new style was partly based on the classical sculpture he had seen at Pisa. He was mentioned with respect by humanists and his work was an inspiration to later generations of Renaissance artists.

If we choose Giotto, however, it is difficult to omit his contemporary Dante. The two men and some of their followers were responsible for an extraordinary 'outburst of creativity' in Florence just after the year 1300.[37] Today, we tend to think of Dante as medieval, but in fifteenth- and sixteenth-century Florence he was closely associated with Petrarch. If the rediscovery of antiquity is to be the criterion for choosing a starting date, we should not forget that Dante's generation was also that of the Paduan writer Albertino Mussato, who wrote drama and history modelled on the classics. In the case of education, too, at least in Italy, it has been argued that the years around 1300 mark a turning-point.[38]

Whatever date is chosen for the beginning of the Renaissance, it is always possible to make a case for going back still further. In the history of painting, for example, we might start in the thirteenth century with Cimabue, or in sculpture with Giovanni and Nicolo Pisano, whose work was inspired at least on occasion by ancient Roman models.[39] Some intellectual historians also stress the importance of changes in the thirteenth century, notably the reception of Aristotle in the West, by Thomas Aquinas and others.

Petrarch and his followers tried to distance themselves from the Aristotelians. In a little book with the Socratic title *On his own ignorance* ('and that of many others'), Petrarch criticized the academic philosophers of his day, 'the crazy and clamorous sect of schoolmen' (*scholastici*), for their exclusive devotion to Aristotle. In the perspective of the long-term, on the other hand, it is difficult to discern any sharp break between Aquinas's interest in Aristotle and Petrarch's enthusiasm for classical writers. Like the humanists later, scholastic philosophers such as William of Conches declared that 'the dignity of our mind is its capacity to know all things.'[40]

Other historians draw attention to parallels between the interests of twelfth-century men of letters such as the Englishman John of Salisbury and their fifteenth-century successors. John was familiar with some of the classics, including Cicero and Seneca, Plato's *Timaeus* and Virgil's *Aeneid*. He accommodated these texts to his culture (consciously or unconsciously) by giving them a moral or religious interpretation, claiming, for example, that Plato knew the doctrine of the Trinity and that the adventures of Aeneas were allegories of the progress of the soul through life. However, some fifteenth-century scholars would offer similar interpretations, as we shall see.

Whether we prefer to speak of 'Renaissance', 'Pre-Renaissance', or simply of preconditions for the Renaissance, the point to emphasize is the survival of the classical tradition. Some ancient Roman writers, the poets Horace and Virgil for example, continued to be read and imitated throughout the Middle Ages.[41] The tradition of Roman law remained vigorous in some regions, such as Italy and the south of France. In the

Italian city-republics of the twelfth and thirteenth centuries, as in ancient Rome, the study of rhetoric, in other words the art of persuasion in speeches and letters, was a necessary preparation for careers in law and politics. Civic virtues and good government were debated with reference to classical writers such as Cicero and Sallust. The unusually urban and secular culture of these republics had obvious affinities with that of antiquity, making classical literature and philosophy unusually relevant to their citizens.[42]

The classical tradition also continued in the visual arts. Pre-Gothic art and architecture is known today as 'Romanesque' precisely because of its debt to that of the Romans. The remains of classical buildings survived in a number of European cities and continued to evoke wonder. Verona had its Roman ampitheatre, Nîmes its Roman temple, Segovia its Roman aqueduct and so on. In Rome itself, there was the temple of the Pantheon, the Colosseum, the Arch of Titus, Trajan's Column and much more. Classical survivals assisted classical revivals. In the age of Charlemagne, the Pantheon inspired the imperial chapel at Aachen. In the twelfth century, it inspired the Baptistery in Florence.

The rediscovery of the classical tradition by the West was assisted by encounters with what have been called its 'sibling' cultures, the Byzantine and Arab world. For example, Byzantine scholars were familiar with a number of ancient Greek authors who were completely unknown in the West. They edited and commented on these texts in the way Renaissance humanists were to do in the fifteenth and sixteenth centuries.[43] The Arabs too played an important role in transmitting Greek tradition, especially from the ninth to the fourteenth centuries. The famous schools of Athens and Alexandria moved to Baghdad. Muslim scholars wrote commentaries on Plato and Aristotle. The philosopher Ibn Sina (known in the West as Avicenna) was a Neoplatonist, while Ibn Rushd (Averroes) was an Aristotelian. A number of ancient writers, including Aristotle, Ptolemy, Hippocrates and Galen, were translated into Latin in the Middle Ages from the Arabic translations of the original Greek.

Petrarch and his Circle

This particular history of the European Renaissance effectively begins with Petrarch, thanks to the breadth of his interests and achievements, as poet, scholar and philosopher; to his enthusiasm for Roman culture; and to his influence on the generations which followed him, not only in Italy but in much of Europe as well. With hindsight, we might say that Petrarch was the first 'humanist', a term which will be discussed below (p. 29).

Petrarch thought of himself primarily as a poet, a second Virgil. The recognition – for himself and for poetry – which he craved, and which he apparently succeeded in obtaining, was to be crowned with laurels on the Capitol in Rome in 1341. The coronation followed a classical precedent recently revived (Albertino Mussato had been crowned in Padua in 1315, and a proposal had been made to crown Dante). Petrarch was important both as an epic and as a lyric poet. His epic poem *Africa* was an account of the life of the Roman general Scipio Africanus, written in Latin and modelled on classical epics by Virgil and Statius. In the vernacular, Petrarch wrote a sequence of lyrics. The bitter-sweet poems of this 'song-book' (*Canzoniere*) present the poet as a lonely and pensive lover (*solo e pensoso*), stressing his torments, his sighs, his 'bitter tears' (*amare lagrime*), and the beauty and cruelty of his mistress.

Petrarch was also a moralist, of the stoic persuasion. His Italian poem the *Triumphs* deals with the successive triumphs of Love, Death and finally of Fame, all described in terms of the processions which celebrated the victories of ancient Roman generals and emperors. His 'Remedies' for both good and bad fortune was written in the form of a dialogue between 'Reason' and four other allegorical figures, 'Joy', 'Hope', 'Pain' and 'Anxiety'. Petrarch the scholar was not far removed from Petrarch the moralist. His *Illustrious Men* was a collection of thirty-four biographies of ancient Romans and figures from the Bible whose example readers were supposed to imitate. In similar fashion he advised the ruler of Padua on the choice of illustrious men to be painted in a hall in his palace. One of his own heroes was Cicero. He owned Cicero's philosophical works, discovered a number of his letters, and wrote his own letters in a similar style.

Petrarch was also concerned with classical antiquity for its own sake. He was interested in Homer and tried unsuccessfully to learn Greek. However, his great enthusiasm was for ancient Rome. The sight of the ruins of Rome made a great impression on him. He collected ancient coins. His passion for personal contact with the ancient Romans is revealed by the fact that he wrote to letters to Cicero and Seneca. He collected and transcribed manuscripts of ancient writers, notably Cicero and Livy. Even in his handwriting Petrarch imitated the ancients, abandoning the Gothic style.

Throughout Petrarch's work runs a new and intense concern for the individual self. The portrait of Laura which he commissioned from Simone Martini has been described as the first known portrait in the modern sense of the likeness of an individual. Petrarch wrote not only biographies but an auto-biography, the 'Secretum', a dialogue between 'Franciscus' and 'Augustinus' in which the author of the *Confessions*, one of his favourite books, represents the author's conscience. His epic *Africa* is a kind of biography, while his lyrics, as has often been noted, are written in the first person and almost exclusively concerned with the lover's feelings. His personal letters were carefully revised so that others might read them.

Petrarch believed that the last few centuries, which we call the Middle Ages, were an age of darkness, in contrast to classical antiquity, which had been an age of light. In his poem *Africa* he expressed the hope that 'When the darkness breaks the generations to come may manage to find their way back to the clear splendour of the ancient past.' Following Petrarch, many scholars wrote of their own time as one of light after darkness, awakening after sleep, return to life after death, restoration or rebirth. It would be a mistake not to take these metaphors seriously, since they gave meaning to the experience of the writers and helped them locate themselves in space and time. However, it would be an even greater mistake to take the phrases literally, and so to dismiss medieval culture.

Petrarch himself, for example, was in many ways a medieval figure. His meditations on fortune were traditional. So was his enthusiasm for St Augustine. St Bernard was another of his models. So was Dante. The poems of the *Canzoniere* form a narrative like those of Dante's *Vita Nuova*, with Petrarch's beloved Laura in the place of Beatrice. It is impossible to contrast a 'modern' Petrarch with a 'medieval' Dante. If he disliked Gothic handwriting, Petrarch admired some Gothic architecture, including Cologne cathedral, which he called 'an uncommonly beautiful temple'.

Petrarch had the gift of inspiring others to share his enthusiasm. His circle included the painter Simone Martini, the physician-astronomer Giovanni Dondi (with whom he exchanged sonnets), the Dominican friar Giovanni Colonna (with whom he viewed the ruins of Rome), the Augustinian friar Dionigi di Borgo San Sepolcro (who gave him a copy of the *Confessions* of St Augustine), the political leader Cola di Rienzo (who tried to restore the Roman republic) and Giovanni Boccaccio.

Like Petrarch, Boccaccio combined the roles of scholar and writer in the vernacular. He participated in the search for manuscripts of ancient authors, and in 1355 he found the *Golden Ass* of Apuleius in the monastery of Monte Cassino. He wrote a treatise on the *Genealogy of the Gods*. As a biographer, Boccaccio did for women what Petrarch had done for men. His *Famous Women* included 106 biographies from Eve to Queen Joanna of Naples, via Semiramis, Juno, Venus, Helen, Artemisia, Portia and Lucretia. The collection of short stories for which Boccaccio is remembered today, the *Decameron*, was only a small part of a varied achievement.

Like Petrarch, Boccaccio may be described as medieval in many respects. He too drew inspiration from the Italian rhetorical tradition, and gave public lectures on Dante. It was only gradually that he abandoned the idea that Dante rather than Petrarch was the reviver of poetry.[44] In similar fashion Petrarch's friend and admirer Giovanni Dondi combined an interest in classical writers such as Pliny and Vitruvius (the author of the only treatise on architecture to survive from ancient times) with the traditional culture of the scholastic philosophers. These more or less unconscious continuities were indeed important, but so too was the sense of change which can be found in the writings of Petrarch and his circle. The idea of renovation or reform, which has been used earlier in an ecclesiastical context, was now applied to the secular world. Petrarch was the first to use such terms in literary context, while Cola di Rienzo applied them to politics. He went so far as to date his letters 'Year One' of the restored Roman republic.

Similar phrases were used to describe changes in painting, notably in the case of the Florentine Giotto di Bondone, whose monumental style impressed contemporaries as well as posterity. He was praised by Dante, by Petrarch (as a 'prince' of painters) and by Boccaccio, who claimed in the *Decameron* that Giotto had 'brought back to light' (*ritornata in luce*) an art which had been 'buried for many centuries'. Boccaccio described Giotto's achievement, as the ancient Roman writer Pliny had described the achievement of Greek artists, in terms of *trompe l'oeil*, writing that people were 'deceived by the things he made, believing real that which was painted' (*credendo esser vero che era dipinto*).

It has sometimes been argued that the trauma of the Black Death in 1348–9, when the plague killed about a third of the population of Europe, led to a return to tradition. However, this counter-trend should not be exaggerated, and in any case it did not last. The movement of innovation gathered force in the next generation.[45]

The Second Generation

Cultural change is often linked to the emergence of a particular generation, a group with common experiences. In this case, a group who had been familiar with Petrarch from their youth turned out to be willing and able to take his ideas further. By the 1430s, the distance from the first generation seemed so great that a minor humanist, Sicco Polenton, could comment in a somewhat patronizing manner on Petrarch's Latin in his history of literature: 'He is not at present appreciated by those who are so fastidious that they do not commend anything that is not absolutely perfect. But they should remember Cicero's words in the *Brutus*, that nothing can be discovered already perfect.'

Florence and Tuscany

In Florence, Petrarch's work was continued by Coluccio Salutati, who had studied rhetoric at Bologna in order to be a notary and became interested in textual criticism.[46] Salutati was a great admirer of the heroes of the Roman republic, from Lucretia to Brutus. He was an enthusiast for the stoics, despite his ambivalence about their emphasis on detachment ('apathy') and his criticism of their insistence on superhuman virtue. He believed that literature (*studia litterarum*) and eloquence had revived in the last generations thanks to Mussato, Dante and Petrarch. In his enthusiasm for Petrarch he went so far as to claim on one occasion that his idol surpassed Cicero in prose and Virgil in verse. Around 1360, Salutati joined a group which met to discuss the work of Petrarch and Boccaccio. In the course of his years in Florence, Salutati gradually made himself the centre of an intellectual circle which included Leonardo Bruni (who arrived in the city in the 1390s), and Poggio Bracciolini, who described the master in a letter to his friend, the patrician Niccolo Niccoli, as 'our father Coluccio'.[47]

Salutati was chancellor of the Florentine republic for more than thirty years, 1375–1406. The chancery, an office concerned with the dispatch, receipt and filing of letters, was a place in which humanists had an opportunity to put their ideas into practice, since letters in classical Latin were becoming a way for a government to impress its rivals. Pope Pius II, himself a distinguished man of letters, noted that the Florentines chose chancellors for 'rhetorical skill and knowledge of the humanities'. Salutati's successors in office included Bruni, who served from 1427 to 1444, and Poggio, who returned to Florence towards the end of his life.[48]

Poggio's correspondence with his friend Niccoli about their 'thirst for books' makes a vivid case-study of this generation's enthusiasm for things Roman. To begin with, there is the handwriting. These friends invented the so-called 'italic' script in the early 1420s, modelling it on manuscripts which they believed to be Roman (cf. figure 2). The content of their letters expresses a similar enthusiasm for antiquity. Poggio complains that Niccolo has kept his Lucretius for ten years: 'I want to read Lucretius but I am deprived of his presence.' He gives the latest news of a sighting of a manuscript of Tacitus in Germany or a manuscript of Livy in Denmark. He describes how he 'sweated for several hours' in the September heat, trying to read Roman inscriptions. He tells of showing the sculptor Donatello his collection of

Roman heads and writes with pride that 'Donatello saw them and praised them greatly.' He responds to the news of the recent discovery of manuscripts of some of Cicero's works: 'Nothing annoys me more than the fact that I cannot be on the spot to enjoy them with you.'

Cicero was indeed a hero to this generation, the exemplar of elegant Latin and the model of a man of letters involved in the active life of republican politics. Bruni's *Dialogues* were modelled on Cicero's. His letters echo Cicero's. He wrote a biography of Cicero. Again, Poggio transcribed Cicero, echoed Cicero, and visited Tusculum, the setting of one of Cicero's most famous dialogues, where he was happy to discover 'a villa which must have been Cicero's'.

Poggio himself found manuscripts of eight speeches of Cicero. He also discovered the *Institutes* of Quintilian and, in a Swiss monastic library, a manuscript of the *Ten Books on Architecture* by Vitruvius. In the last case, if not others, the term 'discovery' needs to be placed in inverted commas. The work of Vitruvius had been known not only to Petrarch and his disciple Dondi, as we have seen, but also to medieval scholars. Vitruvius was discovered in the Renaissance in the sense that it was only then that his work began to affect the practice of architecture.[49]

The rediscovery of Greek culture was also proceeding at this time. Salutati brought a Greek teacher to Florence, Manuel Chrysoloras, who stayed for about five years and taught both the language and the art of rhetoric to Bruni and others (Salutati himself began the course but discovered that he was too old to learn). Poggio wrote to Niccoli that he 'burns' to study Greek, not least 'to escape those horrid translations', though it apparently took him many years to master the language. Ignoring the interest already shown in Avignon and Rome, Bruni claimed proudly that 'the knowledge of Greek literature, which had disappeared from Italy seven hundred years ago, has been recalled and brought back (*revocata est atque reducta*) by our city', so that it became possible to see the great philosophers and orators 'not through a glass darkly but face to face'.

What has a better claim to be considered as new was Bruni's theory and practice of translation, a term (*translatio*) which he was the first to use in this sense rather than its traditional meaning of 'transfer'. Bruni concentrated on the meaning rather than the words, attempting to avoid anachronism and to imitate the different styles of individual authors. In his translation of Aristotle's *Politics*, for example, he used the term *magistratus* of magistrates where his medieval predecessors had written *principatus*, projecting their own monarchical system of government on to ancient Greece. Bruni also translated Demosthenes, Plato and Plutarch. Plutarch, a moralist unknown in the West until the 1390s, was, like Plato, to have a pervasive influence on Renaissance culture, as we shall see. Thanks to Chrysoloras, Bruni discovered the great history of the Peloponnesian War by Thucydides, as well as the encomium of Athens by a late classical rhetorician, Aelius Aristides, which served as a model for his own encomium of Florence, the *Laudatio florentinae urbis*.

Bruni and Poggio were not only chancellors of Florence but official historians of the republic, presenting past as well as present policies in a favourable light. The story they told emphasized Florentine liberty, comparing it to that of republican Rome and Athens. In their form too, these histories followed Greek and Roman models such as Thucydides and Livy, notably in the speeches they put into the mouths of their protagonists as a way of explaining their actions. The humanist interest in analysis, in explaining events, is reminiscent of the leading ancient historians but contrasts with the medieval chronicle, which focused on narrative and vivid description.

In retrospect, the interests and achievements of this group of Florentines, like those of Petrarch, have been described as 'humanist'. The term is an appropriate one, given their interest in what Cicero had called the *studia humanitatis*. As Salutati put it, 'Since it is the characteristic of man to be taught and the learned are more human than the unlearned, the ancients appropriately referred to learning as *humanitas*.' Five subjects were generally considered to form part of the 'humanities': ethics, poetry, history, rhetoric and grammar. The emphasis on ethics is obvious enough, the power to tell the difference between right and wrong being what distinguished humans from animals. Poetry and history were considered to be forms of applied ethics, offering good examples for students to follow and bad ones for them to avoid. It is probably less clear to a modern reader why rhetoric or grammar should have been considered 'humane'. The point was that they were arts of language, and that it was

Figure 1   Sandro Botticelli, *Seven Liberal Arts*, Musée du Louvre (Réunion des Musées Nationaux/Louvre, Paris). Rhetoric (recognizable by her open hand) is presiding.

language which allowed humans to tell right from wrong. The point was fundamental for the treatises on 'the dignity of man', in which humanists, like some of the Fathers of the Church, sang the praises of humanity. There was a significant omission from the intellectual package of the 'humanities': logic. Emphasis shifted from the closed fist of the logician, using force to knock down the opponent, to the open hand of the rhetorician, who preferred persuasion (figure 1).

It went almost without saying that the languages to be cultivated were classical Latin and Greek, and that the texts to be studied were those of the ancient Greeks and Romans (including early Christian writers). For the humanists, the way forward was to go back, to follow the example of the best writers and thinkers in a culture which they considered superior to their own. Hence the effort which from Petrarch onwards they invested in searching for early manuscripts of classical texts, emending the errors of copyists (a process now known as 'textual criticism') and interpreting the meaning of obscure passages. In their self-justifications, the humanists placed great stress on the idea of the 'human condition' (*conditio humana*). As a set of cultural practices, on the other hand, humanism was dominated by philology rather than by philosophy, by the criticism of texts rather than the criticism of society.

Some modern historians describe Bruni and his colleagues as 'civic humanists', stressing their concern with the active rather than the contemplative life and their identification with the Florentine republic. Bruni, for example, declared that 'Dante is of greater worth than Petrarch in the active and civic life,' and praised Cicero for combining philosophy with an active political career. Leon Battista Alberti wrote a dialogue on the family in the vernacular, in which he discussed civic values. The place of humanism in public life was recognized and celebrated in the grand funerals of Coluccio Salutati (1406) and Leonardo Bruni (1444). A few scholars take the political interpretation of cultural change still further. It has been argued that the 'crisis of 1402', when the duke of Milan, Giangaleazzo Visconti, died suddenly in the middle of his campaign to conquer Florence, led to the early Renaissance by making humanists and artists more conscious of the values Florence stood for, such as liberty, and its similarities to ancient Rome and Athens.[50] The idea is an attractive one, which might lead an English reader to wonder whether the 'crisis of 1588' and the failure of the Spanish Armada had similar consequences for the age of Shakespeare. However, in the Florentine case, as in that of other Italian cities, civic patriotism together with praise for the active life of civic responsibility (*vita civile*) is well documented from the fourteenth century if not before. Salutati, Bruni and his colleagues simply gave the civic tradition more of a classical colouring.[51]

This classicism was controversial, as an early fifteenth-century debate shows. The Florentine friar Giovanni Dominici attacked Salutati for encouraging the study of pagan authors. According to Dominici, the study of 'philosophy' of 'worldly literature' (*seculares litterae*) was of no use for salvation. On the contrary, it was an impediment. He also denounced what he called the 'lies' of rhetoric. Another participant in the debate called Virgil a 'liar'. His assumption seems to have been that Virgil's account of the flight of Aeneas from Troy must either be true history or a pack of lies. There was no place in his mental world for the modern idea of 'fiction'.

Salutati replied with a defence of poetry against its 'detractors' which is equally remote from modern assumptions, since it depended (as in the case of John of Salisbury, p. 21), on an allegorical interpretation of classical myths like the labours of Hercules. The skin or shell might be pagan, but the inner meaning was a moral or christian one. Salutati argued that 'The *studia humanitatis* and the *studia divinitatis* are linked so closely that true and complete knowledge of the one cannot be had without the other.'[52]

The problem of the compatibility or incompatibility between classical and Christian wisdom would remain a major preoccupation of humanists as long as the Renaissance lasted, just as it had been a preoccupation for the Fathers of the Church, who belonged to two cultures, classical and Christian, and tried with more or less difficulty to harmonize the two. Clement of Alexandria, for instance, described Plato as the Greek Moses. Lactantius emphasized the compatibility of Plato and Cicero with Christianity. Jerome expressed the fear that he was more of a Ciceronian than a Christian.

The humanists often appealed to the Fathers in their defence. Salutati argued against Dominici that the Fathers had quoted pagan writers. Around the time of this controversy, Bruni translated into Latin and dedicated to Salutati a treatise of Basil the Great, archbishop of Caesarea, advising young men how to study the classics. Basil argued for a selective appropriation of pagan antiquity, following the example of bees, who 'neither approach all flowers equally, nor try to carry away those they choose entire, but take only what is suitable for their work and leave the rest untouched'.

Appropriately enough, Basil's very example was a traditional one which had been developed at some length by Seneca (in a moral context rather than a religious one). Maintaining the argument but changing the metaphor, Jerome claimed that Christians could use the classics as the Israelites had used their pagan prisoners, shaving their heads and paring their nails. In his treatise *On Christian Doctrine* (Book 2, chapter 40), Augustine referred to the 'spoils of the Egyptians', interpreting the biblical description of the people of Israel appropriating the treasure of the Egyptians before their exodus to refer to classical culture. Petrarch cited this passage in defence of the study of the classics in the treatise *On his own Ignorance*, writing that 'Augustine filled his pockets and his lap with the gold and silver of the Egyptians.'

The Fathers offered more than simply an arsenal of arguments against detractors of the ancients. To the humanists they looked like comrades, separated by a thousand years but similar in spirit. After all, Lactantius and Augustine were at one time teachers of rhetoric. No wonder then that Poggio studied Jerome and Augustine, that Nicolo Niccoli owned about fifty manuscripts of the Greek Fathers, or that the monk Ambrogio Traversari, a member of Bruni's circle, was said to have known Jerome's letters by heart.

People like Dominici who did not admire antiquity were often described by the humanists as 'barbarians', in the same class as the Goths and other peoples who had invaded and destroyed the Roman empire. Thus Bruni congratulated Poggio for liberating Quintilian from 'the dungeons of the barbarians', in other words, from the monks who owned the manuscript without appreciating its importance. Bruni also referred to British 'barbarism', by which he meant the philosophy of schoolmen such as John Duns Scotus. The idea of the 'schoolmen' was another invention of the humanists, who saw unity where medieval philosophers themselves had seen difference and conflict. In similar fashion, the humanists coined the terms 'dark ages' or 'Middle Ages' (*medium aevum*) to describe the period before the revival or 'renaissance' of the classical world which they were promoting. They were defining themselves against a Middle Ages which in a sense they had invented for the purpose. This sense of distance from medieval culture, however exaggerated, was an important feature of the group's mentality.[53]

The Visual Arts

Connections between humanism and the crafts may be illustrated by the reception of Vitruvius. As we have seen, Poggio
had discovered a manuscript of this ancient Roman treatise on
architecture in 1414. The treatise was at once a eulogy of architecture as a science based on mathematics, and an explanation
of the way in which to construct temples, theatres and other
buildings, the choice of site, the problems of acoustics and so on.
To interpret a text of this kind called for a combination of
the philological skills of the humanists with the technical
skills of builders (who were coming to be known, thanks to
Vitruvius, as 'architects'). Their practical knowledge was all the
more necessary because the manuscripts of Vitruvius lacked
illustrations.

Florence

In the workshop as well as the study, a revival of antiquity,
faintly perceptible in the fourteenth century, was becoming
more visible in Florence in the early years of the fifteenth. As in
the case of literature and learning, we find a small group of
creative individuals who knew one another well, in this case a
circle centred on the architect Filippo Brunelleschi and including
the humanist Leonbattista Alberti, the sculptors Donatello and
Ghiberti, and the painter Masaccio.

The contrast between the Gothic tradition and the buildings
designed by Brunelleschi – the Foundling Hospital (Ospedale
degli Innocenti), the Pazzi Chapel, and the churches of San
Lorenzo and Santo Spirito – now leaps to the eye. Semicircular
arches replace pointed ones, windows and doors have flat
instead of arched tops, spaces are left empty rather than filled
with decoration. Churches resemble classical temples – or the
early Christian churches which followed the model of temples.
Simplicity and purity are the keynotes of the architecture of
Brunelleschi and his followers, perhaps in reaction against the
luxuriant detail of late Gothic.

In his own day, Brunelleschi was admired more as an
'inventor' (as his epitaph describes him) than as an artist. He was
viewed by his friend, the humanist Alberti, not as the creator of

a new style but as a brilliant technician who had solved the problem of designing the dome of the cathedral of Florence, one of the largest masonry domes ever constructed, 'so ample', in Alberti's words, 'as to cover the whole Tuscan people with its shadow'. All the same, there is evidence of increasing interest in architecture 'in the ancient manner (*alla antica*)'. The phrase was used in Brunelleschi's own time to refer to flat-topped doors and windows, but it widened its meaning in a life of the architect written in the next generation, in which the anonymous author noted how Brunelleschi studied the remains of Roman architecture and learned to distinguish the Doric, Ionic and Corinthian styles.

Brunelleschi was also inspired by buildings of the twelfth century (notably the Florentine Baptistery) and even by works of the fourteenth century. He seems to have thought the Baptistery was ancient Roman, just as Poggio thought that the writing of the scribes of Charlemagne's time was ancient Roman.[54] In any case, Brunelleschi was concerned with principles rather than rules in the strict sense, in other words, with the spirit rather than the letter of antiquity. In similar fashion, Alberti saw the principles of classical architecture in a Gothic structure such as Florence cathedral. He too followed medieval as well as classical models in the buildings he designed. In short, the situation was a fluid one in which Gothic and classical were not yet viewed as alternative or antithetical styles.[55]

In the prologue to his famous treatise on painting, Alberti addressed Brunelleschi and spoke of 'our close friend Donato the sculptor'. According to the fifteenth-century biography of Brunelleschi, Donatello was with him in Rome, digging in the ruins with such assiduity that they were nicknamed 'treasure hunters' (*quelli del tesoro*). Donatello's interest in ancient Roman sculpture is evident in his portrait busts, reliefs, in his David (the first nude figure since antiquity) and in the famous equestrian statue of the professional soldier 'Gattamelata', still visible in Padua. Like Brunelleschi's dome, Donatello's statue was a successful solution to a technical problem, that of supporting the weight of both horse and rider on the four bronze legs.

In painting, Masaccio, despite his tragically early death, was the equivalent of his friends Brunelleschi and Donatello. His fresco of the Trinity showed that he had learned the rules of perspective, while the monumental style of his *Tribute Money* is reminiscent of Giotto. Later in the century the Florentine humanist Cristoforo Landino described his style as 'pure without ornament (*puro senza ornato*)', a phrase which might have been used of Brunelleschi and which parallels the concern for pure Latin expressed by Leonardo Bruni and his circle. Masaccio was also praised by Landino for his skilful 'imitation of reality' (*imitazione del vero*).

Landino's eulogy of Masaccio is a reminder of the links between humanism and the visual arts or crafts in Florence at this time. Brunelleschi's circle of friends included Niccoli, Poggio and Traversari, as well as Alberti, who claimed that some of the artists of his time were equals of the ancients and drew on Cicero's treatises on behaviour and rhetoric in order to discuss decorum, grace and variety in painting the architecture.[56] Long despised by intellectuals because they required manual labour, the crafts, or some of them, were rising in status at this time.

The 'civic humanism' discussed earlier has its parallel in the arts. Public patronage (by the guilds, for example) was important in early fifteenth-century Florence, while art gave expression to civic patriotism. Donatello's St George, his David and his Judith have all been read in this way as symbols of Florence, while the dragon, Goliath and Holofernes symbolize the enemies of the Florentine republic. The most famous works of the early fifteenth century were public buildings like the Foundling Hospital or paintings in public spaces like Masaccio's *Tribute Money* in the church of the Carmine, visible to everyone.[57]

Civic values and themes were much less visible in later fifteenth-century Florence during the sixty years of Medici rule, 1434–94. Where Leonardo Bruni and his friends had praised the active life, the new generation of Florentine scholars in the circle of Cosimo de'Medici and his grandson Lorenzo the Magnificent stressed contemplation and the study of esoteric wisdom. Their favourite philosopher was Plato, in whose honour they founded an 'academy' or discussion group in the 1460s.

Three late fifteenth-century humanists who lived in Florence may be taken to illustrate this trend: Cristoforo Landino, Marsilio Ficino and Angelo Poliziano. Landino, whose praise of

Masaccio was quoted above, is best known for his commentaries on Dante and Virgil. He presented Virgil as a Platonist whose poetry was full of 'mysteries' and 'the deepest secrets of philosophy'. Landino's pupil Marsilio Ficino called himself a 'platonic philosopher' and Plato a theologian, a Greek-speaking Moses.[58] He believed that an 'ancient theology' (*prisca theologia*), a set of secret teachings which anticipated Christian doctrines, could be found in the writings of Pythagoras, Plato and the ancient Egyptian sage Thoth, otherwise known as Hermes Trismegistus.[59] Ficino also claimed that poets (Orpheus, for example) were prophets, who went into ecstasy and were inspired by God to utter truths 'which afterwards, when their fury has lessened, they do not well understand themselves'.

Another member of Ficino's circle in Florence was Giovanni Pico, lord of Mirandola (a town near Modena). He too was interested in occult knowledge, shared by the initiated but hidden from the people. Where Landino offered an allegorical interpretation of Virgil's *Aeneid*, Pico claimed that Homer's *Odyssey* had a hidden philosophical meaning. Today, he is best-known for his *Oration on the Dignity of Man*, the most eloquent of the Italian humanist treatises on the subject, blending the Bible with Plato to produce a creation myth in which God tells Adam that he is free 'to fashion yourself into whatever shape you prefer'. Pico's intellectual ambition is revealed by the 900 theses which he proposed to defend in public debate in Rome in 1486, and which drew not only on Greek and Roman but also on Jewish and what he believed to be Egyptian and Persian traditions, all of which he claimed could be reconciled with one another once their mysteries were understood.[60]

As for Poliziano, he was equally remarkable as a poet, in Latin and Italian, and as a scholar, with a remarkable gift for textual criticism. His *Miscellanea* (1489), a collection of studies on classical literature, are virtuoso pieces of philology, whether they focus on texts (and their corruptions in the course of transmission) or their historical contexts.[61] Where Bruni had been concerned to tell his fellow-citizens about Greek and Roman culture because he believed classical examples to be relevant to his day, Poliziano pursued scholarship for its own sake and wrote essentially for fellow-scholars.

In short, the Florentine 'Neoplatonic' movement, as scholars now call it, was concerned with esoteric knowledge for small groups of initiates. These developments coincided with a shift from public to private art. In contrast to the early part of the century, the most famous works were private commissions such as the Palazzo Medici or Botticelli's *Primavera*, a painting which was visible only to a few and – given its references to classical literature and philosophy – intelligible to even fewer.[62]

Rome, Naples and Milan

The first stage in the reception of the Renaissance was the spread of Florentine innovations to other parts of Italy. The reception was assisted by the 'cultural policies' of Cosimo and Lorenzo de' Medici, who made efforts to place Florentine artists at the courts of Rome, Naples, Mantua, Ferrara and elsewhere.[63] However, it is important to avoid an exclusively 'Florentinocentric' interpretation of the movement which denies innovation to the inhabitants of other regions.

For example, the leading humanists of the early fifteenth century included the Venetian patrician Francesco Barbaro; Pietro Paolo Vergerio, who came from Capodistria, in the extreme north-east of Italy; and Antonio Loschi, who came from Vicenza. For all three men their Florentine years in the circle of Salutati and Bruni were important, but they were already humanists in their interest before they visited Florence. The discovery of ancient manuscripts was not a monopoly of Tuscan scholars. In Lodi, near Milan, for instance, the local bishop discovered Cicero's writings on rhetoric. The Sicilian humanist Giovanni Aurispa brought about 200 manuscripts from Constantinople to Italy in 1420. We should therefore look in turn to Rome, Naples, Milan, the small courts of the north such as Ferrara and Mantua, and finally at Venice.

For a few years at least, in the middle of the fifteenth century, Rome was a more important centre of humanism than Florence.[64] Two humanists became popes in the mid-fifteenth century, Nicholas V and Pius II. Nicholas commissioned a series of translations of Greek classics into Latin, asking Poggio, who had learned Greek at last, to translate Xenophon, and the Roman humanist Lorenzo Valla to translate Thucydides. Nicholas also planned the rebuilding of Rome, and it was to him that Alberti presented his treatise on architecture. The papal chancery was a much larger enterprise than the chancery of the Florentine republic and offered employment to a group of distinguished humanists, allowing scholars from different parts of Italy to meet. Bruni had worked there between 1405 and 1415. Poggio, who also worked in the chancery, spent most of his life in Rome (hence he wrote so many letters to his friend Niccoli in Florence).

So did the scholar Flavio Biondo, from Forlì, whose work in papal service allowed him sufficient leisure to write a number of books. In one of them, *Rome Restored*, Biondo described and evoked the buildings of the ancient city, its temples, theatres, baths, gates, obelisks and so on. In the sequel, *Italy Illustrated*, he extended the approach to the whole of Italy, divided into its fourteen ancient regions. *Italy Illustrated*, completed in 1453, was an exemplary study of what was known as 'chorography', a study of local history, including local worthies, but paying particular attention to material culture, to churches, squares, bridges and so on.[65]

Only one leading humanist was born and educated in Rome: Lorenzo Valla, who also taught at the university there, where his pupils included Pomponio Leto, later a lecturer at the same institution (figure 2). Valla might be described as the enfant terrible of humanism, notorious for his mordancy even in that age of sharp scholarly tongues. He offended philosophers for criticizing Aristotle and the jargon of the schoolmen (to which he preferred ordinary language), lawyers for having dared reject the authority of Bartolus (a fourteenth-century Italian jurist) and rhetoricians (including Poggio) for preferring Quintilian to Cicero. Valla's hypersensitivity to language made him, like Petrarch, an effective textual critic of Livy. In the preface to his Latin grammar, the 'Elegances' (*Elegantiae*), Valla claimed that good Latin flourished along with the Roman empire and also declined along with it as a result of the barbarian invasions. 'Not only has no one spoken Latin correctly for many centuries, but no one has even understood it properly when reading it . . . as if, after the fall of the Roman Empire, it was not fitting for the Roman language to be spoken or to be understood.'

It was his awareness of the changes in Latin over the centuries

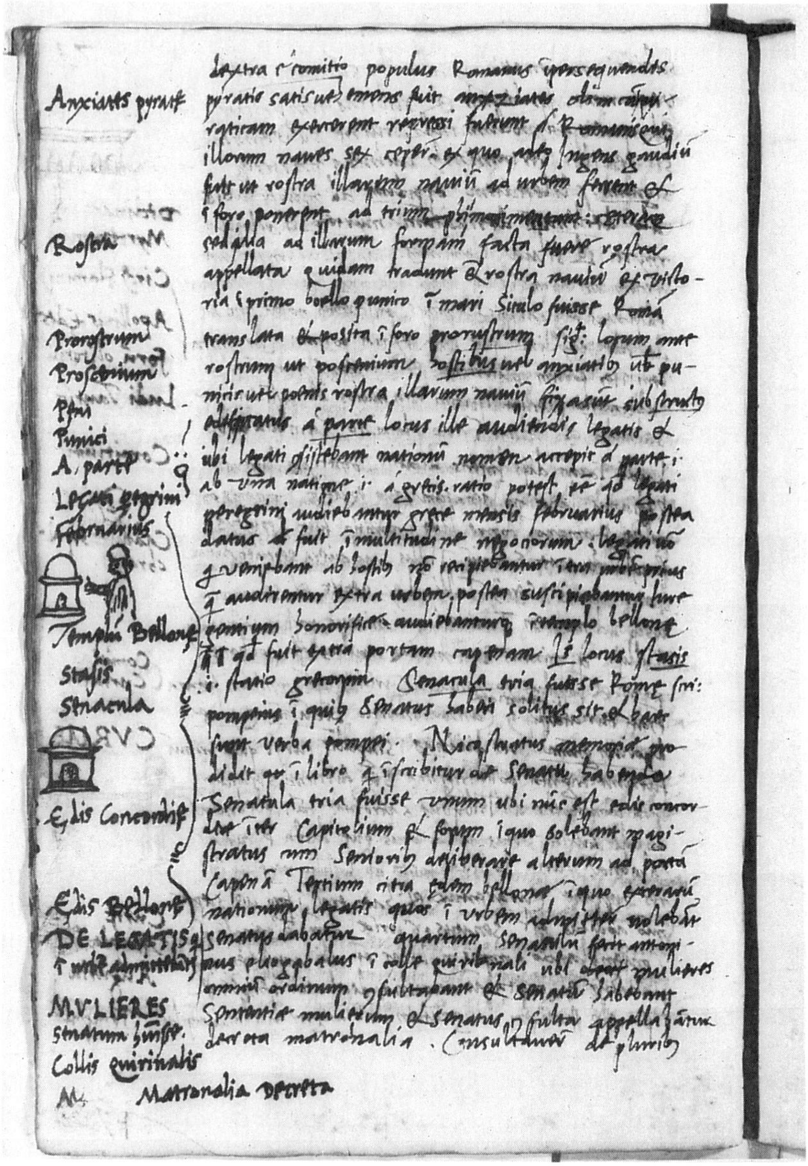

Figure 2   Sketch of teacher in the margin of a notebook of a pupil of
Pomponio Leto (Biblioteca Apostolica Vaticana).

that allowed Valla to see that the famous 'Donation of Constantine', a document according to which the emperor, following his conversion to Christianity, bestowed on the pope the lands later known as the states of the Church, was a forgery written centuries after Constantine's death. Valla was also aware that the ancient Roman legal texts had been corrupted in the course of their transmission over the centuries and offered suggestions for their emendation, claiming that the lawyers of his day did not understand ancient Roman institutions. The constructive side of Valla's philology may be seen in his *Annotations on the New Testament*, dedicated to Pope Nicholas V, in which he clarified the meaning of certain passages thanks to his knowledge of Greek.[66]

Several of Valla's important works were not written in Rome but in Naples, when he was at the court of Alfonso of Aragon in the 1430s and 1440s, employed as a royal secretary. Alfonso was interested in classical antiquity. He had Livy's history of Rome read to him and he collected Roman coins (an ivory box containing the coins of Augustus used to accompany the king on his travels). Alfonso invited to his court a group of talented humanists who competed with one another for his attention. The Sicilian Antonio Beccadelli, for instance, was given 1,000 ducats for compiling a collection of anecdotes (on the model of Xenophon's anecdotes of Socrates), which presented Alfonso as a perfect prince. The Ligurian Bartolomeo Fazio was appointed court historian and wrote a life of the king, as well as a collection of the biographies of the illustrious men of his time. It is interesting to see who qualified as illustrious. Side by side with princes and soldiers we find humanists such as Leonardo Bruni and artists such as Donatello.

Milan was another important centre of humanism in the fifteenth century. Antonio Loschi, for example, chancellor of Milan, wrote against Florence and was the object of invectives by Salutati and Bruni. Piero Candido Decembrio wrote an encomium of Milan in the manner of – and in reply to – Bruni's encomium of Florence. The chancery of Milan under the Visconti and Sforza was a centre of humanist culture. In a letter of 1488, the humanist Jacopo Antiquario recorded finding 'a number of the young clerks neglecting their prince's business, and lost in the study of a book', Poliziano's *Miscellanea*.

The arts too were reformed. For example, the Florentine architect Antonio Avellino, known as 'Filarete', the Greek for 'lover of virtue', arrived in Milan in 1451 and designed the Ospedale Maggiore, a building which – like Brunelleschi's Foundling Hospital in Florence – symbolized a break with the past. Filarete praised Brunelleschi for reviving 'the ancient style of building' and urged his colleagues to abandon what he called 'the modern style' (in other words, Gothic), which the barbarians had introduced to Italy. 'The man who follows the ancient practice in architecture,' he wrote, 'does exactly the same thing as a man of letters who strives to reproduce the classical style of Cicero and Virgil.' Filarete, like his successor Leonardo da Vinci, who arrived in Milan in the 1480s, illustrates the importance of a diaspora of Florentine artists in spreading the classical style throughout Italy. The Colleoni chapel in Bergamo, on the other hand, designed in the 1470s by a Lombard artist, Giovanni Antonio Amadeo, illustrates the importance of local ecotypes. The chapel is classical in many of its details, inspired by Filarete and also, perhaps, by the antiquarian researches of north Italian humanists. However, it could scarcely be more different from the Florentine plain style, every available space being filled with putti, medallions with Roman emperor's heads, and other classical decorative formulae such as acanthus leaves, garlands, urns, and trophies of ancient armour and weapons.[67]

Ferrara, Mantua, Venice

Some of the examples cited in the last section suggest that the new forms of art and literature appealed to princes and republics alike by associating their regimes with the prestige of ancient Rome. All the same, some rulers seem to have been interested in these things at least in part for their own sake, their enthusiasm for antiquity having been kindled when they were still young.

The importance of humanist schools is most obvious in two small courts, Ferrara and Mantua. Guarino of Verona, who had studied in Constantinople, was invited to establish a school at Ferrara in 1429, primarily for the Este family, rulers of the city. Guarino tried to train character as well as intellect with the help of Cicero's moral treatise *De officiis* and of Plutarch. One of his former pupils, Vittorino da Feltre, had already been invited to

Mantua by the ruling family of the Gonzaga in 1423. Vittorino, who taught there for over twenty years, was concerned, like Guarino, with the behaviour as well as knowledge. He too used Plutarch in class. He encouraged his pupils to play games and he tried to make the process of learning as enjoyable as possible. A former student remembered that Vittorino 'gave his pupils a great deal of practice in declamation, pleading imaginary causes in public as if before the people or the senate'.

Thanks to Guarino and Vittorino, the next generation of princes were well acquainted with humanism: Leonello and Borso d'Este in Ferrara, Ludovico Gonzaga in Mantua, and Vittorino's ex-pupil Federico da Montefeltro in Urbino. If their education did not affect the political behaviour of these princes, at least it affected their attitude to the arts. Leonello, for example, wrote poems and collected manuscripts of the classics. Ludovico Gonzaga commissioned Alberti to design a church in Mantua, and invited Andrea Mantegna to be his court painter.

As for Federico of Urbino, he was a professional soldier who tried to combine arms with letters. To symbolize the combination, a portrait of Federigo shows him in armour reading a book. His library of manuscripts was famous in its day. An impression of the breadth of his intellectual interests may be derived from the frieze of figures of illustrious men he commissioned for his study. There were twenty-eight figures, of whom ten were ancients (Plato and Aristotle, Cicero and Seneca, Homer and Virgil, as might have been expected, but also Euclid, Hippocrates, Ptolemy and Solon, representing mathematics, medicine, cosmology and law). Four of the illustrious men were Fathers of the Church, while the moderns included Dante, Petrarch and the duke's old teacher, Vittorino da Feltre. Also among the moderns were the scholastic philosophers Thomas Aquinas and Duns Scotus, a vivid reminder that the contempt for the schoolmen expressed by Petrarch, Bruni and Valla was not universal among humanists.

A familiar figure at these small courts was Pisanello, who worked for Ludovico Gonzaga and Leonello d'Este, as well as Alfonso of Aragon. Pisanello was famous in humanist circles. An epigram by a humanist from Urbino compared him to the ancient Greek sculptors Phidias and Praxiteles. Pisanello's most striking innovation was his series of medals, following the model of ancient Roman coins. Like a coin, the medal was 'struck' by using a mould. What was new was the idea of using the medium to produce personalized images which the owner could present to friends, relatives or clients. There was normally a profile portrait on one side and a symbolic image or device on the other, together with an inscription which allowed the device to be decoded by the viewer.

Pisanello offers a remarkable example of what linguists call 'code-switching', since he alternated between Renaissance and Gothic styles according to the patron and the occasion. A room he frescoed at Mantua in the 1440s illustrated the adventures of knights at the court of King Arthur and may have been furnished with a Round Table. The continuing enthusiasm for chivalry at Italian courts is also revealed by the practice of jousting, by the commissioning of manuscripts of romances of chivalry, and by the names of a number of fifteenth-century princes and princesses such as Galeazzo (Galahad), Isotta (Iseult), Leonello (Lionel) and so on. This enthusiasm coexisted with the passion of some of the same princes for manuscripts of Plutarch, for Roman coins, or for the paintings of Piero or Mantegna.[68]

For more than forty years, Andrea Mantegna was court painter to the Gonzagas in Mantua. His work is impressive for its mastery of perspective and for its monumental qualities, but Mantegna also stands out for his combination of artistic with humanist interests. He was a friend of scholars and shared their enthusiasm for Roman antiquities. This enthusiasm is apparent in his work, above all in the series of nine large canvases known as the *Triumphs of Caesar*. His concern for the precise details of the armour and weapons of Roman soldiers illustrates Mantegna's awareness of anachronism and his careful study of ancient coins and of sculpture such as the reliefs on Trajan's Column in Rome.[69]

Venice has been left to the last because the republic, famous for its stability, was relatively slow to accept change. The Venetian patricians Francesco Barbaro, Ermolao Barbaro the elder and Leonardo Giustinian were all ex-pupils of Guarino of Verona and their humanist interests continued into adult life. Francesco, for instance, combined the active life of diplomacy and public office with book-hunting and writing a treatise on marriage. However, it was only in the later fifteenth century that

Venetians began to make a significant contribution to the *studia humanitatis*. Ermolao Barbaro the younger, for example, was a friend of Poliziano and, like him, a leading textual critic. At the university of Padua he lectured on Aristotle's *Ethics* and *Politics*, returning to the original Greek (as Leonardo Bruni had done in his translations a generation earlier), and attempting to establish what Aristotle had meant by stripping the text of layers of commentary by medieval and Arab philosophers.[70]

In the visual arts too the Venetians resisted the new style for a time, whether from conservatism or because of the alternatives available in that cosmopolitan city. It was in the 1470s that the Bellini brothers, for instance, Gentile and Giovanni, developed their distinctive pictorial style. In the case of Gentile, one of the marks of that style was an interest in the Middle East, encouraged by a visit to Istanbul to paint a portrait of the sultan. It may not be coincidence that at about the time of Bellini's return to Venice, craftsmen began to make use of the decorative formulae known as 'arabesques'. It was from Venice and probably from Spain as well that these formulae spread to other parts of Europe.[71]

It was also in the late fifteenth century that a cluster of buildings *all' antica* (including the church of Santa Maria Formosa), were erected in the city, designed by Mauro Coducci, and all the more impressive because of the dazzling white of the Istrian stone. Some of the churches, such as San Giovanni Grisostomo, followed Byzantine plans. It has therefore been argued that architecture in Venice, which had long had close links with Constantinople, was going through a Byzantine revival, rejecting not only the Gothic style but also the Florentine alternative.[72]

Both cities and courts have been singled out by different historians as environments favourable to the new trends in art and humanism. To decide which milieu was the more favourable is less useful than emphasizing the complementarity of their functions. The inhabitants of city-republics found it easier to identify themselves with republican Romans. Craft-industrial cities, especially Florence, were centres for training artists and establishing what might be called a tradition of innovation. Courts on the other hand were environments to which, if the ruler was interested, gifted people could be attracted from different places.[73]

In the fifteenth century, if not later, courts seem to have offered a more favourable environment than cities for women interested in learning and the arts. It is true that in Florence Alessandra Scala, daughter of the humanist Bartolomeo, was able to study classical literature, like her Venetian equivalent Costanza Barbaro, daughter of the humanist Francesco. Another Venetian, Cassandra Fedele, gave public orations before the doge and the university of Padua. In Verona, the noblewoman Isotta Nogarola had humanist interests. However, these women did not find it easy to be accepted by male humanists.[74]

In courts, on the other hand, women could play roles other than wives and mothers and it mattered less whether male humanists accepted them or not. Cecilia Gonzaga, daughter of Ludovico, the ruler of Mantua, was educated by Vittorino da Feltre and commissioned a medal from Pisanello. Battista de Montefeltro (Federico's aunt), for whom Bruni wrote *De studiis*, came from the ruling family of Urbino. She wrote books and made a Latin speech when the emperor visited the court. Still better-known are the cultural interests of Isabella d'Este (see below, pp. 79–80). Similar opportunities were offered in the courts of other parts of Europe, to be discussed in the following chapter.

2

Reception and Resistance

One more item remains to be added to the list of discoveries in the previous chapter: the discovery of the new Italian culture by the rest of Europe. This discovery was a gradual one.

In the fourteen and fifteenth centuries, European culture was essentially medieval. To return to the three main features described in chapter 1: Gothic art continued to flourish in many regions as if Brunelleschi had never existed. Far from having come to a halt, it was developing new forms such as the 'flamboyant' and 'perpendicular' styles in architecture. Scholastic philosophy too continued to develop in new directions in the age of Duns Scotus and William of Ockham. The values of chivalry were expressed in new romances such as the Catalan *Tirant lo Blanc* and the English *Morte d'Arthur*, both of which were written in the 1460s, in other words, about the time that Mantegna went to Mantua and decades later than the work of Italian humanists such as Alberti, Poggio and Pius II, himself the author of a work of prose fiction, 'The Tale of Two Lovers' (*De duobus amantibus*).

The Italian cultural world described by Jacob Burckhardt thus coexisted with the Franco-Flemish world evoked by the Dutch historian Johan Huizinga.[75] What did the latter world have to do with the Renaissance? In his famous book on the *Autumn of the Middle Ages* (1919), Huizinga was at once following Burckhardt, competing with him and diverging from him. He followed Burckhardt in producing a vividly imagined piece of cultural history in which the social life of the period was viewed through the spectacles of its art and literature. He placed similar emphasis on social rivalries and artistic realism, but argued that Italians were not pioneers in these developments. Huizinga also diverged from Burckhardt in stressing continuity rather than change, the elaboration of medieval traditions such as Gothic and chivalry rather than the pursuit of innovation. He chose his metaphor of the 'autumn' of the Middle Ages with care in order to convey a sense of both ripeness and decline.

One Renaissance or Two?

Some recent historians are more impressed than Huizinga was by the cultural innovations associated with the court of Burgundy, which was a cultural model for much of Europe in the fifteenth century. Oil-painting, for example, like the use of canvas instead of wood, was a fifteenth-century Flemish development, attributed to Jan van Eyck, a leading painter at the Burgundian court.[76] In music in particular, there was a series of important and self-conscious innovations in France and Flanders. From the 1320s on, contemporaries began to refer to the 'new art' of music (*ars nova*) or the 'new school' or the 'moderns'. Even the idea of a 'renaissance' can be found in the writings of the Flemish composer Johannes de Tinctoris, describing the style of composers such as Guillaume Dufay. Other major composers in the polyphonic style of the time were Johannes Ockeghem, Heinrich Isaak and Josquin des Pres.

For these reasons, some scholars speak of 'two Renaissances' in the fifteenth century, with their respective centres in northern Italy and the southern Netherlands, the most urbanized regions in Europe at this time.[77]

As in the case of Italy, the Franco-Flemish movement was influential abroad. In 1431, for instance, the ruler Alfonso of Aragon (not yet the ruler of Naples) sent a painter from Valencia, Luis Dalmau, to Flanders in order to study with van Eyck. The English King Edward IV, who had lived in exile in Bruges before succeeding to the throne, owned an extensive library of manuscripts, the work of Flemish scribes and illuminators. Henry VII of England was also a patron of French and

Flemish artists and writers. Indeed, it has been argued that the English Renaissance owed more to Burgundy than it did to Italy.[78] A more complex example of cultural exchange is that of the painter Michel Sittow, who was born in Reval (Tallinn), trained in Bruges and was active at the courts of Isabella of Castille and Christian II of Denmark, whose portrait he painted.

The idea of two parallel urban renaissances in the north and the south is an illuminating one, provided that we remember two points. In the first place, unlike the circle of innovators in early fifteenth-century Florence, the Burgundian artists and writers did not make any sharp break with what went before them. In that sense Huizinga was right to see change in autumnal terms. Claus Sluter, for instance, a northern Netherlander who made the tomb of Duke Philip the Bold of Burgundy, was one of the great sculptors of his day. Like Donatello (a few years his junior), Sluter was and is memorable for the individuality of his figures and the expression of their emotions. Unlike Donatello, however, he was not inspired by classical statues and for this reason his work looks more traditional.[79]

A similar point might be made about historical writing. The work of Georges Chastellain, who was appointed official chronicler to Philip the Good of Burgundy in 1455, grows out of the tradition of the secular chronicle as exemplified by (say) Jean Froissart, who was writing a century earlier. Chastellain concentrates on narrative and on the vivid description of events, especially ceremonies, rather than offering an analysis of intentions or consequences in the manner of Leonardo Bruni or his ancient models (see above, p. 29). In his memoirs, written in the 1480s and 1490s, the diplomat Philippe de Commynes offered penetrating observations on the political world of his time. His description of the battle of Montlhéry, in which he took part in 1465, is remarkable in two ways. The vividly realistic detail, as in the scene of the archers drinking wine with their boots off before the battle, is reminiscent of Froissart or the Flemish paintings of the period. The general picture of inglorious confusion, on the other hand, may remind a modern reader of Stendhal's Waterloo or Tolstoy's Borodino. The thought of Commynes, like his fascination with political trickery, is sometimes reminiscent of his younger contemporary Machiavelli, and it is not surprising to discover that his work was appreciated in the sixteenth century, when it was translated into Latin, Italian and English. However, the reflections of Commynes lack Machiavelli's constant reference to ancient Rome. His Italian friend Francesco Gaddi moved in the circle of Ficino and Poliziano, but Commynes shows no awareness of Italian humanism.[80]

The second and in some ways opposite qualification to the idea of the two renaissances is that their independence from each other should not be overemphasized. The concern for the revival of the classical tradition was not confined to Italy even in the fourteenth century, as the rise of translations testifies. For example, in 1373 the duc de Bourbon commissioned a translation of Cicero's *Amicitia* into French. Charles the Bold, Duke of Burgundy, was educated by a tutor with humanist interests, who commissioned a scribe in Bruges to copy a manuscript of Leonardo Bruni (together with one of the ancient historian Sallust). Charles himself used to listen to readings from Livy, like his contemporary Alfonso of Aragon. He had inherited a good library which included Cicero, Livy, Ovid, Seneca and other classical authors. A Portuguese at his court, Vasco de Lucena, dedicated to the duke a translation into French of Xenophon's *Education of Cyrus* (a version made not from the original Greek but from the Latin translation by Poggio).[81]

In education the Brethren of Common Life, a group of laity formed in the fourteenth century and living in a community like monks, established a network of schools in the cities of the Netherlands, including Gouda, Zwolle, Deventer and Liège. In their rejection of scholasticism and their concern with Latin literature, the leaders of the Brethren resemble Italian humanists. For that reason it is no surprise that the most famous humanist of all should have been one of their ex-pupils, Erasmus.[82]

In short, a concern with the classical tradition was no Italian monopoly in the fifteenth century, although it was in Italy that this tradition affected the arts, especially the visual arts, most deeply. It is perhaps in this context that we should place another development on the periphery of Europe, the so-called 'Romanesque revival' in fifteenth-century Scotland, the return to cylindrical columns and round-headed windows and doorways in Aberdeen and Dunkeld cathedrals.[83] It may be no more than coincidence that the processional doorway at Melrose Abbey dates from the 1420s, when Brunelleschi was engaged in reforming architecture by returning to Italian Romanesque models which he thought were classical ones. Or were the Scots thinking in the same way?

Whether or not we speak of two renaissances, it is important to remember the cultural exchanges between the north, especially the Netherlands, and the south, especially Italy.[84] Flemish composers, notably Heinrich Isaak and Josquin des Prez (both of whom were employed at the court of Ferrara) and Adriaan Willaert (who worked in Venice) had a great reputation in Italy. When Tinctoris wrote about the Flemish musical renaissance, in 1477, he was living in Naples, so that it may have been in Italy that he became familiar with the metaphor of rebirth.

As for the visual arts, in 1460 the princess Bianca Sforza of Milan sent her painter Zanetto Bugatto to the Netherlands to be trained by Rogier van der Weyden. When a humanist at the court of Alfonso of Aragon, Bartolomeo Fazio (see above, p. 41), wrote a series of biographies of the illustrious men of his time, Jan van Eyck and Rogier van de Weyden were among them. The art of painting on canvas was introduced to Italy from the Netherlands in the 1470s. In the same decade, Justus of Ghent was working at the court of Federico da Montefeltro at Urbino. The altarpiece of the *Adoration* by another master from the Netherlands, Hugo van der Goes, was placed in the Portinari chapel in Florence in 1483.

Cultural contacts between Italian humanists and other Europeans, in person or through their books, were also becoming increasingly frequent. Petrarch visited Paris, Cologne and Prague. The English poet and diplomat Geoffrey Chaucer visited Italy in 1373, and his subsequent poetry reveals his interest in the work of Petrarch and Boccaccio. The French scholar Laurent de Premierfait translated Boccaccio as well as Cicero.

In short, we must not assume that Italy was the centre of cultural innovation in fifteenth-century Europe and that the rest of the continent was mere periphery. On the other hand, it is impossible to ignore the importance of the spread of ideas and cultural forms from Florence, Rome, Venice, Milan and other parts of Italy to other parts of Europe. Where the spread of ancient Greek and Roman ideas and forms were concerned, the role of Italians was particularly important. The twin topics of classical revival and of European responses to Italian culture (or cultures) will be central in the pages which follow.

Early Responses

Scholars from Spain, or more exactly from Aragon and Catalonia, were among the first to show an interest in both classical and Italian culture – another qualification to the idea of the two renaissances. Joan Fernàndez de Herèdia, for instance, the Aragonese Master of the Knights of St John, commissioned translations of Thucydides and Plutarch (texts which had only recently been discovered in Western Europe). His years in Rhodes and other parts of the eastern Mediterranean had awakened Herèdia's interest in Greek culture. It was apparently via his Aragonese version (made by a Spanish bishop in Rhodes) of a modern Greek version (made by a notary from Salonika) that a text of Plutarch reached Italy at the end of the fourteenth century. It was by such indirect routes that the classics travelled in the early Renaissance.[85]

At much the same time, the majordomo to King Joan I of Aragon translated Seneca into Catalan. King Joan himself was a book collector who took pleasure in reading 'the celebrated histories of the Romans and the Greeks', including Livy and Plutarch. He exchanged letters about books with Herèdia and with Giangaleazzo Visconti, Duke of Milan. The Catalan writer Bernat Metge admired both the letters of Petrarch and his *Secretum*. Metge's most famous work, *Lo Somni* ('The Dream') written in 1398, draws on Petrarch and Boccaccio as well as Cicero.[86]

The importance of fourteenth-century Avignon as a mediator between Italy and the rest of Europe also deserves emphasis. Thanks to the presence of the pope and his court between 1309 and 1377, Avignon became a major city, as large as Florence, and a site of international contacts and cultural innovations.[87] Petrarch grew up in Avignon. The Sienese painter Simone Martini worked in Avignon from 1339 onwards. Herèdia lived there for some years. It was in Avignon in 1395 that Metge studied the work of Petrarch and Boccaccio. The cultural role of Avignon only declined around 1400, after the papacy had been re-established in Rome.

From about 1380 onwards, Paris too was a centre of interest in classical antiquity, Italian culture and 'liberal studies' (*studia liberalia*), at least among a small group which included Jean Gerson, Nicolas de Clamanges and Jean de Montreuil. The surviving evidence about this circle allows a case-study to be made of the reception of the Renaissance in the north.[88]

Nicolas de Clamanges, a former secretary in the papal chancery at Avignon, wrote of literary studies in France as 'buried' until they were 'reborn' in his day. He criticized Petrarch for having dared to say that there were no poets or orators to be found outside Italy, but he learned from Petrarch as he did from Cicero and Quintilian in matters of style. He was particularly interested in Cicero's speeches. Clamanges's friend Gerson offered a critique of scholasticism analogous to that made by Petrarch, attacking the Scotists for their oversubtle distinctions.[89]

Another friend of Clamanges, Jean de Montreuil, admired Petrarch, 'the celebrated moral philosopher', as he called him, studied the Latin writings of Boccaccio (at least his *Genealogy of the Gods*) and corresponded with Salutati, 'most famous of teachers', and with Loschi. Like the Italian humanists, Montreuil searched for and studied manuscripts of Cicero and other classics. Even his handwriting was somewhat italianate. He once compared a statue of the Virgin Mary to works by the Greek sculptors Praxiteles or Lysippus (names which he knew only from literary sources). Montreuil is also supposed to have had the laws of the Spartan ruler Lycurgus inscribed on his house. Together with his colleague Gonthier Col, with whom he discussed the relative merits of the active and contemplative lives, he made friends with a man of letters from Milan, Ambrogio de' Migli – until they quarrelled over Migli's criticisms of Cicero and Virgil.

Col and Montreuil were both employed as secretaries by the great patron Jean, duc de Berry, the brother of King Charles V and also of Philip the Bold of Burgundy. The duke also supported Premierfait when he was translating Boccaccio and encouraged the work of Christine de Pisan. He owned some 300 manuscripts, including works by Petrarch, Virgil, Livy and

Terence. Many of the manuscripts were illustrated, for their owner was an enthusiast for the visual arts. Jean loved buildings, tapestries, paintings, goldsmith's work, cameos, coins and medals. He maintained close contacts with Italian merchants and artists. The Italian architect Filarete praised the duke's taste and in particular one Roman cameo in his collection.[90]

In the duke's collection, works in what we call the 'Gothic' style could be found side by side with works *all'antica*. As in the case of Italian artists and patrons before the late fifteenth century, the duke does not seem to have seen these different styles as conflicting. In similar fashion Petrarch was often perceived by the French at this time as a traditional moralist rather than as a critic of late medieval culture.[91]

Contacts with Italy

In the thirty years from 1420 to 1450, contacts between Italian scholars and artists and other Europeans multiplied. Thanks to the Council of Basel, Poggio visited Switzerland and Germany, while Aeneas Sylvius went as far as Scotland. The painter Masolino worked in Hungary (not for a Hungarian patron but for the Italian soldier of fortune Pippo Spano). The humanist Guiniforte Barzizza went to Catalonia to serve Alfonso of Aragon in 1432, before the king conquered Naples. This was the beginning of a trend in which minor Italian humanists became relatively major figures abroad, moving from the periphery of the centre to the centre of the periphery.

There is also plenty of evidence for foreigners visiting Italy. Rogier van der Weyden was in Italy in 1450, for the papal jubilee. Other artists – the Frenchman Jean Fouquet (figure 3), the Fleming Justus of Ghent and the Spaniard Pedro Berruguete – seem to have gone there to work rather than to study, Fouquet in Rome and the other two in Urbino. Their visits reveal more about Italian interest in the north than the other way round. Scholars, on the other hand, went to Italy primarily to attend universities. They might have gone with the intention of studying traditional subjects such as canon law, but on arrival some of them at least made the acquaintance of humanists. In the 1430s the Polish cleric Gregory of Sanok went to Rome for

Figure 3   Jean Fouquet, *Self-portrait*, Musée du Louvre (Réunion des
Musées Nationaux/Louvre, Paris). An early self-portrait by a non-Italian
artist.

ecclesiastical reasons, discovered classical studies there and
encouraged them in Poland when he became archbishop of
Lwów (L'viv) in 1451. His country house became a centre
of humanism.

In the 1440s visitors to Italy included the German Albrecht
von Eyb, the Englishman Robert Fleming and the Hungarian
Janus Pannonius. Eyb, who studied at the universities of Pavia,
Padua and Bologna and was familiar with the work of Valla,
later wrote an encomium of the city of Bamberg, as Bruni had

done in the case of Florence and Decembrio in that of Milan. Fleming studied with Guarino, made friends with Platina, and became the first Englishman known to have learned Greek since the thirteenth-century scholars Robert Grosseteste and Roger Bacon. Janus Pannonius, another pupil of Guarino's, was one of the leading Latin poets of the fifteenth century.[92]

Visitors to Italy often returned home carrying manuscripts. Eyb, for instance, owed manuscripts of Petrarch and Poggio as well as some of the classics.[93] Gregory of Sanok owned a manuscript of Boccaccio's *Genealogy of the Gods* which had belonged to Gonthier Col. Robert Fleming gave some sixty books to Lincoln College, Oxford (which his uncle had founded), including not only classics (including a manuscript of Cicero's *On Duties* which he had copied himself), but also copies of works by Boccaccio, Bruni, Guarino and Valla.[94] A Florentine bookseller of this time, the last generation before printing, Vespasiano da Bisticci, occupied his retirement by writing biographies of the famous men of his day, many of them his customers. Among them were six foreigners who had lived in Italy and acquired fine libraries there. Two were Englishmen, William Grey, Bishop of Ely and John Tiptoft, Earl of Worcester; two were Hungarians, János Vitéz and his nephew Janus Pannonius; one was a Spaniard, Nuño de Guzmán, and one a Portuguese, a certain Velasco.

Some leading aristocrats imported books from Italy. Humfrey, Duke of Gloucester, for instance, the brother of Henry V of England, acquired copies of texts by Petrarch, Salutati, Bruni and Poggio, as well as Apuleius and Vitruvius (who does not seem to have made any impact on English architecture at this time). He gave his books to the University of Oxford. The Spaniard Inigo López de Mendoza, marquis of Santillana, a leading poet of his day in what was described as the 'Italian manner' (*itálico modo*), did not go to Italy himself but he was in touch with Bruni and other humanists and bought manuscripts in Florence via Nuño de Guzmán. His library included Greek classics – Homer, Plato, Polybius, Thucydides – as well as Latin ones and the works of Italians such as Petrarch, Boccaccio and Bruni. His son translated the *Iliad* (from Latin), while his friend Enrique de Villena translated the *Aeneid*. Thanks to Santillana, according to one contemporary, eloquence was brought from Italy to Spain (*trayda a nuestra Castilla*).[95]

Universities, Chanceries and Courts

From the middle of the fifteenth century, universities became important sites for the reception of ideas from Italy. Italian émigrés were sometimes employed as lecturers, as in the cases of Gregorio of Tifernate, Filippo Beroaldo and Fausto Andrelini, all of whom taught at the university of Paris. By this time local humanists were also active in a number of European universities. Gregory of Sanok lectured on Virgil at the university of Cracow. At Heidelberg, Peter Luder announced in 1456 that he would lecture on the *studia humanitatis*. Greek was taught at Paris in the 1470s and at Salamanca in the 1480s. Lectureships in poetry were founded at Leuven (Louvain) in 1477 and at Salamanca in 1484.

Other major sites of the reception of the Renaissance at this time were chanceries and courts. The significance of the Florentine chancery has already been discussed (see above, p. 27), and it was sometimes taken as a model. Petrarch is said to have advised the King of Hungary to keep fewer dogs and to employ someone in the chancery who could write good Latin. The second part of his advice at least was taken by some rulers outside Italy. In the chancery of Richard II of England, someone wrote on one of Salutati's official letters from Florence, 'Note this fine letter (*Nota hic bonam litteram*).'[96] The Catalan chancery under Pere the Ceremonious (father of Joan I) followed the Florentine model. The humanist Alfonso de Palencia, who had lived in Florence, was employed as Latin secretary to Enrique IV of Castille. János Vitéz, archbishop of Esztergom, who sent his nephew Janus Pannonius to study in Italy, introduced classical models into the royal chancery in Hungary.

Before the end of the fifteenth century, however, few rulers outside Italy took a serious interest in Renaissance art or humanism. One of them was René of Anjou, who was in Italy besieging Naples from 1438 to 1441. Like François I after him, he discovered Italian culture while he was on campaign, and became acquainted with Italian scholars and artists. René employed the italianized Croat sculptor Francesco Laurana, who struck medals for him in the style of Pisanello. His friend, the Venetian patrician Jacopo Marcello, presented him with a copy of a book by the ancient Greek geographer Strabo. His library also included works by Plato and Cicero, Herodotus and Livy, Boccaccio and Valla.[97]

Curiously enough, two of the rulers most interested in the new forms of culture were to be found on what might well be considered the periphery of Europe, Istanbul and Buda. Mehmed the Conqueror, the sultan who captured Constantinople, did not reject the classical tradition. The sultan used to listen to readings from classical texts by an Italian, Cyriac of Ancona. One of Mehmed's favourites was Livy, as in the cases of his contemporaries Alfonso of Aragon and Charles the Bold. Despite the official Muslim ban on representational art, the sultan invited Gentile Bellini to Istanbul to paint his portrait, as well as commissioning portraits by Turkish artists.[98] It is unlikely that Mehmed's interests had much resonance outside court circles, but in the early Renaissance this was generally the case in Western Europe and even in Italy itself.

Matthias Corvinus, King of Hungary, had been given a humanist education (by the Pole Gregory of Sanok) and developed into a book collector and a patron of learning. He invited Italian humanists to his court and asked one of them, Antonio Bonfini, to write a history of Hungary. Following the example of Livy, Bonfini called his history the *Decades*. Matthias built up a great library, acquiring books from Florence and confiscating the books of Janus Pannonius after the poet had conspired against him. He appointed an Italian scholar as his librarian. The king was interested in Neoplatonism and was in contact with Ficino.[99]

Matthias was also interested in Italian art, an interest encouraged by his Italian wife Beatrice of Aragon, whom he married in 1476. Beatrice, daughter of the ruler of Naples, had studied Cicero and Virgil and was interested in music (Tinctoris dedicated a text to her). At the Hungarian court she was surrounded by Italians who set the fashion in jewels, clothes, festivals and the arts. Matthias had already invited Aristotele Fioravanti of Bologna to Hungary in 1465, describing him as a 'singular architect' (*architectus singularis*), but after his

Figure 4   Gian Cristoforo Romano, portrait bust of King Matthias. (Castle
Museum, Budapest.) A Renaissance prince represented as a Roman
emperor.

marriage the king employed an increasing number of Italian
artists, including Verrocchio (the teacher of Leonardo da Vinci)
and Filippino Lippi. Some of his books were decorated by
Florentine illuminators. He commissioned busts of himself and
his wife by Italian sculptors such as Gian Cristoforo Romano,
who made him look like a Roman emperor (figure 4). Among
the texts in Matthias's library were the treatises on architecture
by Alberti and Filarete. He put some of their recommendations
into practice, enlarging his palaces of Buda and Visegrád and

visiting the sites to watch the work in progress. The style of these buildings was Tuscan.[100]

The Age of Incunabula

The humanist movement continued to spread beyond Italy in the late fifteenth century, rather than declining like the Carolingian or even the twelfth-century Renaissance. One reason for its success was that it was carried by the new medium of print. Print-making, which began in the early fifteenth century, a few years before the invention of movable type around 1450, involved leading artists in Florence and elsewhere, including Sandro Botticelli, who produced a series of woodcut illustrations for an edition of Dante's *Divine Comedy*. These illustrations were much better-known in the fifteenth century than the same artist's *Birth of Venus* and *Primavera*. Prints were relatively cheap to make and they enabled the work of their designers to reach relatively large numbers of people relatively quickly.

Invented (in all probability) in Germany by Johan Gutenberg, the printing press with movable type spread quickly through Europe. Printers reached Basel by 1466, Rome by 1467, Paris and Pilsen by 1468, Venice by 1469, Leuven, Valencia, Cracow and Buda by 1473, Westminster (distinct from the city of London) by 1476 and Prague by 1477. By 1500 presses had been established in about 250 cities. These presses were often founded by the countrymen of Johan Gutenberg. By 1500 the Germans had founded at least eighty-six presses outside the German-speaking world – thirty-seven cities in Italy, eighteen in the Iberian Peninsula, thirteen in France and seven in the Netherlands (not yet politically divided into north and south).[101] The first press in Italy, for example, was founded at Subiaco in 1465 by two Germans, Conrad Sweynheim and Arnold Pannartz. In Venice, the first printer was the German Johan von Speyer. In Buda Andreas Hess played an important role, in Seville Jacob Cromberger (who arrived in 1500) and so on.

The rapid multiplication of books after 1450 deserves to be emphasized. In Venice alone, where more books were printed than in any other city in Europe, 4,500 editions or about two and a half million copies seems a reasonable estimate. What was printed included many editions of the classics – Cicero, for example. His *De Officiis* was printed at Subiaco. In Paris he became fashionable in the 1470s. 'No one used to read Cicero day and night,' wrote the French scholar Guillaume Fichet, 'as many people do today.' In London, William Caxton printed Cicero's dialogue on friendship in 1481, in Tiptoft's English version. The Greek classics also began to appear in print before the end of the century, thanks in particular to Aldus Manutius of Venice, whose five-volume edition of Aristotle appeared between 1495 and 1498.

The work of some Italian humanists also appeared in print quite early. Petrarch's poems were published in 1470, and were reprinted more than twenty times before 1500. Leonardo Bruni's treatise on education was printed about 1470 and his letters in 1472, while his history of Florence came out in Italian translation in 1476. Lorenzo Valla's *Elegantiae* had its first edition in 1471 and went on to be a successful Latin textbook in humanist schools. Poggio and Ficino were also published in the 1470s. Italian printed books were exported to other parts of Europe, sometimes because they were ordered by expatriate merchants. In 1476, for example, five copies each of the histories of Florence written by Bruni and Poggio were sent to London for the Florentines there.

The spread of humanism was assisted by scholars who turned printers and by printers who were interested in scholarship. For example, it was Guillaume Fichet, a professor of theology and rhetoric, who first established a press in Paris, at the Sorbonne (in other words, the Faculty of Theology). Unemployed humanists sometimes supported themselves by working as correctors of proofs. Aldus Manutius, the famous Venetian printer, and a friend of Erasmus and other scholars, had studied with Battista Guarini, the son of the famous Guarino of Verona. A Venetian contemporary called him 'an excellent humanist and Grecian (*optimo umanista et greco*)'.

Important as the multiplication of copies of the classics was to the success of the humanist movement, printing was more than an agent of diffusion. It also aided and encouraged the process of what might be called 'decontextualization' or 'distanciation', a process which is crucial to all creative reception. Reading about an idea, rather than hearing about it from another person, makes it easier for the receiver to remain detached and critical. The reader can compare and contrast the arguments presented in different texts, rather than being overwhelmed by an eloquent speaker face to face.[102]

Personal contacts between Italy and other European countries continued to be important. The Frisian humanist Rodolphus Agricola, for example, studied in Italy in the 1470s. He learned Greek there and wrote a biography of Petrarch. Again, the young Nuremberg patrician Willibald Pirckheimer (best known today for his friendship with Albrecht Dürer), visited Italy in 1488. Like a good humanist he sketched ancient monuments and copied their inscriptions. Such personal experiences were indispensable to the success of the Renaissance movement. However, they were now supported by the powerful if impersonal medium of print.

Resistance

The spread of Renaissance art and literature was not a smooth process free from obstacles. The new forms and ideas sometimes met with resistance, as we have already seen in the case of Florence itself (see above, p. 31). For another case-study of such resistance we may turn to the eastern periphery of Europe, to Muscovy.

Muscovy's remoteness from the Renaissance was not the result of physical distance alone, important as that factor was in an age of horse transport. Regular contact with the West had been lost in the thirteenth century after the Mongol invasions. Like the Serbs and the Bulgars, the Russians were oriented towards Constantinople rather than Rome. There was a cultural revival in the late fourteenth century, the work – as in the case of Petrarch and his friends at much the same time – of a small group which included St Sergius of Radonezh, the missionary St Stefan of Perm, Epiphanios the Wise (who wrote biographies of Sergius and Stefan) and the painter Andrei Rublev, whose Old Testament Trinity (painted in the 1420s, at the time that Masaccio was active in Florence) is probably the most famous of all Russian icons. What was revived at this time, however, was not the classical tradition but an earlier epoch of Slav culture in the ninth and tenth centuries.[103]

The activities of Ivan III illustrate an interest in Italy and innovation but also the limits of that interest. Ivan took the new title of 'tsar', a term derived from 'Caesar' and implying continuity with ancient Rome. He married the niece of the last emperor of Byzantium, Zoe (Sofia) Palaeologa. Zoe had lived in Rome as a ward of the pope and (like Beatrice in Hungary) she had Italianate tastes. When she married in 1472, the Roman humanist Pomponio Leto, a former pupil of Valla's, visited Moscow as part of her suite. Two years later came the first of three Russian missions to Italy to recruit artists and engineers. Aristotele Fioravanti, who had returned to Italy after working for Matthias, was the first to be brought to Russia. Like Leonardo in Milan a few years later, Fioravanti was employed primarily on account of his expertise in bridge-building and other military skills. However, he also built the cathedral of the Assumption in Moscow. In the 1480s the walls and towers of the Kremlin were reconstructed in the Italian manner, complete with swallow-tail battlements. The façade of the 'Palace of Facets' (*Granovitaia Palata*) in the Kremlin, built between 1487 and 1491, followed the model of the 'Diamond Palace' of Ferrara, while the cathedral of St Michael, built soon after Ivan's death in 1505, combined Russian tradition (the onion domes, for example) with Italian features such as semicircular arches, pilasters and decorative shells.

In the secular sphere, it was possible for italianate forms to penetrate Russian culture. In the religious sphere, on the other hand, the strength of resistance may be illustrated by Tsar Ivan's insistence that in his designs for the cathedral of the Assumption in Moscow, Fioravanti should follow the model of the twelfth-century Orthodox cathedral of the Assumption in Vladimir. Fioravanti's work doubtless embodied his own interpretation of Russian tradition. According to a Russian chronicle of the period, when he saw the cathedral of Vladimir the architect declared that it must be the work of 'one of our masters', in other words, an Italian. All the same, a prestigious foreign architect had been brought to Russia, only to be constrained (unlike his colleagues in Hungary) to work in the traditional local style.[104]

In similar fashion, in the middle of the nineteenth century, the sultan Abdülmecid would invite the Fossati brothers from Italy to Istanbul to work in Aya Sophia in the traditional Turkish style.

In the case of humanism, the career of Maxim the Greek a generation later illustrates similar forces of resistance to innovation. Maxim, who had lived in Italy and moved in humanist circles, was received with enthusiasm by Tsar Vasili III and lived in Moscow between 1518 and 1525. He passed on information about classical antiquity and also about the discovery of America. However, it was not as a humanist but as a monk from Athos translating religious texts that Maxim was welcomed to Russia. It is scarcely surprising that (say) the Florentine debate on the active life should have awakened little interest in Muscovy, where literacy was virtually confined to the clergy. However, even the traditional Byzantine concern with ancient Greek literature and thought seems to have had few echoes in Russia.[105]

These episodes illustrate the power of what Fernand Braudel has called cultural 'refusal'.[106] It was difficult for Italianate ideas and forms to cross the frontier into a world in which the form of Christianity was Orthodox, the alphabet Cyrillic and the language of the liturgy Church Slavonic. Even the printing-press failed to break through the barrier. Tsar Ivan IV brought a press to Moscow, but it was destroyed by rioters in 1565.

Change versus Continuity

How important was cultural innovation in this period? As in Italy, the individuals and groups in other parts of Europe who were most interested in what we view as novelties, the works of Petrarch, for example, often perceived them through the spectacles of tradition. Before 1500 Petrarch's reputation outside Italy was based on his Latin works, and among these the most popular was probably the most traditional, the treatise on fortune known as *De remediis*. Alternatively, an interest in the Greek and Roman classics would be combined with an interest in chivalry (say) rather than replacing it. Like the Este and Gonzaga princes, Joan I of Aragon read not only

Livy and Plutarch but romances such as *Lancelot* and *Giron le Courtois*.

In the arts, what we see (with a few exceptions, such as Buda in the age of Matthias) is essentially *bricolage*, in other words, the borrowing of elements rather than ensembles, the employment of an Italian decorative vocabulary but not of Italian grammar, in the sense of rules for the combination of different items. Innovations were incorporated in traditional structures, literally so in the case of architecture, metaphorically in that of humanism. Sooner or later, however, the traditional order was bound to give way under the strain of the attempt to assimilate an increasing number of new or alien elements. This process became manifest in the next phase of the Renaissance, to be discussed in the following chapter.

3
The Age of Emulation: High Renaissance

The period 1490–1530 has long been known as the 'high' Renaissance, in the sense of the peak of achievement. In Italian art, it was the age of Leonardo, Raphael and Michelangelo; in literature, of Ariosto; in northern Europe, of Erasmus and Dürer. With hindsight, these forty years appear to be an age of what might be called 'crystallization'. The fluidity of the earlier period congealed, the lines between classical and medieval were drawn more firmly and the ambiguities were eliminated.

From an insider's point of view, on the other hand, a better term might be 'emulation'. By this time, some writers and artists were self-confident enough to claim that they or their contemporaries – Raphael and Michelangelo, for instance – could equal or even surpass the achievements of the ancients. It was also at this time that northerners began to claim to rival Italians.

The Centrality of Rome

From a political point of view, the appropriate dates for this chapter are not the deliberately round numbers 1490–1530 but 1494–1527, in other words, the period running from the French invasion of Italy to the sack of Rome by the troops of the

Emperor Charles V. These events made a considerable impact on Italian culture. In the case of 1494, the writings of Niccolò Machiavelli and Francesco Guicciardini, two of the most penetrating thinkers of the period, return again and again and with great bitterness to the shock of the French invasion. It would not be too much to say that the invasion, more especially the lack of resistance on the part of the Italians, coloured if it did not structure the thought of both men, giving it a pessimistic tone together with a new awareness of the common destiny of the different Italian states.[107] As for the sack of Rome by the northern 'barbarians', as Italian humanists viewed them, this traumatic event led to a dispersal of the artists and scholars who had been active there, ending a period in which the city had been a major centre of achievement, influential not only in Italy but also in much of Europe.[108]

Rome of course had it rivals, in Italy as elsewhere. One of the great literary works of the period, indeed one of the masterpieces of Italian literature, the narrative poem *Orlando Furioso*, by Ludovico Ariosto, first published in 1516, was produced in Ferrara, one of the small courts discussed above (p. 42). Ariosto set out not so much to imitate as to emulate Virgil. He did this by combining the classical tradition of epic with the medieval tradition of the romance of chivalry. He neither identified with chivalric values nor rejected them, but treated Orlando (Roland) and other paladins with a kind of affectionate irony. Ariosto's patron was the duke of Ferrara, Ercole d'Este, whose passion for warfare did not prevent him from taking an active interest in the arts, including architecture, painting and music as well as literature.

In Florence this was the age of republican revival, from the time of the expulsion of the Medici in 1494 to their return in 1512, and again from 1527 to 1530. Once again the importance of small groups in cultural innovation is clearly visible, the group in question including Niccolò Machiavelli, the future historian Francesco Guicciardini, the diplomat Francesco Vettori, Donato Giannotti (best known for the analysis of the Venetian political regime which he published in 1540) and Bernardo Rucellai, whose gardens (the 'Orti Oricellari') were the locale in which the group met regularly in order to discuss the best form of government and other topics.

Machiavelli wrote his *Prince* in isolation on his country estate in 1513, after the Medici had returned to power. *The Prince* is a self-consciously original book which sometimes recommends exactly the opposite of the conventional political wisdom. All the same, in tone and language alike, it resembles a number of texts of the period (letters, confidential reports and so on). In his *Discourses on Livy*, parts of which the author read to his friends in the Rucellai gardens, Machiavelli was once again expressing the attitudes of a generation of Florentines who had been deeply marked by the invasion of 1494 and the events which followed it. He argued the need for taking the example of antiquity seriously in political life as well as in the arts. Ancient Rome could teach modern Florence and other states how to preserve their independence.[109]

The restoration of the Florentine republic also affected the arts, with a return to public commissions. Michelangelo's *David* (1501) is often thought to be a personification of the republic. The statue was made for public display, originally on a buttress of the cathedral, and it was first erected on Piazza della Signoria. Leonardo and Michelangelo were commissioned by the new regime to decorate the hall of the Great Council (a new institution following the Venetian model) with scenes glorifying past Florentine victories. The two artists began working on their rival frescoes in 1504, though neither painting was ever completed. Leonardo's showed a group of horsemen fighting for a standard at the battle of Anghiari, while Michelangelo's represented soldiers being attacked while bathing in the Arno before the battle of Cascina. These unfinished works 'served as a school for all the world' while they remained intact, as the goldsmith Benvenuto Cellini, who had seen them in his youth, wrote in his memoirs.[110]

In Venice as in Florence, this period was a time of heightened civic consciousness, of identification with republican Rome and public patronage of literature and the arts. From 1516 onwards, the Venetians began to appoint official historians, the first of them being the patrician humanist Andrea Navagero and the second his friend Pietro Bembo, both chosen for the elegance of their Latin. State patronage of the arts was also important. The Bellini brothers and, a generation later, Titian were commissioned to paint scenes from Venetian history in the

Doge's Palace (works which were destroyed in a fire in 1577). Titian's painting of the battle of Cadore was apparently modelled on Leonardo's unfinished battle of Anghiari. However, the Venetians, Titian included, had begun to make their distinctive contribution to Renaissance painting, a contribution described at the time as an emphasis on colour in contrast to the Florentine emphasis on draughtsmanship (*disegno*).

All the same, from a European point of view (that of the Europeans of the time, in particular), it is on Rome that the Italian section of this chapter ought to concentrate. Rome was often described as the centre or 'head' of the world (*caput mundi*). This kind of hyperbole must not be taken too seriously. All the same, Rome did become a centre of innovation in this period, especially between 1503 and 1521, during the reigns of Popes Julius II and Leo X (formerly Giovanni de' Medici), both of them connoisseurs of the arts.

The centre of the centre was a remarkable group of artists and humanists, rivals in creativity to the Brunelleschi circle in Florence a century earlier. Michelangelo went to Rome after the Medici were driven from Florence in 1494 and remained there till 1501. He returned to Florence, as we have seen, but was back in Rome from 1505 onwards, painting the ceiling of the Sistine Chapel from 1508 to 1512, and making the statue of Moses for the tomb of Julius II around the year 1513. The Florentine sculptor Andrea Sansovino arrived in Rome in 1505, summoned by Pope Julius II. Leonardo da Vinci was in Rome between 1513 and 1517. Donato Bramante arrived around 1500 and began the new St Peter's in 1506. Raphael arrived around 1508. He was presented to the pope by Bramante (who came, like Raphael, from the town of Urbino), and soon afterwards began work on frescoes for the apartments of Julius II in the Vatican, including the Parnassus and the so-called 'School of Athens'.

The cohesion of this group must not be exaggerated. Leonardo was not a sociable man. Indeed, according to Raphael, he was 'as lonely as a hangman'. Michelangelo had his own friends. All the same, the members of this Roman circle learned from one another. 'Look at Raphael's paintings,' Pope Leo is said to have remarked a few years later. 'As soon as he saw Michelangelo's work he suddenly dropped the style of Perugino and followed Michelangelo as closely as he could.'[111]

The Florentine painter Rosso, who arrived in Rome in 1524, both criticized Michelangelo and imitated him.

Today, the Rome of this period is best remembered as the milieu of Michelangelo and Raphael. At the time, on the other hand, it was equally celebrated as a centre of poetry in Latin. Humanism flourished, especially in the reign of Pope Leo, an ex-pupil of Poliziano's who was interested in literature and scholarship and collected manuscripts of the classics. Greek scholars were summoned to Rome. Pietro Bembo arrived in 1512 and was appointed papal secretary by Leo in 1513, together with his friend Jacopo Sadoleto (humanists were still welcome in chanceries). The patrician Andrea Navagero, a humanist who wrote Latin poetry and edited Ovid's works for his friend Aldus Manutius, was the Venetian ambassador in Rome until 1516. Another humanist diplomat, Baldassare Castiglione, the author of the dialogue *The Courtier* (1528), was in Rome from 1513 onwards.

Some members of this group became close friends. For example, Castiglione showed the manuscript of his dialogue to Bembo and Sadoleto so that they could suggest improvements. He helped Raphael write a report to the pope on the need to preserve the antiquities of the city. Again, a letter of Bembo's describes an expedition to view the emperor Hadrian's villa at Tivoli, not far from Rome, in which Raphael, Castiglione and Navagero also participated. Thanks to this group of artists and humanists, the dream of emulating or even surpassing antiquity appeared to have come true.

The means to successful emulation, so it was widely believed, was to follow rules, like those formulated by Marco Girolamo Vida, another protégé of Leo X, in his *Art of Poetry* (1527), a creative adaptation of Horace's poem on the same subject. More influential, however, was Pietro Bembo. Bembo might be described as a pope of culture, laying down the law in language and literature. Following classical precedents, he distinguished three styles, the high, middle and low, each appropriate for particular kinds of subject, but he stressed the superiority and purity of the high style. In the case of Latin, Bembo argued that prose should follow the model of the 'majestic style' of Cicero, with its complex sentences and ornamental phrases. Verse, on the other hand, should follow the example of Virgil – as Vida did in his *Christiad*, an epic of the life of Christ commissioned by Leo X. However, the imitation recommended by Bembo was not slavish. He emphasized the need for the complete assimilation of the model and declared that 'emulation should always be joined to imitation (*aemulatio semper cum imitatione coniuncta sit)*'. Bembo was not the first Ciceronian. Poggio had attacked Valla for lack of respect for Cicero, as we have seen (p. 39). In the 1490s, the Roman humanist Paolo Cortesi had argued the case for imitating Cicero, to which the Florentine Poliziano had replied advocating a more eclectic approach. All the same it was Bembo's formulation, or his example, which was to be influential in the next generation.

Bembo also offered a model of pure and elegant writing in the vernacular. This Venetian patrician living in Rome devoted considerable effort to the establishment of Tuscan as the literary language of Italy. However, Bembo's ideal was not the Tuscan of his day. In his *Prose della volgar lingua*, a poetics of the vernacular, Bembo argued in favour of archaism (as linguistic purists often do), on the grounds that it was, in one of his favourite terms, 'majestic'. For poetry, his model was the language of Petrarch and Dante, and for prose, that of Boccaccio's *Decameron*. These authors were for him what might be called 'classics' of the vernacular, a new idea at that time but one destined to be influential (see below, pp. 104, 139). Bembo himself wrote dialogues in Italian and sonnets in the manner of Petrarch which became literary models themselves, not only in Italy but in France, Spain and elsewhere. Like Petrarch's, his poems were set to music, and his views on style were translated into musical terms by composers such as Willaert.[112]

Bembo's views of language were sometimes contested, but he had a powerful ally in his campaign for Tuscan. The spread of printed books, each copy identical with the rest, assisted the standardization of language. Print also facilitated what might be called the 'canonization' of exemplary vernacular authors, who began to be edited as if they were Greek or Latin classics. Bembo himself showed the way with his editions of Petrarch (1501) and Dante (1502), both published by Aldus Manutius of Venice, the humanist printer best known for his editions of ancient writers. Ariosto (figure 5) would soon receive similar treatment.[113]

In the visual arts, a similar trend to the formulation of rules is

Figure 5   Portrait of Ariosto, woodcut from the Spanish translation of
Orlando Furioso (Venice: Giolito, 1553). (Private collection.) Compare the
image of the poet crowned with that of the Emperor Augustus (figure 7).

also visible. Indeed, the vocabulary for describing and judging
works of art, which was still under construction in this period –
terms such as *grazia* (grace), *facilità* (facility), *maniera* (style),
ordine (order), *contrapposto* (in the sense of antithesis) and so
on – was derived to a large extent from that of ancient literary
criticism, especially Cicero, Quintilian and Horace's *Art of
Poetry*. The very idea of artistic 'style', together with the distinction between the high, middle and low, was derived, directly or
indirectly, from classical rhetoric.[114]

In the case of painting, ancient models were not available,
apart from a few fragments of fresco, but some modern painters
were canonized. Giotto was sometimes described as the equivalent of Dante, while Masaccio played the role of Boccaccio.
Leonardo, for instance, acknowledged the importance of both
these predecessors. In his collection of biographies of Italian
painters, sculptors and architects, first published in 1550 but
written earlier, the Tuscan artist Giorgio Vasari formulated the

influential idea of the rebirth (*Rinascità*) of the arts, using this noun for the first time, distinguishing three ages of progress towards 'perfection' and identifying the last age with the work of three masters, Leonardo, Raphael and, above all, his own teacher Michelangelo.

This period was also a time of increasing enthusiasm for ancient sculpture. The interest in classical statues on the part of humanists such as Poggio and artists such as Mantegna has already been noted, but it was at this time that collecting sculpture became fashionable in Rome and elsewhere. The popes set an example, Julius II having the sculpture court of the Vatican laid out to display his collection. New discoveries such as the Apollo Belvedere and the Laocöon (unearthed in 1506), both in the papal collection, helped to fuel enthusiasm. Sadoleto wrote a Latin poem on the Laocöon, praising its expression of emotion and presenting the rediscovery of the statue as a symbol of ancient Rome's return to light, in other words, of the Renaissance itself. Michelangelo, who was one of the first people to see the Laocöon, emulated it in a number of his works. Such statues were used to establish a canon in the arts equivalent to the literary classics.[115]

In architecture, the report written by Raphael (or at least in his name) to Pope Leo X in 1519 reads like a manifesto for the classical style. It condemned 'the German style of architecture' (*la maniera dell'architettura tedesca*), in other words, what we now call 'Gothic', as well as the buildings of the Goths themselves, 'completely lacking in style' (*senza maniera alcuna*). It claimed that architecture had now 'awakened', and called on the pope to equal and 'go beyond' the ancients, *superarli*.

The equivalent of Ciceronianism in architecture was what might be called 'Vitruvianism'. The Roman architect Vitruvius had emphasized the importance of what he called *decor*, in other words, the right combination of elements, the 'severity' of the Doric column being appropriate for temples of male gods, for example, while the 'delicacy' of the Corinthian was appropriate for goddesses. Architects designing three-storey palaces would now use Doric columns or pilasters on the ground floor to symbolize strength, Ionic on the first floor and the delicate Corinthian at the top. The 'grammar' of classical architecture, that is, the rules for the correct combination of different elements, had now been mastered. The flexibility of the age of Brunelleschi, whether it was the result of ignorance or creativity, had been lost.[116]

Print was as important for the formation of the visual as for the literary canon, including editions of Vitruvius and engravings of the works of Leonardo, Raphael and Michelangelo. The first edition of Vitruvius was published in Rome around 1490, while the first illustrated edition came out in 1511 and an Italian translation in 1521. Leonardo's *Last Supper* was more widely familiar in its engraved version (figure 6) than in the original.[117] The engraver Marcantonio Raimondi, who worked in Rome, made a reputation for himself – and for his friend Raphael – by his 'translations' of Raphael's paintings into prints, working from preparatory drawings as well as the finished paintings and imitating in a creative, emulative sense rather than merely reproducing. He also made prints of famous classical statues.[118]

The 'high' Renaissance owes its name not only to the heights of achievement reached by Leonardo, Raphael and Michelangelo but also to the emphasis on what Vasari and others called the 'high style' (*grande maniera*). The aim, to use Bembo's term, was 'majesty', and one means to this was the exclusion of 'low' elements, such as everyday objects or colloquial expressions. All the same, it was impossible to keep the arts completely free from these elements, grotesque as they seemed to Bembo and his friends.

Indeed, it was in Rome and in the circle of Raphael, who headed a team of artists decorating the loggias of the Vatican, that the so-called 'grotesque' developed, a new type of ornament emulating the decoration of ancient Roman underground chambers or 'grottoes', notably the recently rediscovered Golden House of Nero.[119] Vitruvius had criticized what he called 'monstrosities' (*monstra*) like heads on stalks, as signs of the decline of painting. All the same, this style of decoration, with its animals, flowers, fruit, sphinxes, satyrs, centaurs and so on, was much admired and would soon be imitated in many parts of Europe (see below, p. 179). An equivalent style flourished in literature, showing that the interest in the grotesque was not a simple response to the discovery of the Golden House. At the very time that Bembo was trying to write like Cicero, an Italian monk called Teofilo Folengo was writing comic poetry in what

Figure 6 Marc Antonio Raimondi, engraving of Leonardo, *Last Supper*.
(Copyright © British Museum, London). An early example of the
mechanical reproduction of a work of art.

has become known as 'macaronic' Latin, a rustic style in which
a Latin vocabulary was combined with Italian syntax, or Italian
words were given Latin endings.

It is tempting to speak of a 'counter-attack' of the low in this
period, in reaction against the literary dictatorship of Bembo
and his stylistic mannerisms, sometimes referred to contemptu-
ously as *Bemberie*. In this counter-attack, a leading figure was
Pietro Aretino. Aretino was socially an outsider, the son of a
craftsman at a time when most writers were the sons of nobles
or merchants. He came to Rome around 1517 and soon made
a reputation for himself as a satirist. His targets included
courtiers, the courtly behaviour recommended by Castiglione,
and the elegant style of writing and speaking recommended by
Bembo. In similar fashion the poet Francesco Berni, another
Florentine who came to Rome to seek his fortune at this time,
wrote mock eulogies of drunkenness, plague and thistles and
parodied one of Bembo's sonnets.[120]

The conflict between the classicism and the anti-classicism of this period should not be misunderstood. The two styles were complementary opposites, which sometimes appealed to the same people in different settings, on different occasions or in different moods. Each needed the other as a foil against which to define itself. Anti-classicism was not a movement so much as an attitude of playful disrespect which could coexist with admiration for the canon. However, it was impossible to confine the low style within these limits. It broke through the barriers, especially in the years after 1530, as we shall see. Looking back, the high Renaissance seems a moment of brief and unstable equilibrium.

Things were never quite the same after the death of Leo X in 1521, but the end of the period is generally dated to the sack of Rome by the troops of the Emperor Charles V in 1527. By this time Clement VII (another Medici) was pope, Raphael and Bramante were already dead, Leonardo and Sadoleto had gone to France, and Bembo had returned to Venice. All the same, this traumatic event, viewed by humanists as the return of the barbarians, was interpreted at the time as the end of an epoch. There was looting and vandalism. An unknown German soldier scratched the name LUTHER in capital letters on a fresco by Raphael in the Vatican. A number of artists and scholars fled the city, never to return.[121] In future, the Renaissance movement would be polycentric. Indeed, according to some non-Italian artists and scholars, it already was.

Literature and Empire

A serious challenge to the primacy of Italy was mounted by foreign humanists at this time, as the Longueil affair illustrates. Christophe Longueil, or Longolius, was a Frenchman who went to Rome in 1516 and became a friend of Bembo. An ardent Ciceronian, he was made welcome in Roman circles until the discovery that before he left for Italy he had delivered an oration on the superiority of French culture. The case of Longueil's 'treason' was tried in the presence of Leo X. The defendant was acquitted, but all the same he thought it better to leave Italy.

Longueil's views were not exceptional for their period.

Erasmus, for example, once declared that Latin literature had been 'carried off by the northerners, provoking a Florentine humanist, Giovanni Corsi, into writing a *Defence of Italy* (1535) in which he offered a long list, beginning with Bembo, of Italians who were 'most eminent in every genre of the arts'. The biographer of Erasmus, the humanist Beatus Rhenanus, described his hero as taking to Italy the learning 'which others have been accustomed to bring back from that country'. The English scholar John Leland described the muses crossing the alpine snows to Britain (*Musas transiliisse nives*), and claimed that the poet Sir Thomas Wyatt was equal to Dante and Petrarch (*Anglus par Italis*).

The Spanish, French and German humanists Antonio de Nebrija, Claude Seyssel and Conrad Celtis each claimed the primacy of their own region by associating the flourishing of literature with the flourishing of a modern empire, just as Lorenzo Valla had done in the case of ancient Rome, (see above, p. 39).

Nebrija, who had spent ten years in Italy, saw himself as a grammarian fighting the barbarians. The prologue to his Spanish grammar (the first grammar of a modern European language), published in 1492 and addressed to Queen Isabella, argued like Valla that language is 'the companion of empire', rising, flourishing and falling with it. Nebrija supported his argument with the examples of Hebrew (at its apogee in the age of Solomon), Greek (in the age of Alexander) and Latin (in the age of Augustus). He told the queen that the turn of Spanish had come and that it had to be accepted by the 'barbarous peoples' under Isabella's rule. This reference to the taking of Granada and the incorporation into Spain of the last of the Muslim ('Moorish') kingdoms in the peninsula has come to be read in the light of the discovery of America, just as the date of Nebrija's book now seems symbolic.[122]

The royal counsellor Claude de Seyssel, in the introduction to his translation of the ancient writer Justin's history of Rome, addressed to King Louis XII, made a similar point, asserting that the Romans tried 'to make their Latin grand, rich and sublime' (*magnifier, enrichir et sublimer leur langue latin*). Indeed, according to Seyssel (again echoing Valla), the Roman empire was maintained by the 'practice and authority of the

Latin language' (*usance et authorité de la langue latine*). Thanks to the recent French conquests in Italy, French was spreading in a similar way. He praised Louis because, so he told the king, 'you are working to enrich the French language and make it more important' (*enrichir et magnifier la langue française*). Like his eulogies, Seyssel's translation of a history of Rome was doubtless his way of encouraging the king to follow Roman examples.

The poet Konrad Celtis was crowned by the Emperor Frederick III in Nuremberg in 1487, the first non-Italian to receive the honour of which Petrarch had been so proud. Celtis was most famous in his time for his creative imitations of Horace, including odes, epistles and his best-known work, the *Amores*, in which he gave his poems local colour by describing four women from four regions of Europe, associating Hasilina with the river Vistula, Elsula with the Rhine, Ursula with the Danube and Barbara with the Baltic. He tried to emulate the achievements of modern Italy as well as ancient Rome. A scholar no less than a poet, he planned a *Germania illustrata*, a study of Germany in the manner of Flavio Biondo's chorography of Italy. In a letter of 1487, Celtis had already claimed that the Italians would soon 'be forced to confess that not only the Roman empire and arms, but also the splendour of letters has migrated to the Germans' (*litterarum splendorem ad Germanos commigrasse*).

In an oration delivered at the university of Ingolstadt in 1492, the year of Nebrija's *Grammar*, Celtis went even further in comparing modern Germany to ancient Rome. As the Romans became cultured by ruling Greece, the Germans could do the same by ruling Italy. Dedicating a volume of poems to the emperor, Celtis described Maximilian as 'a second Caesar' who 'restores classical learning with empire' (*Romanas et Graecas litteras cum imperio restituis*). Where the Italians identified themselves with the Romans and the northerners with the barbarians, Celtis identified the Germans with the victorious Romans and the Italians with the effete Greeks.[123]

The Arts

This account of the arts begins with patrons, because it was usually the patron rather than the artist who chose the subject and sometimes even the style of a building, painting or statue. Isabella d'Este, for example, was Marchioness of Mantua and one of the best-known patrons of art of the period. A collector of classical sculpture who owned replicas of the Laocöon and the Belvedere Apollo, she also did her best to acquire works by living artists such as Giovanni Bellini, Mantegna, Perugino, Leonardo da Vinci and Michelangelo, as ornaments for her grotto and her study. Said to speak Latin better than any other woman of her time, Isabella's encouragement of the humanist Mario Equicola to write on love resembles the encouragement of humanists and men of letters such as Bembo and Castiglione by Elisabetta Gonzaga, Duchess of Urbino.

It was in the early sixteenth century that a substantial number of patrons outside Italy began to commission works in the classical manner. Generally speaking these patrons were high in status, whether they were rulers, churchmen or other aristocrats. Such aristocrats had played an important role in fifteenth-century Italy, as we have seen, but they were less dominant. In Florence and Venice in particular, civic patronage and the patronage of individual citizens, often merchants, left its mark on the arts. It is too simple to speak of 'bourgeois' patronage, as social historians of the Renaissance used to do. The adjective 'urban' might be better. All the same, the contrast between the Italian situation and that in other countries is palpable. We might therefore speak of the 'aristocratization' of the Renaissance as it spread beyond Italy and became more closely associated with the courts of kings or great nobles.

Three princes of the Church, all three of them expected by some contemporaries to obtain the papacy, lived and spent with particular magnificence at this time, and their visits to Rome ensured their awareness of the new trends. Cardinal Tamás Bakócz, a man of humble origin who became the primate of Hungary, knew Italy well. His chapel in the cathedral at Esztergom was made in the local red marble but in a pure Florentine style. His portrait medal also bears witness to his interest in Italian art. The second figure in this trio was Cardinal

Georges d'Amboise, a connoisseur of art with a particular admiration for the work of Mantegna. His château at Gaillon, which was constructed by an Italian architect, included a loggia, a study, a chapel decorated by an Italian artist and a fountain made in Genoa. A special road was constructed in order to bring the fountain to the château.

Cardinal Thomas Wolsey, like Bakócz of humble birth, was a rival of the Cardinal d'Amboise in patronage as in other domains. Wolsey's Hampton Court was grander than the king's court, as the satirist John Skelton was not slow to point out. The cardinal has been described as 'one of the greatest patrons of the arts in English history', and he was certainly interested in the latest trends. His magnificent services of plate included a number of pieces in what were known at the time as 'antique work', in other words, the Renaissance style. Wolsey also commissioned a tomb with costly materials (gilt bronze and marble) and an Italian sculptor.[124]

One of the cultural consequences of the French invasion of Italy was that the Italians – like the Greeks in the days of the Roman empire – took their conquerors captive. The process began early. The artist Guido Mazzoni returned to France in the suite of King Charles VIII as early as 1495, together with the paintings, statues and tapestries which had been looted from Italy. Florimond Robertet, an official who took part in Charles VIII's expedition, developed a taste for Italian art while he was there, acquiring a statue by Michelangelo and a painting by Leonardo. However, the trend became more pronounced in the early sixteenth century, as foreigners were increasingly convinced of the artistic superiority of the Italians. As the French printer Geoffrey Tory, who had lived in Italy, declared in his *Champ Fleury* (1529), the Italians were 'sovereign in perspective, painting and sculpture . . . we have no one here to be compared with Leonardo da Vinci, Donatello, Raphael of Urbino or Michelangelo'.

His king would have agreed. Like Charles VIII, François I discovered Italian art by invading Italy. The king saw the *Last Supper* at Milan, was impressed, and would apparently have taken the painting home if it could have been detached from the wall. The king invited Leonardo to France, where he used to converse with him, as he later did with the goldsmith Benvenuto

Cellini (François had learned Italian from his mother Louise of Savoy). Michelangelo too was invited to France. François was also interested in sculpture and architecture. According to the Venetian amabassador, the king asked the pope to give him the Laocöon, though he had to make do with a copy. The royal castle of Chambord was designed by an Italian, Domenico da Cortona, though the work was carried out by French masons. A new wing was added to the château at Blois, with loggias imitating those designed by Bramante at the Vatican. The palace of Fontainebleau was also designed in an Italianate style, with a gallery decorated by the Italian painter Rosso. One of his frescoes, *The Expulsion of Ignorance*, symbolizes the Renaissance itself.[125]

The palace of Fontainebleau was begun in 1527, shortly after Charles V's new palace at Granada and apparently in competition with it. The King of France and the emperor were rivals in patronage as in politics and war. The palace of Granada was designed by Pedro Machuca, who had recently returned from Italy. The pure Roman classicism of this circular palace makes a spectacular contrast with its neighbour, the Moorish palace of the Alhambra. It has been suggested that the style of the palace should be read as a statement of Western values as opposed to 'oriental' ones, but it is equally possible to interpret the building as a claim by the Spaniards to be the equals of the Italians, whether ancient or modern.[126]

Whether the emperor was interested in the style of his palace, *a lo romano* as they said in Spain, is open to doubt. At the time he commissioned it, he had not been to Italy. Much the same point may be made about his patronage of painting and sculpture. Charles took Jan Vermeyen to Tunis with him to paint his victories over the 'Moors'. He also ennobled a number of artists, including his court painter, Titian, but he was much less of a connoisseur than François, or the two female relatives (from whom he took over Vermeyen, Titian and other painters), his aunt Margareta of Austria and his sister Maria of Hungary.

Margareta of Austria was a patron of painters, sculptors and architects. The Italian artists Jacopo de' Barbari and Pietro Torrigiano spent some time at her court. She was fond of music, especially that of Ockeghem and Josquin. Maria of Hungary was also a patron of music. She inherited her aunt's art collection and added to it. She commissioned some twenty paintings from Titian, but she was also interested in fifteenth-century Flemish painting and owned the Arnolfini portrait by Jan van Eyck which now hangs in the National Gallery in London. Her intellectual interests as revealed by her library will be discussed below.[127]

Italian architects and sculptors were in demand in other part of Europe at this time. In England, Torrigiano made the tombs of Lady Margaret Beaufort (1511) and King Henry VII (1512), while Giovanni da Maiano (figure 7) and Benedetto da Rovezzano worked for Wolsey. In Poland, the rebuilding of the royal palace on the Wawel hill in Cracow (figure 8) was directed by a certain 'Francesco the Florentine' (*Franciscus florentinus*). The Wawel impressed a French visitor in 1573 because it had 'three times as many loggias as the Louvre' (*trois fois autant de logis que le Louvre*). The future Zygmunt Stary of Poland discovered Italianate architecture when he spent three years in Buda at the court of his brother King Wladislaw and became familiar with the works which had been commissioned by the king's predecessor, Matthias Corvinus. His personal interest in architectural details is revealed in a letter of 1517 concerning the chapel he was building in Cracow cathedral: 'The Italian was here with the model of the chapel which he will build for us and we liked it well, but we ordered him to change a few things.'[128]

Artists as well as humanists went to Italy to study in this period. The German painter Albrecht Dürer visited Venice twice. The Spanish painter Alonso Berruguete spent about fourteen years in Italy and was impressed by Michelangelo's unfinished painting of the battle of Cascina. Machuca studied in Rome and Florence. The Dutch painter Jan Scorel lived in Venice and Rome. The later work of these artists is evidence of the imprint of classical and Italian models on their imagination. The export of engravings allowed artists who lacked the opportunity to visit Italy to become familiar with the new style. In Spain in the 1520s, for example, more than one artist imitated Raimondi's prints after Raphael.

It was at this time that some painters from Germany and the Netherlands turned for the first time to the secular subjects, especially ancient history and classical mythology, which Italian

Figure 7 Giovanni da Maiano, terracotta roundel with head of Augustus, Hampton Court, *c*.1521. (Photograph reproduced by kind permission of Dr Philip Lindley.) An early example of the fashion for images of Roman emperors.

masters such as Raphael had made famous. Lukas Cranach of Wittenberg, for example, made paintings of Venus and Lucretia. Albrecht Altdorfer painted Alexander the Great at the battle of Issus as part of a series of battle-scenes commissioned by Duke Wilhelm IV of Bavaria. Hans Holbein of Augsburg produced his famous series of portraits, including Henry VIII and Thomas More.

The revival of antiquity in the arts did not please everyone. Two Dutchmen who are not often considered together, Erasmus and Adrian of Utrecht (later Adrian VI), shared a suspicion of classical forms as expressions of paganism. Others accepted

Figure 8　Wawel Castle, Cracow, courtyard. (Copyright © Wawel Castle, Cracow.)

the classical style, but not he predominance of Italy. The idea of emulation was gaining ground at this time. The French poet Nicolas Bourbon called Holbein 'the Apelles of our time'. The royal palace of Fontainebleau was described as a 'second Rome' because of the fine collection of antiques assembled there.[129] In a dialogue by the humanist Cristóbal de Villalón, *Ingenious Comparison between the Ancient and the Modern* (*Ingeniosa comparación entre lo antiguo y lo presente*, 1539), not only Raphael and Michelangelo but also Spanish artists such as Alonso Berruguete and the sculptor-architect Diego de Siloe were supposed to have 'surpassed the ancients' (*exceden á los antiguos*).

Emulation might take different and even opposite forms. In Portugal, for instance, King Manoel I sent two artists to study in Italy. Yet the so-called 'Manueline' style in architecture, named (in the nineteenth century) after the king and exemplified by the Jeronimite monastery at Belém, just outside Lisbon, is distinguished by the exuberant use of ornaments which are as distant from classical and Italian examples as they are from Gothic. These ornaments, playful references to the Portuguese seaborne empire, include hawsers, capstans, seaweed, coral, lotuses and crocodiles. Whether or not they are inspired by Muslim or Hindu art, as some scholars have suggested, they constitute a remarkable declaration of independence from both traditional and contemporary models.[130]

For a case-study of creative imitation and emulation in this period we may return to Dürer. His sketches of Italian paintings tell us something of what he learned in Venice, especially from Giovanni Bellini, whom he met there. He enjoyed unusual fame in his own day. The Emperor Maximilian described him as 'renowned above other masters in the art of painting'. Celtis, Erasmus and other northern humanists sang his praises. Luther quoted him in his *Table-Talk*, while Luther's colleague, the humanist Philip Melanchthon, cited Dürer as an example of the grand manner in painting, the equivalent of the high style in rhetoric.

Dürer's reputation spread all the more widely thanks to prints. Dürer's own woodcuts and the prints of his paintings made by Raimondi made his work influential in Italy. Vasari declared him to be 'so universal' that if he had only been born in Tuscany, 'he would have been the best painter in our land', which was praise indeed from an Italian. Dürer's treatises on proportion and on geometry (including perspective) also added to his international reputation. These treatises were translated into Latin by the German humanist Joachim Camerarius, who also wrote his life, the first northern European biography of an artist.[131]

Humanists

Humanists too needed the patronage of rulers, just as rulers needed the advice of humanists, as Erasmus and Budé pointed out in parallel treatises on the education of princes, addressed to Charles V and François I respectively and presented to these monarchs in 1516 and 1519. Budé carried out research on the rewards of writers in the ancient world in order to support his claims, pointing out, for example, that Virgil had received the equivalent of 250,000 *écus* for his work. Paraphrasing the Roman poet Martial, Budé declared that 'it is said today that for lack of Maecenases there are no more Virgils and Horaces' (*dit-on aujourd'hui que par faute de mécenates il n'est plus de Virgiles ni de Horaces*). As in the case of the fifteenth-century courts described earlier (pp. 42–3), the humanist education of princes seems to have had some effect on their later interests. François had Greek and Roman classics read aloud to him, and asked his ambassador to Venice (Lazare de Baïf, himself a humanist), to buy Greek manuscripts for the royal library. Charles was no great intellectual, but one of the few books which is supposed to have interested him was the history of Rome by the Greek writer Polybius.

The role of Renaissance princesses as patrons of learning as well as the arts deserves to be emphasized. Queen Bona, for example, the wife of Zygmunt I of Poland, had been given a humanist education at the court of Milan and was said to speak Latin well. She learned Polish and encouraged writers. Queen Isabella of Castile also knew Latin, which she was taught by Beatriz Galindo, nicknamed 'La Latina', a learned lady who also wrote a commentary on Aristotle. Isabella encouraged Hernando del Pulgar to write a history of Spain and ordered Nebrija to translate it into Latin. The queen also corresponded with the female humanist Cassandra Fedele. Isabella's daughter, Catherine of Aragon, received a good education from a humanist tutor and was able to speak Latin extempore. As queen, Catherine was the patron of her compatriot Luis Vives (who lived for some years in England) and also of the humanist physician Thomas Linacre, the tutor to her daughter Mary Tudor. Most important of all was Marguerite de Navarre, sister of François I. Marguerite herself wrote poems, plays and stories, as well as acting as the patron and protector of a number of humanists.

Princes were increasingly interested in attracting Italian scholars to their courts, whether to teach their children or to write laudatory accounts of their deeds or those of their ancestors in an elegant Latin style, as Antonio Bonfini had done for King Matthias. Thus Paolo Emili of Verona wrote a history of France for King Louis XII. Polidoro Vergilio of Urbino wrote a history of England (the *Historia Anglica*) for Henry VIII. The Lombard Pietro Martire d'Anghiera was appointed chronicler (*cronista*) to Charles V, and wrote a history of the discovery of the New World, entitled *Decades* in homage to the Roman historian Livy.

There was even more traffic in the opposite direction. In the 1480s, for example, humanist visitors to Italy included Konrad Celtis, Thomas Linacre, who studied with Poliziano in Florence, and Johan Reuchlin, who met Ficino and Lorenzo de'Medici. In the 1490s they included the Frenchman Jacques Lefèvre d'Etaples, the Englishman John Colet, and the Poles Piotr Tomicki and Nicholas Copernicus. Lefèvre's concern with the need to 'drink from the fountain of a purified Aristotle', in other words, to study the texts of the master in the original Greek, followed his meeting with Ermolao Barbaro. Colet's famous lectures on St Paul, delivered at Oxford, followed his acquaintance with Ficino's circle in Florence. Tomicki introduced a classical Latin into the royal chancery after his return to Poland. Copernicus's Platonism, which encouraged him in his heliocentric theory (see below, p. 132), dated from the time when he was a student in Bologna.

After 1500 foreign visitors to Italy are too numerous to list, so that a few famous examples will have to suffice. The biography of Erasmus by his disciple Beatus Rhenanus described his hero's 'great desire' to see Italy, remarking that 'no place in all the world is more cultured [cultius] in every way than this region.' In 1511 the poet Jean Lemaire noted the discovery of the 'magnificence, elegance and sweetness' of the 'Tuscan language' by Frenchmen 'frequenting Italy' (frequentans les Ytalles). Among German visitors, there were the satirist Ulrich von Hutten and the magician Heinrich Agrippa. Among Frenchman were the humanist lawyer Guillaume Budé and the philosopher Symphorien Champier, who fought in the French army as well as studying at Padua university. Among Spaniards were the poet Garcilaso de la Vega and the scholar Juan Gines de Sepúlveda, who stayed in Italy for twenty years.

Despite the continuing enthusiasm revealed by these pilgrimages, it was at this time, around 1520, that the Italians lost their supremacy in humanist studies. This was not only the age of Erasmus, Reuchlin and Budé, but also that of the Spaniard Luis Vives and the Englishman Thomas More. To some members of this group, a new age seemed to have dawned. Bliss was it in that dawn to be alive. Erasmus at fifty declared in 1517 that he 'could almost wish to be young again' because of 'the near approach of the golden age'. The German humanist Ulrich von Hutten told his friend Pirckheimer that it was good to be alive at a time when studies and creativity flourished (*vigent studia, florent ingenia*). This was also the time when the term 'humanist' spread beyond Italy. Lefèvre, for example, was called *humanista theologizans*. The followers of Reuchlin in Germany were sometimes described as *humanistae*. The term 'Middle Ages' (*media antiquitas, media aetas*) was in use by some German humanists at this time, as it had been by fifteenth-century Italians.

As in the case of Italy, new ideas and techniques were often developed in small groups. Konrad Celtis, for instance, was an acquaintance of Dürer's and a friend of Johan Trithemius, a Greek and Hebrew scholar who was abbot of a Benedictine monastery, first at Sponheim and later at Würzburg. Celtis led a wandering life, but in some of the cities in which he stayed, including Cracow, Heidelberg and Vienna, he founded discussion groups of *sodalitates*. Trithemius offered hospitality in his monastery to a number of humanists, including Celtis, Reuchlin, Agrippa, and two Frenchmen, Gaguin and Charles de Bouelles.[132] In Paris, Lefèvre's circle of pupils, friends and acquaintances included Gaguin, Bouelles, Budé and Beatus Rhenanus.[133] In the new university of Alcalà (figure 10), a team of scholars headed by Nebrija and supported by Cardinal Jiménez de Cisneros edited a polyglot Bible, juxtaposing Hebrew, Aramaic, Greek and Latin texts.[134]

In similar fashion, the letters exchanged between humanists made an important contribution to their ideal of an international 'republic of learning' (*respublica litteraria*). The phrase goes back to the early fifteenth century, but it was at this time that international scholarly contacts began to give this imagined community some semblance of reality.[135] The republic of learning was also held together by print. In this field too, Italian (or more exactly Venetian) dominance was challenged after 1500 by Paris, Basel and other centres. The scholar-printer Aldus Manutius had a number of emulators outside Italy. In Basel the scholar-printers included Johan Amerbach, a friend of leading German humanists, and Johan Froben, once Amerbach's apprentice and later the friend as well as the publisher of Erasmus. In Paris they included Jodocus Badius, a Netherlander who had studied (like Aldus) with Battista Guarini in Ferrara. Badius, who was called to Paris by the humanist

Robert Gaguin and became printer to the university in 1507, wrote books himself, including a treatise on letter-writing, and published not only the classics but also books by Valla, Ficino and Poliziano. His shop was a meeting-place for the Lefèvre circle of humanists.

Another locale in which the humanist movement was able to flourish was the university. In Italy before 1500, the movement had developed largely outside the universities and even to some extent against them. After 1500, on the other hand, a number of European universities, including two new ones, Wittenberg and Alcalà, offered favourable environments for the new learning. This claim may be illustrated by the history of three subjects of study: poetry, Greek and Hebrew.

Poetry was one of the main interests of the humanists in the circle of Marsilio Ficino, especially Poliziano, a fine poet in both Latin and Italian, and Landino, who claimed that poetry was above the other liberal arts. As we have seen (see above, p. 37), Ficino himself compared the inspiration of poets with that of prophets. From the late fifteenth century onwards, the study of poetry began to be institutionalized in universities outside Italy. A chair of poetry was founded at the university of Leuven in 1477, and at Salamanca in 1484. The professors gave their lectures on Latin and Greek poets. At Salamanca, for example, the Lombard humanist Pietro Martire of Anghiera lectured on Juvenal, and was received – so he tells us – with great enthusiasm. Celtis lectured on his favourite poet Horace when he was teaching at the university of Ingolstadt, and on Homer at the university of Vienna. He also persuaded the Emperor Maximilian to found a Poet's College.

Greek studies, which had been virtually confined to Italy before 1500 (apart from small groups in Paris in the 1470s and in Salamanca in the 1480s), also spread more widely in this period. Erasmus learned the language from a Greek in Paris around the year 1500. Thomas More learned it from William Grocyn (who had acquired his Greek in Italy) in 1501, while his friend Colet began to study the language a little later at the age of about fifty. The teaching of Greek was established in the universities of Cracow (*c.*1500, by two Italians), Alcalà (*c.*1513), Leipzig (1515), Paris (1517), Wittenberg (1518) and elsewhere.[136]

Greek was studied not only because it was the language of Homer, Aristotle and Plato, but because it was the language of the New Testament. It was also at this time that the language of the Old Testament began to be taken seriously by an international circle of Christian scholars. In 1311 the Church council of Vienne had ordered chairs in Hebrew to be established in five European universities, but the order was not implemented. A few fifteenth-century Italian humanists had been interested in Hebrew. Pico della Mirandola, for instance, took lessons from the Jewish scholars Elia del Medigo at Padua and Jochanan ben Isaac Alemanno in Florence. In the early sixteenth century, however, the study of Hebrew was established in a number of European universities. Alfonso of Zamora taught Hebrew at Salamanca in 1511. In 1517 the famous 'trilingual college' was founded at the university of Leuven to teach the three languages of scripture, Latin, Greek and Hebrew. A similar college was founded at Alcalà. Hebrew was taught at the university of Heidelberg from 1519, at Basel from 1529, and at the new Collège Royal in Paris, founded by François I at the suggestion of Guillaume Budé, from 1530 onwards.

It was not only to understand the Old Testament that Hebrew was studied. For a number of humanists, from Pico onwards, a major goal was to understand the Kabbala, in other words, the secret or 'occult' tradition of Jewish scholars. The word Kabbala means 'tradition', and was sometimes translated into Latin in this period as 'reception' (*receptio*). More precisely, the Kabbala was a mystical tradition, an attempt to reach God through meditating on his many names. The students of the Kabbala believed that Hebrew was the original language, the language of God, in which words were more than mere signs for things but had their own power. By using their secret names, kabbalists were able to summon angels. It is not difficult to explain the enthusiasm of humanist philologists or 'word-lovers' for such a doctrine.[137]

The appeal of this Jewish tradition to Christian humanists was similar to the appeal of Zoroaster, Hermes Trismegistus and to some extent Plato. The texts of this 'ancient theology' (see above, p. 37) were viewed as foreshadowing and so confirming Christianity (needless to say, Jewish scholars found this use of their tradition quite absurd). Thus Pico claimed that 'no science proves the divinity of Christ as well as magic and the Kabbala.'

In Italy, kabbalistic studies began to flourish in the early sixteenth century. In Rome, for example, Cardinal Egidio da Viterbo, a former disciple of Ficino, became an enthusiast for what he called 'Jewish truth' (*Hebraica veritas*). He told Pope Leo X that biblical studies would come back to life in his time 'as if from their ashes', just as Greek studies has been revived in the age of Lorenzo de'Medici. In Venice, the Franciscan friar Francesco Giorgi (or Zorzi) used the Kabbala as evidence of the harmony of the cosmos. As an expert on harmony, he was consulted on the construction of the church of San Francesco della Vigna.[138]

In Germany, Johan Reuchlin published a book about the Kabbala in 1517, dedicating it to Pope Leo X. He claimed that this Jewish tradition gave access to the lost 'symbolic philosophy' of Pythagoras, who had derived his wisdom from the East. Pythagoras, he declared, was now reborn , since Reuchlin was able to expound his ideas in the same way that Ficino had expounded the philosophy of Plato and Lefèvre that of of Aristotle. Reuchlin's disciple Heinrich Cornelius Agrippa was already lecturing on Reuchlin in 1509, the year in which he visited Trithemius and conversed 'about alchemy, magic, Kabbala and the like'. Agrippa went on to write a book *On the Occult Philosophy* which was finally published in 1531.

Like the Neoplatonists of late fifteenth-century Florence, with whom Reuchlin had studied, the German humanists were trying to attain the knowledge of ancient mysteries. Like the Florentine circle, they associated poetry, prophecy and the dignity or what Agrippa called the 'dignification' of man. Like the Florentines, they emphasized the compatibility between Christianity and the secret doctrines of the ancients. On the title-page of Agrippa's book stood a quotation from the Gospel of St Matthew (10: 26): 'there is nothing covered, that shall not be revealed; and hid, that shall not be known.' However, the German group took Jewish culture more seriously than their predecessors, making many respectful references to the learned rabbis who had studied the Kabbala before them.[139]

Greek was studied as a key to two antiquities, the pagan and the Christian. As an example of the links between the two, and the uses of ancient Greek culture to the humanists of this time, the reception of Lucian makes an illuminating case-study.

Lucian, who lived in the second century AD, was the author of lively, colloquial and satirical dialogues. They are often set in heaven, the classical Olympus, or in hell, the classical Hades. The Olympian viewpoint allows the philosopher Menippus, one of Lucian's protagonists, to look down on earth from a distance so great as to make human activities seem of no importance. The function of Hades is to show once-important men stripped of their wealth and power. The souls have to leave everything behind before they enter the boat which will take them across the River Styx to the underworld. The boatman, Charon, like Menippus, comments on human folly.

Lucian's works were published in the original Greek in the 1490s. Latin translations of some of the dialogues were made early in the sixteenth century by Erasmus, More, Reuchlin and Budé. The dialogues also inspired a number of humanists, including Erasmus, Hutten and Valdés, to imitate or emulate the Greek satirist. 'If you could look down from the moon, as Menippus once did,' says the protagonist of the famous *Praise of Folly* by Erasmus, 'on the countless hordes of mortals, you'd think you saw a swarm of flies or gnats quarrelling among themselves.' Olympus and Hades became the Christian Heaven and Hell. In the anonymous *Julius Exclusus*, almost certainly the work of Erasmus, the warlike pope appears at the gates of heaven and tries to open them with his keys. There follows a dialogue with St Peter, who is amazed at the worldly appearance of his successor. 'It's a very different thing nowadays to be bishop of Rome,' Julius explains.[140]

Hutten and Valdés were among those who followed the example of Erasmus. Indeed, Hutten was described by the printer Johan Froben as 'Lucian reborn'. In Hutten's *Inspicientes* ('The Onlookers'), the observers in the heavens, Sun and Phaeton, look down on ant-like humans 'leading out great armies over trifles, dying for an empty name'. They comment on the corruption of Pope Leo X, squeezing money out of the German people under the pretence of a crusade against the Turks, and the arrogance of his legate Cardinal Cajetanus. Hutten himself translated this dialogue and three others into German in order to reach a public wider than that of his fellow-humanists. For the same reason, Alfonso de Valdés, 'more Erasmian than Erasmus' according to a humanist colleague, wrote in

Spanish.[141] His dialogue *Mercury and Charon* combined political with moral and religious themes. Mercury comes down to Hades to give Charon the latest news of the world above. Having heard that Charles V and François I are at war, Charon has bought a new galley, fearing that his old boat would not hold all the dead who are about to descend on him. Mercury describes the war to him from Charles's point of view (Valdés was the emperor's secretary). In the course of the conversation, the souls of the newly-dead arrive, to be interrogated about their past lives by the two main speakers. The souls include a former ruler, a minister, a priest and a theologian, all evil and bound for hell. The form of this dialogue may follow Lucian, but the tone is very different. It is much more earnest, adapting or accommodating the Greek satirist to the political and religious mood of the late 1520s.

The anti-Italian tone of these dialogues should be noted. The critique of papal Rome had national (if not 'nationalist') overtones. National rivalry and scholarly competition were closely entwined. In France, for example, among the humanist students of Roman law, the emulation of Italy turned into a rejection of the 'Italian method' (*mos italicus*) in favour of a native one, the *mos gallicus*, a distinction which goes back to the middle of the sixteenth century. The 'French method', the interpretation of Roman law by replacing it in the context of ancient Roman culture, had actually been the method employed by Valla and Poliziano, but the practice was taken further in France in this period. Guillaume Budé's *Annotations on the Pandects* (1508) was a technical but also an exemplary piece of philology in which the author historicized Roman law by showing it to be the product of a particular period. Like earlier humanists who had studied classical literature and philosophy and the New Testament from this point of view, Budé attempted to 'restore' Roman law by emending corrupt texts and stripping them of layer after layer of misinterpretation.[142]

Conflicts

It will be clear that by this time there were deep divisions within the humanist movement. One humanist even referred to the 'civil war between Ciceronians and Erasmians'.[143] The contrast between (say) Bembo, with his enthusiasm for elegant literary form, and Egidio da Viterbo, who lived in Rome in the same period but considered Latin a 'barbaric' language by comparison with Hebrew, could hardly be more obvious. These conflicts should not be reduced to personal or local rivalries, important as these were. They made manifest the latent contradictions within the humanist enterprise. Erasmus put his finger on the difficulties. How could one reconcile respect for pagan antiquity with Christianity? Should one follow the letter or the spirit of the classical tradition? If the humanist movement did not fragment completely at this time, the credit should probably be given to its enemies, whom we might call the 'Trojans', following the example of Thomas More in his defence of Greek studies at Oxford. The Oxford conservatives were not alone. At much the same time at the university of Leuven there was a similar attack on Greek and Hebrew studies and on the philology of Valla and Erasmus. In France, the Sorbonne (in other words, the Faculty of Theology) opposed the new approaches of the *lecteurs royaux*. In Spain, Erasmus had many enemies as well as disciples.

Two notorious controversies of the period reveal the hostility to humanism which persisted in some quarters: the Pomponazzi case and the Reuchlin affair. Pietro Pomponazzi was a professor at the university of Bologna, lecturing on the philosophy of Aristotle. Although he was not a Greek scholar himself, like Ermolao Barbaro (see above, p. 45), he participated in the movement to rediscover what Aristotle had originally meant, as opposed to what later commentators (Averroes, for example) had claimed he was saying. In 1516 Pomponazzi published a book *On the Immortality of the Soul* which claimed that Aristotle had asserted that the soul was mortal. This little book stirred up a great controversy. Although Pomponazzi had declared that neither the mortality nor the immortality of the soul could be demonstrated by natural reason, he was attacked as if he was himself a 'mortalist'. His book was burned in Venice and a number of theologians wrote against him. Pomponazzi did not suffer: the university doubled his salary. All the same the reception of his book reveals the strength of the obstacles to the reception of humanism.[144]

In the Reuchlin affair, anti-humanism was entwined with anti-semitism. Reuchlin was first attacked for arguing against the suppression of Jewish books. When he defended himself, his own work, especially his book on the Kabbala, became the target. The dispute gradually broadened, intellectually and internationally. Reuchlin came to believe that his 'barbarian adversaries' were trying to discredit Greek and Hebrew scholarship in order to defend their own puerile studies. Erasmus wrote to Reuchlin to assure him of support against the 'malevolence' of his enemies, and a postscript to the letter listed Reuchlin's friends in England, including More, Colet, and their friends Linacre and Grocyn.[145]

In Germany, the dispute was presented in *The Letters of Obscure Men* (*Epistolae Obscurorum Virorum*, 1515) as an attack on humanism by the forces of barbarism. A collective enterprise in which Hutten played a central role, these imaginary letters to and from scholastic philosophers in German universities such as Cologne and Mainz paint a collective portrait of the clerical enemies of poetry and 'new-fangled Latin', who are also the defenders of 'good old books' by Peter of Spain, Thomas Aquinas and so on. The writers are made to condemn themselves as ignorant, stupid, greedy, authoritarian and anti-semitic, in the act of condemning Reuchlin as 'a secular poet and an arrogant man withal, who putteth himself, in opposition to four universities, on the side of the Jews, and . . . is not versed in Aristotle or Peter of Spain' (a thirteenth-century writer on logic). The language of the letters is a hybrid. The Latin in which they are written, reflecting the culture or lack of culture of the writers, is medieval rather than classical, and it has been contaminated by the vernacular. The style or lack of style of the letters would have been enough by itself to make humanist readers fall about laughing.

Soon after the publication of the *Letters of Obscure Men*, the Spanish humanist Luis Vives delivered a direct and impassioned attack on the scholastic philosophers or 'sophists' of the University of Paris, *Against the Pseudologicians* (*In Pseudodialecticos*, 1520). In language reminiscent of Valla and Erasmus, Vives denounced the Parisians for their 'vain and futile' studies, 'the most trivial of trivialities' (*nugacissimas nugas*), for failing to distinguish words from things, for

replacing ordinary language with a barbarous jargon of 'suppo-
sitions', 'restrictions', 'appellations' and so on, and for following
Peter of Spain rather than Cicero or Quintilian. Instead, Vives
advocated the study of 'those disciplines which are worthy of
man and are therefore known as the humanities'.

The humanists also criticized chivalry. Erasmus, Vives and
More were all critics of the romances so widely read in their day,
the stories of Arthur, Lancelot, Tristan, Roland and so on,
because they were badly written, 'wholly unlearned, stupid and
silly' (as Erasmus wrote in his *Enchiridion*), and because they
glorified war and love outside the framework of marriage. The
rejection of the romances was also linked to the critique of
warfare in More's *Utopia* and in Erasmus's commentary on the
proverb *Dulce bellum inexpertis*, 'Sweet is war to those who
have not experienced it.'

The protests had little effect. The Spanish romance *Amadis de
Gaula*, first published in 1508, went on to be a best-seller in
many parts of Europe in the sixteenth century, with virtually
innumerable continuations as well as translations into French,
Italian, German and English. Although Erasmus had warned
him against this kind of reading in *The Education of a Christian
Prince*, among the few books known to have interested Charles
V was a romance of chivalry, *Le chevalier délibéré*, which he had
translated into Spanish. François I was not very different from
Charles in this respect. He commissioned a poem from an Italian
writer at his court, the exiled Florentine Luigi Alamanni, but the
subject he chose came from a French romance of chivalry. In
captivity in Spain the king read *Amadis*, and liked it so much
that on his return he commissioned a translation into French.

In the visual arts too the contact and conflict between styles
produced a hybrid culture. Cardinal Georges d'Amboise and his
brothers commissioned buildings not only in a Renaissance style
but also in Gothic, including the Palais de Justice at Rouen and
the Hôtel de Cluny in Paris. When Diego de Siloe was designing
the new cathedral in Granada, some people appealed to the
Emperor Charles V to forbid the architect to build it *a lo
romano*, insisting on *el modo moderno*, in other words, the
Gothic style.[146] Charles was apparently of two minds in this
matter. The emperor, François I, and a number of artists and
men of letters of this time lived simultaneously in what we might

describe as the world of Huizinga and the world of Burckhardt.

To complicate matters a little further, some humanists outside Italy came to see the despised Middle Ages as the equivalent in their regions of the Roman past. Their sense of rivalry with Italy encouraged positive attitudes to the 'barbarians'. German humanists were delighted by the praises of their ancestors in the *Germania* of Tacitus. Celtis wrote an epic about Theodoric, the ruler of the Ostrogoths, and edited the plays of the tenth-century nun Hrotsvitha. The later Middle Ages also became an object of sympathetic interest. The Emperor Maximilian commissioned an edition of medieval German epics. The Alsatian humanist Jacob Wimpheling praised the architecture of Strasbourg cathedral, its Gothic tracery, columns and statues.

Erasmus the Arch-Humanist

To pull the threads of this chapter together it may be helpful to take a closer look at Erasmus, the northern equivalent or rival of Bembo. Erasmus shared the general humanist contempt for the scholastic philosophers, the 'brawling Scotists' and 'stubborn Ockhamists', with their 'slovenly and barbarous Latin' and their 'cobwebbed subtleties'. He denounced barbarism. He shared the general admiration for the two antiquities, pagan and Christian, especially the latter. He learned from Cicero and (as we have seen) from Lucian, as well as editing the works of a number of Fathers of the Church. He believed in the revival of learning, writing in 1517 that 'Polite letters, which were almost extinct, are now cultivated and embraced by Scots, by Danes and by Irishmen' (in other words, on what he regarded as the periphery of Europe). He admired earlier humanists, notably Rudolphus Agricola, whom he described as 'one of the first to bring a breath of the new learning from Italy', and Lorenzo Valla, whose *Annotations on the New Testament* he was the first to publish.

Unlike the earlier humanists, however, Erasmus grew up in the age of print. He enjoyed good relations with his printers, notably Aldus Manutius in Venice and the Froben family in Basel. Thanks to the new medium, as well as his own gift for articulating humanist ideals more clearly and more persuasively than his colleagues, he became what might be called the 'arch-humanist' of his day, the most successful and the most respected all over Europe. His *Enchiridion* or 'handbook of a Christian soldier', a manual of piety for the laity, had twenty-six Latin editions between 1503 and 1521, as well as being translated into Czech (1519), German (1520), English (c.1522), Dutch (1523), Spanish (1524), French (1529), Italian and Portuguese. The *Praise of Folly*, the satire for which Erasmus is perhaps best known today, went through thirty-six Latin editions between 1511 and 1536, and was translated into Czech, French and German.

As a result, Erasmus enjoyed an international reputation on a scale matched by no scholar before him – and not so many since. He made a triumphal progress up the Rhine in 1514. He was invited to Spain by Cardinal Cisneros, to France by François I, to England, to Bavaria, to Switzerland, to Hungary, to Poland where, according to an English witness in 1527, 'no day passes without many references to Erasmus.' Despite his claim that he would make no 'Erasmians', he had many followers. In England, his friends and disciples included Thomas More and John Colet. In France, they included Lefevre d'Etaples, Marguerite de Navarre and Rabelais, who wrote a letter of homage to the master. Among Spaniards, Vives and Valdés were his most famous disciples. A lecture on the *Praise of Folly* was given at Wittenberg University in 1520, an unusual tribute to a living scholar. Statues of Erasmus were erected in Basel and in his birthplace, Rotterdam, at a time when only rulers, soldiers or saints normally received this honour. A biography of Erasmus was written shortly after his death by his disciple Beatus Rhenanus.[147]

This international reputation was especially appropriate for a man who once wrote (to Ulrich Zwingli in 1522) that 'I should like to be a citizen of the world' (*Ego mundi civis esse cupio*). By 'the world' he effectively meant the European common-wealth of learning. He corresponded with fellow-humanists in many countries, once confessing to writing so many letters that 'two wagons would hardly be equal to carrying the load.' Among his most frequent correspondents, leaving aside his fellow-Netherlanders, were Germans (Beatus Rhenanus and the lawyer Ulrich Zasius), Englishmen (More and Colet), Frenchmen (Budé), Italians (Ammonio), Spaniards (Vives), Portuguese (Damião de Gois) and Hungarians (Miklós Oláh).

Erasmus was as untypical in his success as he was in the sheer amount that he published. In later life he had secretaries and other helpers in tasks such as proof-reading, so that he should perhaps be regarded as the literary equivalent of Raphael, the head of a humanist workshop. As for his attitudes, by this time there were too many conflicts inside the movement for any individual to be regarded as typical. Erasmus supported the study of Hebrew as one of the three languages needed to return to the 'sources' of Christianity, but he never learned Hebrew himself, explaining in a letter to Colet that 'the strangeness of the language' repelled him. He supported Reuchlin in 1516, as we have seen, but he disliked the tone of the *Letters of Obscure Men* and he had serious reservations about the study of occult philosophy. 'Talmud, Kabbala, Tetragrammaton, Portae Lucis – empty names,' he wrote to a German colleague in 1518. 'I had rather see Christ infected by Scotus than by that rubbish.'

Erasmus was also ambivalent towards Italian humanism. It was from the Italians that he learned the importance of philology. He admired and published Valla's *Annotations on the New Testament*, which he found an inspiration. On the other hand, his visit to Rome in 1509 did not fill him with enthusiasm. On the contrary, it inspired his later rejection of the Roman humanists in his dialogue the *Ciceronianus* (1528), which reads like an answer to Bembo's discussion of imitation fifteen years earlier. As the author confessed, it 'offended quite a few Italians, as I rather thought it would'. In this dialogue, Erasmus presents a foolish pedant, Nosoponus, who refuses to use words or even inflections which cannot be found in the writings of Cicero. Nosoponus and other 'apes of Cicero' (*Ciceronis simii*) are criticized by another speaker, Bulephorus, who distinguishes imitation from emulation, the first concerned with following a model and the second with surpassing it. According to Bulephorus, a good orator will 'accommodate' the past to the present. Erasmus skilfully turned Cicero's central idea of *decorum* or appropriateness against the Ciceronians.[148]

Erasmus's dialogue dramatized a tension within the humanist movement, the tension between the desire to imitate the example of antiquity and the sense of historical perspective, in other words, the awareness of the cultural distance between past and present. However, the *Ciceronianus* has other levels of meaning. the dialogue is not purely concerned with Latin style but has political and religious overtones. Published in 1528, a year after the sack of Rome, it expresses the fear that paganism had been revived by Bembo and his circle. What inspires the imitation of Cicero, says Bulephorus, is *paganitas*. This reverence for a pagan author is a kind of 'superstition' and the Ciceronians are a 'new sect'. In language, their superstition takes the form of describing God as Jupiter or the pope as the ancient Roman *flamen* or high priest. In the visual arts, it means portraying Christ in the form of Apollo (as Michelangelo was in the course of doing in the Sistine Chapel).

However, Erasmus suffered a double rejection by later reformers of the Church, whether Protestants or Catholics. Luther and his supporters viewed him as too ambiguous (an 'eel') or too timid. Dürer wrote in his diary in 1521: 'Oh Erasmus of Rotterdam, why dost thou not come forward . . . Hear, thou knight of Christ, ride forward . . . attain the martyr's crown.' Erasmus's enthusiasm for some aspects of classical antiquity was also criticized. The man who criticized high Renaissance Rome as too pagan was himself described by Luther as 'a mocking Lucian' and even an 'atheist'.

Adding to the ironies, Erasmus was viewed by Catholics as too close to Luther. In France, the Sorbonne condemned his *Colloquies* in 1526. In Spain, the followers of Erasmus began to be viewed as 'luteranos' from about 1530 onwards. In Italy, a generation later, Erasmus was again described as a Lutheran.[149] These examples may give the impression that the Renaissance came to an end around 1530. That this view is mistaken is one of the points to be argued in the following chapter.

4

The Age of Variety: Late Renaissance

It was once assumed that the transition from Erasmus to Luther marked a 'crisis' or even the end of the Renaissance. The famous controversy between Erasmus and Luther in the 1520s about the freedom of the will used to be taken to symbolize the conflict between Renaissance and Reformation, with Erasmus representing the defeated humanist view of the 'dignity of man'. In similar fashion it has been argued that English humanism was 'arrested' in the 1530s. In the case of Catholic countries, it has often been claimed that the Council of Trent, called to reform the Church in response to Luther's challenge, brought the Renaissance to an end. After all, the trilingual project was defeated. The Council reaffirmed that the traditional Latin translation of the Bible, known as the Vulgate, was the official version, a major defeat for the project of a return 'to the sources'. The works of leading Renaissance writers from Erasmus to Machiavelli were placed on the *Index of Prohibited Books*.

Attempts have also been made to launch the idea of a 'Counter-Renaissance'. In art history in particular the 1530s have often been viewed as a turning-point, the age in which the Renaissance was replaced by 'Mannerism', defined as a reaction against harmony, against proportion and even against reason, expressing a spiritual and political crisis which is sometimes compared to that of the early twentieth century.[150]

There are no objective frontiers between periods in history. Periodization always involves a choice of what one considers important or significant. It is hard to deny that the 1520s and 1530s marked some kind of turning-point in European cultural history. Whether this turning-point is best described as the end of the Renaissance is another matter. For example, the idea that humanism ended in the early sixteenth century depends on the assumption that fifteenth-century Italian humanism was pagan, in contrast to northern 'Christian humanism' which paved the way for a Reformation which swept away humanism altogether. As we have seen (above, p. 99), Erasmus seems to have shared the view that the Italians were pagans, but this was a northern European misunderstanding of the south. Another reason for the appeal of the idea that the Renaissance ended in the 1520s may well be the assumption that history is the story of dramatic events rather than general trends. It was taken for granted that only one important historical actor could be on stage at a given time. Enter the Reformation: exit the Renaissance. The sack of Rome by an army which included German Protestants offered a vivid illustration of the sudden end of the movement.

An alternative view, to be developed in this chapter, is that the Renaissance continued unabated for another century, until the years around 1630. Mannerism, for instance, may be seen not as an anti-Renaissance but as a late phase or variety of Renaissance art, in which the rules of Cicero or Vitruvius were so well known to producers and consumers alike that artists both took and gave pleasure by breaking these rules or playing with them, subverting the expectations of viewers or readers, as in the famous case of the Palazzo del Tè at Mantua, designed and decorated by Raphael's pupil Giulio Romano, where the triglyphs seem to be slipping from the frieze and the ceilings to be about to crash onto the spectators.[151] New varieties of humanism were produced in the course of coexistence and inter-action with Protestantism and reformed Catholicism. In art, literature and music, some of the most thorough and successful attempts to emulate the examples of Italy and antiquity came in this period, not before. It was less a new period than an 'autumn' of the Renaissance, or even an Indian summer.[152]

Expressions of equality with the ancients reveal increasing cultural confidence in different parts of Europe.[153] Thus the dramatist Gil Vicente was known as the Portuguese Plautus, the humanist Jerónimo Osorio as the Portuguese Cicero, and the historian João de Barros as the Portuguese Livy. The historian Johannes Aventinus was the Bavarian Herodotus, while Pieter Corneliszoon Hooft was the Dutch Tacitus. The English Ovid was Michael Drayton, the Czech Ovid Simon Lomnický. Gaspara Stampa was the new Sappho. The playwright Nicodemus Frischlin was the German Aristophanes. The neo-Latin lyric poet Johannes Secundus was the Propertius of the Netherlands. The satirists Joseph Hall and Francisco Quevedo were new Senecas. The poet Luis Góngora was the Spanish Homer. The architect Hans Vredeman de Vries was the Flemish Vitruvius, and the astronomer Tycho Brahe was the Danish Ptolemy. The French poets, including Pierre Ronsard, known as the 'Pléiade' – another example of the place of small groups in innovation – were named after a group of Alexandrian poets.

Italy, on the other hand, posed more of a threat to the self-confidence of artists and writers elsewhere because the Italians did not take the achievements of others seriously enough. The German writer Johann Fischart, for example, complained about Vasari's discussions of German art in his *Lives of the Artists*. A resentment stemming from an unrequited love for Italy is a significant element in what might be called the 'Italophobia' of the period (see below, p. 173).

Variety

One reason for the title of this chapter is the stress on *varietas* in so many discussions of art and literature in the later sixteenth century. The inspiration or at least the legitimation of the trend to variety was the Roman orator Quintilian. It was common to quote or paraphrase the famous passage in Book X of Quintilian's treatise, in which the author argued that there are multiple standards of excellence in oratory, not one correct pattern.

It is true that some critics continued to stress the importance of unity in a literary work, and to criticize Ariosto, for example, because his *Orlando Furioso* lacked this formal unity. Again, it is true that print was promoting cultural standardization, and also that in the visual arts we see the rise of an international Italianate style at the expense of regional styles. All the same, this was the period in which classical or Italian models were interpreted in a self-consciously free and creative manner. There were also reactions against the Italian manner, Italophobia as well as Italophilia.

In other words, the conflict between the making and breaking of rules which has been discussed already (p. 70) was still sharper in this period than before. In literature, rules for different genres were formulated on the basis of Aristotle's *Poetics*. Aristotle was interpreted as saying, for instance, that tragedy dealt with protagonists of high status but comedy with ordinary people, and that plays should observe the unities of time, place and action. The Venetian publishing house of Giolito in particular spread Bembo's idea of a literary canon by producing editions of the modern classics, especially Petrarch, Boccaccio and Ariosto, presented to the public with the care and the critical apparatus previously reserved for ancient writers, with glossaries, commentaries and so on. Bembo himself was given the same treatment in the early 1560s.[154]

Giorgio Vasari encouraged the idea of an artistic canon through the judgements he made in his *Lives of the Artists*, first published in 1550 and in an enlarged edition in 1568. In architecture, Vitruvianism continued. The Venetian patrician Daniele Barbaro, a former pupil of Bembo, published an influential translation of Vitruvius in 1556 with a commentary on the text. Vitruvius became widely known outside Italy at about this time. A French translation of his work was published in 1547, with illustrations by the artist Jean Goujon, and a German translation came out in 1548. The architects Sebastiano Serlio (a former assistant of Raphael's) and Andrea Palladio helped establish the Vitruvian rules in their treatises *Five Books of Architecture* (1537–47) and *Four Books of Architecture* (1570). These books too were influential outside Italy. Serlio, for example, was translated into five languages in this period. Vasari was not translated but his book was in the libraries not only of fellow-architects such as Juan de Herrera and Inigo Jones but also of the magician John Dee and the painter El Greco. Palladio was not yet as important as he would become in the eighteenth century (see below, p. 235), but he too was known abroad. The Earl of Arundel, for instance, took his copy of Palladio to Italy in 1613.

However, the tyranny of the rules must not be exaggerated. Some playwrights disobeyed Aristotle. Anti-Petrarchism was a fashion as well as Petrarchism. The Dutch artist Karel van Mander challenged Vasari's Tuscan model of artistic excellence and defended the relativity of standards, pointing out that in Java, contrary to Europe, white stood for sorrow and black for joy.[155] Vasari himself left a place in his theory for what he called 'caprice' or 'licence', as in the case of the later career of his master Michelangelo, who 'departed a good deal from the kind of architecture regulated by proportion order and rule'. All the same, according to Vasari, 'all artists are under a great and permanent obligation to Michelangelo, seeing that he broke the bonds and chains that had previously confined them to the creation of traditional forms.' Thirty years later, in a treatise on music, Vincenzo Galilei (Galileo's father) compared the composer Cipriano de Rore with Michelangelo as an example of someone who knew when to break the rules. Giulio Romano was another. Again, Serlio's appropriately titled *Libro estra-ordinario* (1551) was concerned not so much with rules as with 'licence'. Palladio too, in the villas he designed for Venetian patricians, allowed himself to depart from his Roman models in important respects.[156]

In any case, there were conflicts between rival models. In painting, the great battle was the one between Florence and Venice, design versus colour. In the dialogue, there were the competing models of Plato, Cicero and Lucian. In literature more generally, the civil war was between Ciceronians and anti-Ciceronians. Many writers and teachers still accepted Cicero as a model of speaking and writing in Latin and the vernacular, but others now preferred models associated with the later Roman writers Seneca and Tacitus. The brevity and the biting phrases of Tacitus, and the relaxed, conversational style of Seneca both had their devotees.[157]

In practice, variety was necessarily the keynote of a time when cultural developments in France, Spain, England and elsewhere were more and more self-consciously independent than before. In the world of printing, the former dominance of Venice gave way to a situation of competition in which Antwerp, Lyons and Basel (together with Venice) were the front-runners. One might call this period an age of 'polycentrism'.

Peripheries

It was also in this period that Renaissance forms and ideas spread not only to certain 'peripheral' parts of the continent but even beyond Europe altogether.

In the arts, a diaspora of artists from the Netherlands was particularly important in spreading and adapting the Italian style. Hans Vredeman de Vries, originally from Friesland, was active in Frankfurt, Wolfenbüttel, Hamburg and elsewhere, and the printed pattern-books which he published travelled still further. In Prague in the age of Rudolf II (see below, p. 157), the emperor's artists included the sculptor Adrian de Vries and the landscape painter Roelandt Savery. In England, the Italian artists active in the age of Wolsey were succeeded by the portrait painter Hans Eworth (from Antwerp), and the sculptors William and Cornelius Cure (from Amsterdam) and Maximilian Colt (from Arras), who made the polychrome monument to Queen Elizabeth in Westminster Abbey.

Artists and humanists from the Netherlands also played a crucial part in the reception of the Renaissance in the Baltic region, writing history, teaching in colleges, painting portraits, carving tombs, designing fountains and so on.[158] For example, the expatriate Dutchmen Johannes Meursius and Johannes Isaacszoon Pontanus both wrote humanist histories of Denmark. In the case of funeral monuments, two sculptors from Mechelen were particularly important, Willem Boy and Willem van den Blocke. Boy made the tomb of Gustav Vasa in Uppsala, with recumbent effigies of the king and queen and four huge obelisks at the corners. Blocke was active at the Prussian court at Koenigsberg before he settled in Gdańsk, where he accepted commissions from the kings of Poland and Sweden. In some respects these sculptors from the Netherlands followed Italian models, notably the tombs in Rome made by Andrea Sansovino, but in other ways they diverged. The 'four-poster' style of free-standing funeral monument, resembling a marble bed, was a northern innovation. So was the decoration in the form of 'strapwork' (see below, p. 179). Polychrome monuments came into fashion, with brightly painted coats of arms as well as coloured marble and alabaster.

The Renaissance even spread beyond the limits of Europe, carried by merchants and missionaries. This was the time that some Asian painters discovered Renaissance art, whether in the form of Italian paintings or Flemish prints. In Isfahan, for instance, the traveller Pietro della Valle saw Italian paintings on sale in the shop of a Venetian merchant. In India, the Jesuits gave the Mughal emperor Akbar engravings and religious paintings in the Renaissance manner, including a print after Heemskerk, and Akbar ordered his artists to copy them. In China, the engravings by the Wierix brothers of Antwerp introduced by the Jesuit Matteo Ricci apparently inspired Chinese landscape painters not exactly to copy them but to modify their style in response to these alien images.[159]

Ricci was sufficiently steeped in classical culture to see China through Greek and Roman eyes. Chinese philosophy reminded him of the doctrines of Pythagoras, and the scholarly habit of retiring to the country to study made him think of Cicero in his villa at Tusculum. Ricci's humanist training made him receptive to the ideas of Confucius, whom he described as 'the equal of the pagan philosophers and superior to most of them'.[160] In return, he introduced the Chinese to the philosophy of Plato and the stoics and to the classical art of memory.

The Renaissance also affected the New World at this time. A Mexican bishop not only owned a copy of More's *Utopia* but also tried to translate it into practice in some Indian villages in his diocese.[161] There were Petrarchists in Peru in the 1590s, a group of them centred on the Academia Antártica in Lima. Conversely, knowledge of the New world affected views of paganism. Vicenzo Cartari's *Images of the Gods*, a handbook intended for artists, was extended in its 1615 edition to include the gods of Mexico. The two cultures were combined or mixed in the churches built in Spanish America after the conquest. These churches, especially their decorated façades and door-ways, included classical elements mediated by the Spanish Renaissance, which have been interpreted as at once a repre-sentation and a reinforcement of Spanish cultural superiority.

The sculptors, however, were often Amerindians accustomed to working in other styles, and hybrid forms inevitably resulted.[162]

The most remarkable case of cultural hybridity is surely that of the 'Inca humanist', Garcilaso. His mother was an Inca princess, while his father was a Spanish conquistador. Garcilaso left Peru for Spain in 1560, and lived the life of a man of letters. He frequented a circle of Spanish scholars and his library included books by Ficino and Bembo as well as Ariosto's *Orlando Furioso* and Castiglione's *Courtier*. Garcilaso began his literary career by translating into Spanish the Italian dialogues on Neoplatonic love by a Jewish physician who himself lived in two cultures, Leone Ebreo (see below, p. 206). He went on to write a history of Peru before the coming of the Spaniards which expressed his nostalgia for the lost empire of the Incas. The relation of his history to the reception of the Renaissance is apparent in the author's use of the language or languages of Western humanism, from philology to Neoplatonism, to criticize Western claims to cultural superiority.

Garcilaso was concerned to rebut the Spanish claims that the Amerindians were barbarians and idolaters. He discussed the importance of philosophers and poets in Inca times and claimed that the inhabitants of Peru already believed in one God and in the immortality of the soul before the arrival of the Spaniards. At first sight, Neoplatonism might seem to have little to do with the history of Peru, but in Garcilaso's work they are linked. His history implies that Peruvian culture fitted the pattern of the venerable antiquity and the ancient theology discussed by Ficino and others. Neoplatonists had a cult of the sun, and the sun was also worshipped in Peru, as the temple in Cuzco bears eloquent witness. Thus one form of syncretism, between pagan and Christian cultures in the first centuries after Christ, was used to justify another, with the humanists of the Renaissance as the mediators between the two.[163]

Classical Models

Ancient Roman models remained influential in this period, as the examples of Cicero and Virgil reveal. Cicero was not only reprinted but translated into the vernacular. For example,

between 1513 and 1603 his dialogue on friendship was translated three times into Spanish, twice into French and English,
and once into Czech, Italian, Portuguese, German and Polish.
The Ciceronian debate rumbled on. The supporters of the
imitation of the master included the French scholar-printer
Etienne Dolet and the German humanist Johann Sturm. Sturm
was an orthodox Christian Ciceronian, but Dolet, who would
later be burned for heresy, launched a characteristically violent
attack on Erasmus which was also a defence of Longolius and
of secular art.[164] On the other side, the critics of Cicero included
Petrus Ramus, the iconoclastic professor at the university of
Paris who also criticized Aristotle, and the leading humanist
of the second half of the century, the Netherlander Justus
Lipsius.

The critics of the Ciceronian model did not reject the example
of antiquity. Lipsius, for example, proposed an alternative
model, based on the Roman writers of a later period than
Cicero, the so-called 'silver age', such as Tacitus and above all
Seneca. This style, which following Quintilian Lipsius called
'Attic' as opposed to the 'Asiatic' style of the Ciceronians, aimed
at simplicity and brevity, tolerated irregularities, and was
characterized by the frequent use of parentheses and what
Lipsius called *acumina*, 'pointed' turns of phrase. This model of
Latin prose became fashionable in the 1570s and spread to the
vernacular, as we shall see (below, p. 142).[165] In verse, the
supreme model remained Virgil. The *Aeneid* was published in a
number of European vernaculars in this period, including
Italian, Spanish, German, French, English and Scots, translated
on occasion by practising poets such as Joachim Du Bellay or
the Earl of Surrey. In the drama, which was becoming more
important in cultural life in this period (see below, p. 148) the
Romans Plautus and Terence inspired a host of imitators.

However, in this age of variety some writers turned to Greek
exemplars as well as to Roman ones. In Paris, the humanist Jean
Dorat introduced his pupils (who included Ronsard) to Greek
literature, including Homer. Ronsard was impressed and would
claim later to have modelled his epic the *Franciade* 'on the spontaneous facility of Homer rather than the self-conscious
diligence of Virgil' (*plutôt sur la naïve facilité d'Homère que sur
la curieuse diligence de Virgile*). Homer was translated into

Italian, French, English and German in this period. The Greek playwrights Sophocles and Euripides (though not Aeschylus) also attracted interest at this time. The *Electra* of Sophocles, for instance, was translated into Spanish, French and Italian and adapted into Hungarian. The *Hecuba* of Euripides was translated into Latin (by Erasmus), Spanish, French and more than once into Italian. The ancient Greek romance by Heliodorus, the *Aethiopica*, was translated into French, Spanish, Italian and English.

In lyric poetry, a great discovery of this period was Pindar, especially his odes, praises of Olympian athletes in the high style, which had been published in the original Greek by Aldus in 1513. 'Ode' became a fashionable word at this period, used in Italian by Ariosto, in French by Ronsard and others, and in English by Shakespeare. The genre also became fashionable and was translated from the world of ancient Greek athletics to the world of the Renaissance court in order to give a short poem, especially a praise-poem, the dignity of epic. Ronsard, who admitted having 'pindarized' (*pindarizé*), also described himself as 'building' an ode, comparing the elevated style to the columns and the marble of a royal palace. He wrote in praise of King Henri II, the victory of 1544 and the peace of 1550. In Spain, Fernando de Herrera wrote odes to celebrate the victory of the Christians over the Turks at the battle of Lepanto and to mourn the death of King Sebastian of Portugal at the battle of Alcazarkebir (El-Ksar-el-Kebir). Mikołaj Sęp-Szarzyński wrote an ode in Polish to King Stefan Báthory, a 'royal hymn' of praise for his triumph over the 'the terrible tyrant' (*straszny tyran*) of Muscovy (Tsar Ivan IV, who has gone down in history as 'Ivan the Terrible'), while Jan Kochanowski celebrated the same victory in Latin.

An even more striking example of the appeal of classical models was the attempt made in a number of countries at this time to write poetry in classical metres. In Italy, for example, the attempt was made by Claudio Tolomei and Giangiorgio Trissino; in France, by Jean-Antoine de Baïf, a poet in the circle of Ronsard, with what he called his 'measured verses' (*vers mesurés à l'antique*), replacing quantity (the contrast between long and short syllables) by stress. In England, Spenser's friend Gabriel Harvey tried to naturalize the Latin hexameter. In

Germany, Martin Opitz admired measured verses (*gemessene Reime*), and wrote in alexandrines. No wonder then that contemporaries sometimes spoke of the 'reform' of poetry in this period, in the sense of progressing by going backwards, returning to classical models.

Needless to say that attempts to follow these models raised problems. Attempts to write in classical metres, ignoring differences in sound and structure between the ancient languages (in which the distinction between long and short syllables was important) and the modern vernaculars, generally led to criticism and disappointment. Harvey, for example, was mocked for his pains. The term 'ode' was criticized by some contemporaries as an unnecessary foreign word. Some writers thought that the imitation of Plautus was absurd, since comedy is concerned with manners and customs, and these customs change over time. As the dramatist Anton Francesco Grazzini put it, 'In Florence we no longer live as they once did in Athens and in Rome: there are no slaves, adopted children are not common.'

It was less problematic to take ancient Rome as a theme for poetry, as had been done from the time of Petrarch onwards, but never so often as in the later sixteenth century. After spending four years in the city, Joachim Du Bellay devoted a whole volume of poems to *Les Antiquités de Rome* (1558). One of the most famous admonishes the newly-arrived traveller in search of past glories that there is nothing but ruins remaining, a contrast with the former pride of the city which reveals the inconstancy of earthly things. *Nouveau venu, qui cherches Rome en Rome / Et rien de Rome en Rome n'apperçois . . .* This justly famous poem should be placed in a sequence. Like so many Roman buildings, it includes fragments of earlier constructions and was in its turn to become a quarry. Du Bellay's opening lines are translated from the Latin of a poet from Sicily, Janus Vitalis: *Qui Romam in media quaeris novus advena Roma / Et Romae in Roma nil reperis media.* Edmund Spenser then translated Du Bellay, 'Thou stranger, which for Rome in Rome here seekest / And naught of Rome in Rome perceiv'st at all'. There followed a Polish version (by Mikołaj Sęp-Szarzyński), and a Spanish one (by Francisco de Quevedo).[166]

Visits to Rome had other purposes besides meditating on the

inconstancy of human affairs. More and more artists went to study, measure and sketch the classical remains there (Greece being less accessible and attracting less attention). Among the testimonies to the interests of painters are the graffiti in Nero's Golden House, which include the names of Maarten van Heemskerck, Frans Floris, Karel van Mander and Bartholomeus Spranger.[167] Three artists have left us particularly rich evidence of the impression made on them by ancient Rome, the evidence of their sketchbooks. Heemskerck, who was in Rome in 1536, made drawings of the Colosseum, the Arch of Constantine, the Forum and the Pantheon. The Portuguese artist Francisco de Holanda, who was sent to Italy by King João III in 1538, also sketched the Colosseum, the Arch of Constantine and the Pantheon, as well as Trajan's Column, the decoration of the Golden House, the Belvedere Apollo, the Laocöon and the equestrian statue of Marcus Aurelius. The British architect Inigo Jones, in Italy in 1613 with the art-loving Earl of Arundel, took notes on classical costume, theatres and squares, sketched classical statues and annotated his copy of Palladio, comparing the illustrations with the original buildings such as the Pantheon.

Italian Models

As in earlier generations, Italian expatriates played an important role in presenting the Renaissance abroad. Rosso, Serlio and Primaticcio all spent much of their careers in France. Primaticcio was active not only as a painter and decorator but also in obtaining items from Italy for the collections of François I and other important people such as Cardinal Granvelle (see below, p. 161). The architect-painter Pellegrino Tibaldi spent nearly a decade in Spain, while the painter Arcimboldo spent a quarter of a century in Central Europe.

As for the foreigners who visited Italy in this period, they are so numerous that it might be simpler to list those who did not go. The reasons for the visits are better-documented than before and they include an interest in modern Italy as well as the antiquities. The journal of Sir Thomas Hoby, the translator of Castiglione into English, shows that he was in Padua in 1548 to study Italian and 'humanitie'. Jacques-Auguste de Thou, the future historian, recorded in his journal his excitement on visiting Italy in 1573. Besides meeting scholars and buying Greek texts, he viewed Isabella d'Este's collection at Mantua and spoke with Vasari in Florence. His friend Montaigne admired the Piazza San Marco in Venice, the display of statues on the Belvedere in Rome, the Palazzo Pitti in Florence and the monuments to Bembo and Ariosto in Padua and Ferrara.

In the case of the visual arts, Heemskerck's sketchbook reveals his interest in the decoration of the Vatican loggias by Raphael and his workshop, and also in the Palazzo del Tè at Mantua, while Francisco de Holanda made drawings of the equestrian monuments of Gattemelata in Padua and Colleoni in Venice. The rise of Netherlands Mannerism owes a good deal to the years which Frans Floris spent in Italy, studying and copying the work of Michelangelo and Giulio Romano. John Shute was sent to Italy in 1550 by his patron the Duke of Northumberland (as he reminded the duke in the dedication to his treatise on building), not only to look at ancient monuments but also 'to confer with the doings of the skilful masters in architecture'. In 1586 the Duke of Bavaria sent Martin Weiss 'to learn the praiseworthy art of painting more firmly in Italy' (*in Welschland die löbliche Malerkunst noch fester zu lernen*).[168] When Inigo Jones was in Italy, he sketched paintings by Raphael, Michelangelo and Parmigianino as well as classical remains, made notes on the design of piazzas and on the church of San Pietro in Montorio by Bramante, in the form of a circular temple, which he says he 'observed often'. In similar fashion, now that the Italians had finally become the models in music as well as in the other arts, musical pilgrimages to Italy began, to Venice in particular. Hans Leo Hassler left Nuremberg for Venice in 1584 and became a pupil of Andrea Gabrieli. Christian IV sent four of his musicians to Venice in 1599 to study with Andrea's nephew and pupil Giovanni Gabrieli. The Landgrave Moritz of Hesse-Kassel followed Christian's example and sent the composer Heinrich Schütz to Italy in 1609, again to study with Giovanni Gabrieli.

In literature too Italy remained a model to emulate. In the early part of the century, personal contacts seem to have been necessary to encourage this emulation. For example, the English poet Sir Thomas Wyatt was sent on a mission to Italy in 1527, and when he was in that country, in the words of a later sixteenth-century critic, he 'tasted the sweet and stately measures and style of the Italian poesie'. In similar fashion, it was during his years in Italy that Francisco de Sá discovered the sonnet and the eclogue, and he introduced these poetic forms to Portugal on his return.

Alternatively, Italians abroad spread the knowledge of the new forms. The diplomat Andrea Navagero, the friend of Bembo (see above, p. 75), met the poet Joan Boscán while on a mission to Spain in 1526. As the latter testified in the preface to his poems, 'one day in Granada with Navagero . . . discussing intellectual and literary matters with him, especially the variations between languages, he asked me why I did not try to write in the Castilian tongue some sonnets and other literary forms employed by the good authors of Italy' (*estando un día en Granada con el Navagero . . . tratando con él en cosas de ingenio y de letras y especialmente en las variedades de las muchas lenguas, me dixo por qué no provara en lengua castellana sonetos y otras artes de trobas usadas por los buenos authores de Italia*). Boscán went on to do precisely this.

Personal contacts allowed foreigners to understand more quickly and more fully what the Italians were doing. Print, on the other hand, spread the new models more widely and also allowed foreigners to distance themselves more easily from these models. The example of Lyons may reveal the complexities of the process and the number of intermediaries involved. In Lyons the community of Italian merchants and bankers provided a substantial demand for books in Italian which local printers supplied. Jean de Tournes, for example, a friend of a number of French poets as well as their publisher, also printed many books in Italian, including Dante and Petrarch. Guillaume Rouillé, who had been apprenticed to Giolito in Venice, married an Italian and published Castiglione, Dante, Petrarch and Ariosto in Italian. Once in circulation, the books also attracted the interest of French readers.

Printed music too spread the knowledge of Italian models abroad. The madrigals of Roland de Lassus, for example, which set to music lyrics by Petrarch, Sannazzaro and Ariosto, were first published in 1555. By this time music publishing was established outside Italy, in Antwerp, for example, where Pierre

Phalèse published a collection of Italian madrigals, *Harmonia celeste*, in 1583. The next stage was to publish Italian madrigals in translation. In England, for example, Nicholas Yonge did this in his *Musica Transalpina* (1588), Thomas Watson in his *First Set of Italian Madrigals Englished* (1590) and Thomas Morley in his *Madrigals* (1594).

Translations from Italian as well as translations from the classics were becoming more and more numerous in the later sixteenth century, in France, for example, and in England. The discovery of Italy by foreign travellers encouraged translation, and translation in turn encouraged readers to discover Italy for themselves. Among the Italian authors most translated were Ariosto, whose *Orlando Furioso* appeared in French, Spanish, English and Polish; Castiglione, whose *Courtier* was rendered into Spanish, French, English, Latin and German; and Tasso, whose *Jerusalem Delivered* was published in Spanish, English, French, Latin and Polish, while his *Aminta* appeared in Latin, English and in two separate versions in Croat. Translations also helped spread the knowledge of Italian art. Alberti's treatise on architecture, for example, was published first in Italian translations (1546, 1550) and then in French (1553) and Spanish (1582). Serlio's treatise on architecture was even more successful, appearing in Dutch, French, Spanish, Latin and English versions as well as the original Italian.

Architecture

Thanks to these treatises the new term 'architect' entered a number of European vernaculars at this time. In France, for instance, Bramante was described as an *architecte* in 1529 by the printer Geoffroy Tory (who knew Italy at first hand). Serlio was described in 1541 as the king's *architecteure ordinaire*. Philibert de l'Orme opened his treatise with the claim that 'There are few true architects today' (*il y a aujourd'hui peu de vrais architectes*), since the majority are simply master masons. The true architect knows *lettres* as well as *oeuvres manuelles*. A little later, the term was used in Spanish to describe Juan de Herrera, 'Architecto de su Magestad'. In England, John Shute, who had studied in Italy, described himself as an 'architect' in 1563, while

Robert Smythson was called an 'architector' on his funeral monument in 1614.

As in the previous period, new palaces gave architects an opportunity to show their mettle. In Paris in the 1540s, Pierre Lescot was put in charge of the Louvre, at that point a palace for François I and his successor Henri II. In Heidelberg in the 1550s, elector Otto Heinrich of the Palatinate commissioned a place known after him as the Ottheinrichbau (figure 9). In Florence in the 1560s, Cosimo de' Medici commissioned the Uffizi from Vasari to serve as offices for his growing bureaucracy – hence its name – as well as a place to display his collection of works of art. It was also in the 1560s that Juan Bautista de Toledo and Juan de Herrera were building the Escorial for Philip II. In the 1570s, Uraniborg was constructed on the island of Hveen on the orders of King Frederik II for the use of the astronomer Tycho Brahe. Uraniborg has been described as an early scientific 'research institute', complete with library, laboratories and the famous observatory, but it should also be viewed as a Renaissance palace, with towers, galleries and so on. Brahe himself was familiar with the work of Vitruvius, Serlio and Palladio. He decorated Uraniborg with elegant Latin inscriptions. For its neighbour Stjerneborg he commissioned a 'Hall of Illustrious Men' in traditional Renaissance style (see above, pp. 23, 43), with portraits of famous astronomers, including Ptolemy, Copernicus and himself.[169]

By this time classical or Italianate models of building appealed not only to rulers and their courts but also to urban patriciates and to rural nobilities. The civic Renaissance had not completely withered away. In Italy, the new Library of St Mark at Venice was designed by Jacopo Sansovino and described by Andrea Palladio as 'perhaps the richest and most ornate building since the time of the ancients'. Palladio himself designed the Basilica (that is, the town hall) and the Teatro Olimpico, both in Vicenza. It is no accident that all this work was carried out on the territory of the last important Italian republic. Town halls in the new style were also built outside Italy, in Antwerp, for example, in Toledo and in Poznań, where the architect was an Italian from Lugano. Other imposing civic buildings from this period include the University of Alcalà (figure 10); the Cloth Hall of Cracow, rebuilt in the 1550s with the help of an Italian architect; the Arsenals of Augsburg and Gdańsk; and the Bourse of Copenhagen, begun in 1620 by Hans II Steenwinkel, yet another example of the Netherlands diaspora.[170]

Antwerp Town Hall makes a good example of the use of Serlio's designs. Its façade included a triumphal arch, obelisks (a symbol of eternal fame) and the inscription SPQA, 'The Senate and the People of Antwerp' thus presenting the city – like so many cities in this period – as a new Rome (figure 11).[171] The Town Hall has been interpreted as 'an expression of Antwerp's struggle for freedom'. Some contemporaries agreed even if they disapproved, like the leading churchman who wrote that 'It would be a very good thing to make them erase their SPQA which they inscribe everywhere on their buildings and edifices, pretending to be a free republic, and that the prince cannot command them without their consent.'[172] When the humanist Johannes Goropius dedicated his study of the origins of the city to the 'senate and people' of Antwerp in 1569, he may have been offering something more than a conventional homage to classical antiquity.

In England, by contrast, the municipal authorities in Leominster, for example, or in Titchfield resisted the Renaissance

Figure 9 Ottheinrichbau, Heidelberg. (Copyright © Roger-Viollet, Paris.) It is difficult to say whether the deviations from the classical norm are self-consciously 'mannerist' or simply provincial.

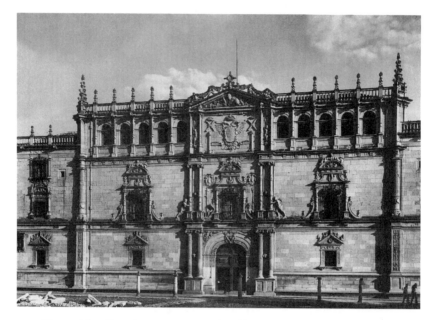

Figure 10 Façade to entrance of Collegio de S. Ildefonso, Alcalà.
(Copyright © Institut Amatller d'Art Hispanique.)

and commissioned new town halls in the traditional vernacular style. It was only after 1660 that they discovered the dignity of classical architecture.[173]

In the countryside this was the age of the villa, a self-conscious revival of an ancient Roman practice (see below, p. 176). The ruins of the Emperor Hadrian's villa at Tivoli, not far from Rome, were studied, measured and even excavated. It was also in this period, especially from the 1540s to the 1570s, that Andrea Palladio built his famous villas for Venetian patricians, such as the Villa Foscari, the Villa Rotonda near Vicenza and the Villa Barbaro at Maser, commissioned by the editor of Vitruvius, Daniele Barbaro, together with his brother Marcantonio. A combination of farms with country retreats for the summer, these originally modest residences were given a new dignity by Palladio's variations on classical themes, adapting grand porticos from Roman temples and other features from Roman baths.[174]

In other parts of Europe, Italian villa and palace designs were

Figure 11   Town Hall, Antwerp, façade. (Architectural Association Photo
Library; photograph copyright © Hazel Cook.)

themselves adapted to suit not only local traditions but also the
needs of aristocracies who preferred hunting to farming or, on
the other hand, lived in the country for most of the year rather
than the summer months alone. The results include the
châteaux of the Loire, the country houses of Elizabethan
England and the 'pleasure houses' (*Lusthäuser*) of central
Europe, from Stuttgart to Kratochvile ('pastime') in southern
Bohemia. The Bohemian castles of the later sixteenth century
with their arcaded courtyards, often the work of Italian architects, have been described as 'more italianate than the
better-known French *châteaux* of the Renaissance'.[175] One of
the most remarkable of these châteaux was at Anet, a palace in
the form of a hunting lodge, or a hunting lodge in the form of
a palace, designed by Philibert de l'Orme for Diane de Poitiers,
mistress of Henri II of France, and described in poems by
Ronsard and Du Bellay. The sculptured dogs and deer on the
gateway, like the fountain of Diana within, simultaneously
alluded to the king's love of the hunt and identified Diane with
the goddess Diana.[176]

In England, this was the age of the great Elizabethan country houses, such as Longleat in Wiltshire, Hatfield in Hertfordshire and Hardwick in Derbyshire ('Hardwick Hall, more glass than wall'). The place of these houses in the history of European architecture remains the subject of debate. On one side it has been argued that 'posthumously and at long range', the Italian Sebastiano Serlio 'influenced English architecture more than any other single man'. After all, Hatfield and other houses have loggias, an Italian invention ill-suited to the English climate. Chimneys, more necessary than in Italy, were sometimes disguised as classical columns and decorated with Ionic capitals. On the other side, it has been claimed that the new house designs were 'totally independent of developments elsewhere in Europe'. For example, the plans reflected not Italian models but the social functions of the house, the centrality of the great hall, for example, in which the owner of the house ate himself, offered hospitality to guests and oversaw his servants.[177]

In the case of decoration, it is sometimes difficult for a historian to tell whether divergences from the classical model are conscious or unconscious, provincial misunderstanding or fashionable mannerism.[178] They may even be both at once, as in the case of the Ottheinrichbau in Heidelberg (figure 9), supposedly combining 'solecisms' with 'mannerist elements'.[179] In the case of Poland, it seems impossible to distinguish between an Italian Mannerism (defined as self-conscious and complex) and a Polish Mannerism (defined as naif and spontaneous).[180] Similar points could be made about England. The language of architecture was both classical and vernacular. Some critics see it as no more than a mixture, others regard it as 'a true synthesis, a style in its own right'.[181] There are no precise criteria for distinguishing a mixture from a synthesis, but it is worth adding that what from a lender's point of view is 'misunderstanding' or 'solecism' may be creative variation when looked at from the standpoint of the borrower.

Only at the end of the period did the classical elements become dominant, as in the case of Inigo Jones. In his case it is possible to combine the evidence from buildings with that of his reactions to Italian architecture, as recorded in the Roman sketchbook of 1614 and the notes he made in a copy of Palladio's *Four books*, a volume which its modern editor describes as 'used almost to

Figure 12   Andrea Palladio, Palazzo Chiericati, Vicenza. (Private
collection.)

destruction'. The house – or palace – he designed for the Queen
at Greenwich makes a good example of creative imitation,
taking a design from Palladio (Palazzo Chiericati in Vicenza)
and turning it in a sense inside out (figures 12, 13).[182]

Painting and Sculpture

In this period, both classical themes and Italian styles spread
more and more widely in Europe, whether carried by expatriate
artists or imitated by local talents. In the case of painting, a
single genre may be taken to illustrate these developments:
scenes from classical mythology, which often followed Ovid's
poetic descriptions in his *Metamorphoses*, a book translated in
this period into English, French, German, Spanish and Italian.
Titian's mythologies or, as he called them, his *poesie*, appealed
to patrons outside Italy, notably to Philip II of Spain. Some of
these mythologies circulated in engraved reproductions and
inspired imitation. Veronese represented the pagan gods at Villa

Figure 13   Inigo Jones, Queen's House, Greenwich. (Photograph A. F. Kersting.) Jones's adaptation of Palladio's Palazzo Chiericati is a good example of creative imitation.

Maser, especially in the Stanza di Bacco and the Sala di Olimpo. At Fontainebleau, Primaticcio produced a series of paintings of Ulysses at much the same time that Dorat was introducing Ronsard to Homer. The so-called 'school of Fontainebleau' also painted the goddess Diana (on occasion with the features of Diane de Poitiers) and the transformation of Actaeon into a deer, so dramatically recounted by Ovid. In Prague, Bartholomaeus Spranger painted Venus, Mars, Vulcan, Mercury and Hercules for the Emperor Rudolf II. In Antwerp, Frans Floris produced a series of paintings of the Labours of Hercules.

Even Pieter Brueghel, whose work might seem to have nothing to do with antiquity, has a place in this trend. Brueghel belonged to a circle of Antwerp humanists which included the geographer Abraham Ortelius. His *Icarus*, for example, at first sight a landscape painting without a deeper meaning, turns out to be an illustration of a passage from Book 8 of Ovid's *Metamorphoses* describing the flight of Icarus and his father

Daedalus. 'Some fisherman perhaps, plying his quivering rod, some shepherd leaning on his staff, or a peasant bent over his plough caught sight of them as they flew past.'

In the case of sculpture, the new trends may be illustrated by two genres of increasing importance, the fountain and the equestrian monument. Elaborately sculptured fountains became more and more common ornaments of city squares and palace courtyards. The themes were generally taken from classical mythology. In Italy, to cite only the most famous examples, there was the Neptune fountain in Florence by Bartolomeo Ammannati and the Neptune fountain in Bologna by the most celebrated sculptor of the later sixteenth century, the Italianized Frenchman Giambologna (Jean de Boulogne). The Bologna fountain illustrates a passage in Virgil's *Aeneid* about the god calming the waves and may be read as an allegory of the pope's rule over the city. In Germany, there was the Apollo fountain at Nuremberg and the Hercules fountain at Augsburg. In France, the most famous was the Fontaine des Innocents in Paris, by Jean Goujon, with reliefs of nymphs which are reminiscent of Hellenistic art and were made at the very time that Ronsard was drawing inspiration from Greece.

Equestrian statues on the Roman model – more specifically the model of the statue of Marcus Aurelius in Rome – were revived in fifteenth-century Italy to honour mercenary leaders. Donatello made the famous 'Gattamelata' at Padua (see above, p. 35), and Leonardo's master Verrocchio made the monument to Bartolomeo Colleoni, erected in Venice. In the sixteenth century, on the other hand, this kind of monument became the privilege of princes, including Grand Duke Cosimo de'Medici of Florence, whose statue on Piazza della Signoria was the first on a public square, a powerful symbol of dominance in what had once been republican space. Foreign rulers also began to commission equestrian statues – from Italian artists. For example, an equestrian statue of Louis XII was placed over the gateway to his palace at Blois. Catherine de' Medici asked Michelangelo for such a monument to her late husband Henri II. He refused but recommended his pupil Daniele de Volterra, who produced what has been called 'the first great bronze horse since Verrocchio'.[183] Still concerned with the rider, Catherine asked Francesco de' Medici to lend her his sculptor Giambologna but her request was refused. Henri IV had better fortune. His statuette by Giambologna was produced in his lifetime and the monument itself, by Pietro Tacca, was finished shortly after his death and erected at the Pont-Neuf in Paris in 1614. At much the same time a statue of Philip III by Tacca, a present from the Grand Duke of Tuscany, was erected on the Plaza Mayor of Madrid.

Varieties of Humanism

Like 'architect', the term 'humanist', recorded in Latin in the previous chapter, came into use at this time in a number of vernaculars. In Spanish the word was in use by 1552. In French the term is recorded in 1554, when the municipal authorities of Grenoble were looking for a 'humaniste' as a schoolmaster. A generation later, Montaigne contrasted 'les humanistes' with the theologians. In Portuguese, the term was used around 1578 by Diogo do Couto in his dialogue *O Soldado prático*. In English it is recorded by 1589.

Some of the leading humanists of fifteenth century Italy continued to enjoy a great reputation. The works of Bruni, Poggio and Valla were reprinted in the sixteenth century in Basel and elsewhere. Valla attracted particular interest. His critique of the Donation of Constantine was a useful weapon in the hands of Protestants and endeared him to Luther as it had to Ulrich von Hutten. His philological approach to the New Testament interested the Sozzinis, Italian heretics who gave their name to 'Socinianism'. Petrus Ramus, who took a similar pleasure in shocking the philosophical establishment with a criticism of Aristotle, was another admirer of Valla's.[184]

All the same, the humanist movement was changing. A greater variety of interests and attitudes can be found at this time. 'Variety' is a polite word for what may also be seen as fragmentation. The reader may well ask at this point whether humanism was a movement any longer. Probably not. The ideals which a small group had fought for in the early fifteenth century were now taken for granted in many circles. Indeed, they affected the everyday life of a substantial minority of Europeans, as the following chapter will attempt to show. The price of this success was a certain loss of intellectual cohesion. In philosophy, for example, the Neoplatonic movement now had to compete with a revival of epicureanism, scepticism, and above all of stoicism (see below, p. 207). Late humanists took an interest in more antiquities, not only Greek and Roman but also the barbarian wisdom of the Celtic druids, the Persian magi and the Indian Brahmins or 'gymnosophists'.

There was also an increasing interest in Arab culture.[185] Pico della Mirandola had studied Arabic in the 1480s as part of his plan to master human knowledge, followed by his nephew Gianfrancesco Pico and Egidio da Viterbo. The French humanist Guillaume Postel learned Arabic in Istanbul in 1536, while the Netherlander Nicolas Clenardus learned it a few years later in Granada and Fez (buying a Moroccan slave to assist his studies). Spaniards were for obvious reasons interested in a language spoken in their own peninsula, and adepts included Antonio Nebrija and Diego Hurtado de Mendoza. A chair of Arabic was established at the university of Salamanca in 1542. One reason for this interest was the hope of converting Muslims to Christianity, but some scholars became interested in Islam more or less for its own sake. The Italian Protestant humanist Celio Secundo Curione wrote a *History of the Saracens*.

An interest in ancient Egypt and its esoteric wisdom went back to late fifteenth-century Italy, notably to the circle of Ficino, who studied the ancient treatise on hieroglyphs by a certain 'Horapollo', to the entourage of Alexander VI, who was supposed to be a descendant of Osiris, and to *The Dream of Poliphilo*, a romance set in a landscape of ancient ruins. Horapollo's *Hieroglyphics* and *The Dream of Poliphilo* were published in French translation in the mid-sixteenth century. The fashion for emblems from the 1530s onward (see below, p. 205) owed something to the discussions of the meaning of hieroglyphs, which Greek philosophers had interpreted as moral symbols rather than a form of writing. In turn, emblems affected the way in which hieroglyphs were perceived. Egyptian obelisks also attracted interest. The word 'obelisk' (*obelisco*, *obelisque*) entered Italian, French and English at this time. Interpreted as symbols of eternal fame, these obelisks multiplied on tombs and country houses or stood by themselves, as in the case of the obelisk erected by Henrik Rantzau at Segeberg in honour of Frederick II of Denmark (figure 14). The fascination of Egypt

Figure 14   Obelisk from H. Rantzau, *Hypotyposis* (1592), p. 117. (By
permission of the Syndics of Cambridge University Library.) Only a few
years after the erection of obelisks in the Rome of Sixtus V, the fashion had
spread to Denmark.

continued to be felt in the later sixteenth century, among
orthodox and heterodox alike. Pope Sixtus V had an obelisk
erected in Rome in 1587. The Dominican friar Giordano Bruno
was burned for heresy in the same city in 1600, charged among
other things with attempting to revive the religion of the ancient
Egyptians. Around 1600, the humanist Nicolas-Claude Fabri

de Peiresc and his friends among the magistrates of Aix-en-Provence were collecting Egyptian antiquities, including mummies, with enthusiasm.[186]

Still more important was what might be called the humanist 'rehabilitation' of the Middle Ages, linked to the spread of humanism beyond Italy. This may look like a reversal of all the movement had stood for, given the way in which fifteenth-century Italian humanists had defined themselves in opposition to what they called the 'Middle Ages'. However, it may be more illuminating to regard this rehabilitation as one example among others of the conflict between the spirit and the letter of the revival of antiquity. The literalists argued for building in the Roman style irrespective of climate, for example, or writing poetry in classical metres, whatever the differences between Latin and French (say) or Polish. Their opponents argued for the accommodation of classical and Italian culture to local circumstances. Did not the Romans of Cicero's day reverence their past? If sixteenth-century Italians followed Petrarch, why should the English not follow Chaucer?

In France, for example, there was a kind of Celtic revival at this time. Humanists praised Vercingetorix the Gaul rather than his enemy Caesar and investigated the philosophy of the Druids.[187] In his poem the *Galliade* (1578), Guy Lefevre de La Boderie claimed that ancient Gaul had been the birthplace of the arts and sciences, to which they were returning in his own day. Medieval French literature was discussed and celebrated by French scholars such as Montaigne's friend Etienne Pasquier. The English, or at least some scholars in the circle of Archbishop Matthew Parker, notably Laurence Nowell and William Lambarde, discovered their Anglo-Saxon past. Parker, a scholar himself, commissioned his printer John Day to design type in Anglo-Saxon characters so that documents could be printed in the original language. In Italy itself, Tasso chose the Crusades as the theme of his epic poem *Jerusalem Delivered*, while the humanist Carlo Sigonio wrote an important study of the history of Italy between 560 and 1200.

The interest in the non-classical past was especially marked on the periphery of Europe, which might be defined in this case as the area which the Romans never conquered. The Hungarians identified themselves with the Huns, the Poles with the

Sarmatians, the Danes with the Cimbrians, and the Spaniards and the Swedes with the Goths. For example, Johannes Magnus, Archbishop of Uppsala, went into exile in Rome after the Swedish Reformation and used his leisure to write history. His *History of the Goths* (posthumously published in 1554) contradicted the traditional humanist view by presenting the Goths as pious, liberty-loving, and even as enemies of barbarism. Johannes traced the descent of the Swedes from the Goths, after Magog son of Noah had migrated to Scandinavia. This history, which was not well received in Denmark (where the king commissioned a historian to refute it) led to a cult of the Goths in Sweden. King Erik XIV liked to be known as 'the restorer of the Goths' and commissioned tapestries illustrating the deeds of Magog, Gothus and other early kings of Sweden. His successors Johan III and Karl IX also took an interest in the Goths, an interest which stimulated historical research. The scholar-official Johan Bure travelled Sweden in the 1590s collecting runic inscriptions in the way in which earlier humanists had collected Roman ones, and publishing them in 1624 with the title *Monumenta Sveo-Gothica*. Johannes Messenius, a professor at Uppsala, also transcribed runes and wrote plays about Sweden in Gothic times.[188]

Humanism, Music and Natural Philosophy

Disciplinary varieties of humanism are as striking in this period as regional ones. Music has so far received little attention in these pages, apart from the idea of a musical renaissance, suggested by Tinctoris, or Ficino's attempts to draw down planetary influences by playing the appropriate notes. The reason for this omission is simple. The musical achievements of the fourteenth and fifteenth centuries had little to do with the main themes of this book, the reception of classical and Italian culture.[189] On the contrary, in the case of music it was the Italians who admired foreign products, especially those of Josquin (see above, p. 51). A character in Castiglione's *Courtier* remarked acidly that 'a certain motet that was sung before the Duchess pleased no one and was not thought good until it was known to be by Josquin des Prez' (Book 2, chapter 35).

From the 1570s onward, on the other hand, there were attempts to revive ancient Greek music by humanists such as the Florentine Girolamo Mei or the Frenchman Jean-Antoine de Baïf, whose interest in classical metres has already been mentioned. Baïf intended his poems to be sung and founded an Academy of Poetry and Music under royal patronage.[190] The most thorough student of the classical sources describing the music of ancient Greece – the differences between the Dorian, Phrygian and Lydian modes, for instance – was Mei. He did not publish his discoveries himself but communicated them to Vincenzo Galilei. Vincenzo, the father of Galileo, wrote a *Dialogue on Ancient and Modern Music* in which one speaker claimed that after the barbarian invasion of Italy, people 'took as little notice of music as of the West Indies'. Only recently had scholars begun 'to seek to rescue it from the darkness in which it had been buried' and to restore it to its ancient state.

These scholarly researches had important practical consequences. Mei, Galilei and their friends criticized polyphonic music, in which the different voices followed independent lines, and advocated monody, the *canto fermo* as they called it. Once again we find that a small group played a crucial role in innovation. The centre of the group, which became known as the *Camerata*, was Count Giovanni de' Bardi, who attempted to reconstruct a Greek musical festival in his *Victory of Apollo over the Serpent*, performed in 1589 as part of the entertainments for the wedding of Ferdinando de' Medici. It was in Bardi's house that the members of the Camerata met.

This group included Galilei; the singer Giulio Caccini, who invented what might be called a conversational style of singing, the *stile recitativo* or *rappresentativo*; and Jacopo Peri, who composed the music for a musical drama in the new style, *Euridice*, performed in 1600 and now regarded as the first surviving opera (another, *Dafne*, had been performed in the house of Bardi's rival Jacopo Corsi in 1598). Monteverdi was among the visitors to Corsi's house and was inspired to write in the new style, the 'second practice' as he called it (*seconda prattica*), in which words dominate the music rather than the other way round. Monteverdi's *Orfeo* was performed in 1607, his *Arianna* in 1608.[191] A few years later, in 1627, the German composer Heinrich Schütz composed a new version of *Dafne*, this time with a German libretto by the poet Martin Opitz. The international opera was launched. In the course of seeking to revive something old, the humanists had helped to invent something new.

A similar paradox characterizes the role played by humanists in the study of nature. For the circle of Leonardo Bruni there was no such role, since the *studia humanitatis*, as we have seen (p. 29), focused on the human not the natural world. All the same, the humanist movement did have consequences for the 'natural philosophers', as they were called at the time ('scientist' is a nineteenth-century term). The point was that ancient writers were treated as authorities in these fields: Hippocrates and Galen in medicine, for example, Ptolemy in geography and cosmology, and Aristotle virtually everywhere. Hence the humanist enterprise of going back to the sources and of editing texts from the best manuscripts was important for natural philosophy, as some fifteenth-century scholars realized. One was the famous philologist Ermolao Barbaro (see above, p. 45), who emended the text of Pliny's *Natural History*. Another was the German astronomer Regiomontanus, who studied Ptolemy in the original Greek.[192]

Natural philosophers shared the humanist reverence for classical antiquity. Like the poets, they wanted a 'reform'. Some of them, including Francis Bacon at the time of his early work *The Wisdom of the Ancients*, believed that the progress of knowledge depended not on new discoveries but on the recovery of what the ancient sages had already known. This esoteric knowledge was communicated to the few in the coded form of myth. The German alchemist Michael Maier held similar views. His book *Atalanta Fleeing* (1617) followed the same procedure by presenting 'the secrets of nature' in the form of fifty emblems (a genre discussed below, p. 230). The title itself alluded to the myth of the fleet-footed girl who would only accept a suitor who defeated her in a race, and lost because she stopped to pick up the three golden apples he dropped on the way. The belief in the wisdom of the ancients gives a more precise meaning to the praise of Regiomontanus and Copernicus for their 'restoration' of astronomy. Copernicus was also described as having 'emended' astronomy, as if it were a corrupt classical text. Or as the Lutheran humanist Philip Melanchthon put it, 'celestial philosophy is reborn' (*renata est haec philosophia de rebus coelestibus*).[193]

In this domain the gap between learned and popular culture was less wide than it was in the humanities. Just as Alberti learned from builders, so the German humanist Georgius Agricola derived from the miners of Bohemia much of the information he published in his treatise *On Metals* (1556). The gap between the 'two cultures' of arts and sciences was also much narrower than it later became, if such a gap existed at all at this time. On one side, leading natural philosophers such as Johan Kepler and Galileo Galilei showed great interest in the humanities. Kepler, for instance, wrote poetry. His treatise *The Harmony of the World* (1619) referred to the political theorist Jean Bodin in its 'digression' on harmony in the state. He explained astronomical references in classical texts for the benefit of humanist friends and acquaintances.[194] As for Galileo, he had characteristically strong views on literature, painting and sculpture. He approved of Ariosto, for instance, but disapproved of Tasso.[195] Again, the German Andreas Libavius stressed the importance of the cultivation of *humanitas* for the 'chemist' (*chymicus*).[196]

On the humanist side, we might point to the vogue of the scientific poem at this period, on the model of Lucretius on *The Nature of the Universe*. The poet-mathematician Jacques Peletier, for example, described the cosmos and celebrated the human desire for knowledge, while the Calvinist Guillaume Salluste Du Bartas put a great deal of scientific information into his epic on the creation, *La Semaine* (1578), a poem so popular that it had reached its forty-first French edition by 1623.[197] We might also appeal to the evidence of libraries such as that of Sir Walter Raleigh, who owned works on zoology, medicine, botany, physiognomy, astronomy (including Copernicus) and chemistry (including Libavius). In similar fashion, the 'cabinet of curiosities' (see below, chapter 6) would normally contain antiquities, such as coins and medals, juxtaposed with the remains of unusual animals, birds or fish.

Enthusiasm for the contribution of the ancients to natural philosophy coexisted with an increasing readiness to criticize them when the evidence made this inevitable. The two famous cases are those of Copernicus and Vesalius, whose books on astronomy and medicine respectively were both published for the first time in 1543.

Copernicus shared the humanist interests of his day. He claimed that it was in the course of reading Cicero and Plutarch that he discovered references to ancient philosophers who believed that the earth moved. His description of the central position of the sun would have pleased Ficino. 'In the middle of all sits Sun enthroned. In this most beautiful temple could we place this luminary in any better position from which he can illuminate the whole at once? He is rightly called the lamp, the mind, the ruler of the universe; Hermes Trismegistus names him the visible God, Sophocles' Electra calls him all-seeing. So the sun sits as upon a royal throne ruling his children the planets which circle around him.' We are not very far from the Neoplatonic world of Garcilaso the Inca (see above, p. 108), describing the Peruvian cult of the sun.

How well known the theories of Copernicus were in this period it is not easy to say. His book had only three editions between 1543 and 1617. However, summaries of the heliocentric theory were also in circulation.[198] The theory was also discussed at universities. At the university of Salamanca, for example, the new statutes of 1561 named Copernicus among the authors who could be used in the study of astronomy. Casual references suggest that the name Copernicus was generally associated with heliocentrism, or at least with novelty. Montaigne, for example, refers to the heliocentric theory in one of his essays. John Donne, who described Copernicus as going to hell as a penalty for having turned the cosmos upside down, was himself known as a 'Copernicus in poetry', presumably for his stylistic innovations.[199]

Copernicus owes his later fame to the fact that in the last resort he was prepared to diverge from the opinions of Ptolemy. In similar fashion, Vesalius was prepared, reluctantly, to correct Galen, who had based some of his statements about human anatomy on dissections not of humans but of monkeys. Vesalius presented his work as a contribution to the revival, restoration or rebirth of medicine. 'In this fortunate age,' he wrote, 'medicine, like every other study, has for some time been beginning to revive and to raise its head from the deepest darkness into which it had been plunged . . . We have seen medicine successfully reborn, (*medicinam prospere renasci vidimus*). All the same, his book, illustrated by a pupil of Titian's, reveals a shift from texts to experience. The attempt to recover the wisdom of the ancients was producing new knowledge.[200]

The Rise of the Vernaculars

Yet another sign of variety or fragmentation was the humanist critique of Latin. In his dialogue on language, Sperone Speroni, a follower of Bembo, put into the mouth of his master the remark that Latin was not a spoken language but 'only paper and ink' (*carta solamente ed inchiostro*). In another dialogue on the subject, Benedetto Varchi's *Ercolano*, Greek and Latin were described as 'exhausted' (*spente*) while Florentine is 'alive'. In other words, the idea of a 'dead language' was first formulated by the humanists. For some of them following Cicero no longer meant writing in his language, Latin, but writing, as he had done, in the vernacular. Whether a reaction against the freezing of Latin, or an expression of a new cultural self-confidence, the later sixteenth century was a great age of what the literary theorist Mikhail Bakhtin called 'heteroglossia', a diversity of languages and speech styles in interaction or dialogue with one another.[201]

A number of voices were raised in praise of the vernaculars at this time. The most famous was that of the poet Joachim Du Bellay. His *Défense et Illustration de la Langue française* (1549), rejected the description of French as a 'barbarous' language. Ironically enough, this declaration of independence itself followed a foreign model, that of a dialogue on language published in 1542.[202] Du Bellay was supported by the scholar-printer Henri Estienne, who declared in his *Precellence de la langue françoise* (1579) that France had no less gravity and grace than Latin and was capable of greater eloquence than other languages. The Spaniards claimed that their language was the closest to Latin, while Estienne in return claimed that French was the closest to Greek. The Italian Corbinelli, commenting on Estienne, noted the different excellences of Spanish, Italian and French, but considered the last of these as only a 'language for speech' (*lingua parlativa*).[203] Etienne Pasquier, on the other hand, contrasted the 'proud and ceremonious vernacular' of 'the arrogant Spaniard' with the 'soft and effeminate vernacular' of the Italians, 'having degenerated from ancient Roman virtue'.[204]

Other tongues were also heard in this European debate. João de Barros published the praises of Portuguese. The German writer Johann Fischart declared that 'our language is also a language, and can call a sack a sack as well as the Latin saccus' (*Unser sprache ist auch ein sprache und kan so wohhl ein Sack nennen als die Latiner saccus*). The English poet Edmund Spenser asked rhetorically 'Why a God's name may not we, as else the Greeks, have the kingdom of our own language?'[205] Lukasz Górnicki discussed the relative advantages of the different Slav languages in his *Polish Courtier*. Balint Balassa's prologue to his *Hungarian Comedy* declared his desire 'to enrich the Hungarian language with this comedy, so that all may realize that what can exist in other languages can also exist in Hungarian'. The painter-poet Lukas de Heere praised Jan Baptist van der Noot for showing that Dutch was not inferior to French as a language for poetry. A Netherlander, Simon Stevin, described 'the wonderful hidden qualities of the Dutch language' in the dedication to his *Life of a Citizen*. The Antwerp humanist Johannes Goropius went so far as to claim that Flemish (rather than Hebrew, as most scholars thought) was the original human language.

The rhetoric of the vernacular was encouraged by rhetoric in the vernacular, by textbooks such as Thomas Wilson's *Art of Rhetoric*, Fouquelin's *La rhétorique française* and Lorenzo Palmireno's *Rhetorica*, which brought the knowledge of the rules of writing to a wider audience than before.[206] This was also the age of the first grammars of vernacular languages (apart from Nebrija's early grammar of Spanish; see above, p. 77), of the first histories of the vernacular – a history of Spanish was published in 1606 – and of debates about the best way to spell Italian, French and English.

Still more important was translation, whether it is taken as a sign of the development of the vernacular, a result of its development, a stimulus to its development, or all three. The importance of translations into Latin, the language of the international republic of letters, must not be forgotten. More than 200 translations from the different languages of Europe into Latin were made between 1530 and 1600.[207] However, the number of translations into the vernacular was far greater and the cultural consequences of these translations more important. The translations of Cicero, Virgil, Vitruvius and Homer into various vernaculars have already been mentioned, a significant development because it made these texts accessible to a wider audience, including a female audience, to whom Latin, let alone Greek, was usually unknown. Many other ancient writers were translated at this time. A number of Plato's dialogues, for example, were rendered into Italian and French in the middle of the century. Ovid's poem the *Metamorphoses* – an inspiration for artists, as we have seen – was published in Italian, Spanish, French, English and German.

Translations from modern Latin included not only the work of Erasmus, discussed earlier, but also Thomas More's *Utopia*, which appeared in German in 1524, Italian in 1548, French in 1550, English in 1551 and Dutch in 1562. Finally there were translations from texts in modern European languages, especially Italian. In France, over 600 translations were published between 1525 and 1599, mainly from four languages (Greek, Latin, Italian and Spanish).

A number of what later generations regarded as 'classics' of translation were produced in this period, not only from ancient writers from Homer to Plutarch but also from modern ones. In Spanish, for example, one thinks of Boscán's version of Castiglione's dialogue on the perfect courtier, *El Cortesano*. In German, there was Fischart's translation of Rabelais, the *Geschichtsklitterung* (1575), which reached its seventh edition in 1631. In English, there was the translation of Montaigne's essays made by an Anglicized Italian, John Florio. In Polish, there were translations of Ariosto and Tasso by Piotr Kochanowski, the younger brother of the famous poet.

The frontier between translation and creative imitation was easily crossed. Fischart amplified the text he was supposedly translating, especially the already long lists dear to the original author, like the 200 odd games played by the young giant Gargantua. Fischart never used one word when three would do, out-Rabelaising Rabelais and inventing a grotesque multi-syllabic language of his own. A Latin version of the French poem on the creation by Guillaume du Bartas boasted on the title-page that it was 'freely translated and in many places amplified'. The Polish version of Castiglione by Lukas Górnicki transposed the dialogue from Urbino to Cracow, thus turning it into the 'Polish Courtier'. The translation of a dialogue on civil life by Giambattista Cinthio Giraldi, made by another Anglicized Italian, Ludowick Bryskett (whose name was originally Bruschetto), transposed the setting of the conversation from Italy to Ireland, to the translator's 'little cottage' near Dublin, and introduced English participants, including his friend Edmund Spenser.[208]

Translation enlarged the vocabulary of the vernaculars. When Alberti's treatise on architecture was translated into French in 1553, the dedication to the king drew attention to the translator's enrichment of the language. Fischart invented many German words in order to translate Rabelais. In his version of Montaigne, as the preface explained, Florio coined such new English terms as 'conscientious, endear, tarnish, comport, efface, facilitate, amusing, debauching, regret, effort, emotion'. Poets allowed themselves the same licence. A contemporary biography of Pierre Ronsard describes him as both a collector and an inventor of French words. The language of the Pléiade group was indeed full of words taken from the Greek: *anagram-matisme*, for example, *analytique*, *anapeste* and *astronomique*, all neologisms at this time.

The other side of the coin was awareness of the poverty of the vernaculars which made neologisms necessary. In the prologue to his translation of Virgil, Juan del Encina complained of 'The great lack of words in Castillian, compared with Latin' (*el gran defecto de vocablos que ay en la lengua castellana, en com-paración de la latina*). Thomas Elyot wrote of the 'insufficiency' of English.[209] In his book on the education of the prince, written in French, Guillaume Budé argued that writing in an ancient language gave notable actions and sayings 'more elegance, authority, charm and grace' (*plus d'élégance, d'authorité et venusteté et de grace*). Even Joachim Du Bellay, in his famous apologia for French, admitted that the language was 'poor and sterile' (*pauvre et stérile*) compared to the riches of Latin and Greek.

The rise of the vernaculars led some writers to borrow from

Latin and other languages and others to denounce this process. In Italy, a Latinate vernacular had been fashionable in the fifteenth century, but in this period the Accademia della Crusca, so called because its members were supposed to separate the linguistic wheat from the 'chaff', reacted against Latinization in the name of linguistic purity. In similar fashion in France, the printer Geoffroy Tory complained about the 'skimmers of Latin' (*escumeurs de Latin*), as he called them, who turned 'Let us cross the Seine' into 'transfretons la sequane'. Rabelais elaborated on this passage in *Pantagruel* (chapter 6), in which the giant hero is so irritated by a student from the Limousin who uses this and similar Latinate expressions that he throttles him until the man begs for mercy in his own dialect. In England, there was a critique of what were called 'inkhorn terms', words invented by writers without regard to the spoken language. The Englishman Sir John Cheke and the Dutchman Jan van de Werve attacked the corruption of their respective languages by foreign words, especially Italian and French. In France, François Malherbe tried to purify the vernacular from Latin words and dialect words alike.

Some European languages lagged behind others. That German was a latecomer on the vernacular scene may be illustrated by the history of translations. Although Boccaccio's *Decameron* had been translated as early as 1473, the wave of translation into German began a whole century later, with versions of Rabelais (1575), Jean Bodin on demons (also by Fischart), Giovanni Botero on reason of state, the stoic moralists Guevara and Lipsius, and five romances: *Lazarillo de Tormes*, *Don Quixote*, Montemayor's *Diana*, John Barclay's *Argenis* and Philip Sidney's *Arcadia*. For an equivalent to Du Bellay's *Defense*, the Germans had to wait until 1617, when the poet Martin Opitz lamented *The Contempt of the German Language* – in a book written in Latin. In 1624 there followed his 'Book of German Poetry' (*Buch von der deutschen Poeterey*). Opitz was stimulated by the desire to emulate not only Petrarch and Ariosto but also Ronsard, Sidney and the Dutch poet Daniel Heinsius. Not only did he read all these languages, he also made translations from Latin, Italian, French and English.

Opitz was not the only polyglot. The composer Roland de Lassus, a Frenchman trained in Italy and working in

Bavaria, wrote songs in Latin, Italian, French and German and corresponded with his patron in a mixture of languages. The Hungarian poet Balassa knew Italian, German and Turkish. The German poet Georg Rudolf Weckherlin wrote in Latin, German, French and English. Netherlanders in particular were at home in a variety of tongues. Jan Baptist van der Noot wrote poems in Dutch and French, sometimes translating himself, and commented on them in Italian and Spanish. In his youth, at the end of the period, the polymath Christian Huyghens wrote poems in eight languages: Greek, Latin, Italian, French, Spanish, English, German and his native Dutch.[210]

Italian was of course well known among the upper classes all over Europe, and the inventories of libraries suggest that Spanish and French came not too far behind. However, the knowledge of most European vernaculars was virtually confined to a single region. Huyghens translated some poems by John Donne into Dutch, but few people outside Britain would have been acquainted with the plays and poems of Shakespeare, which were not translated into any foreign language until the eighteenth century. Few people outside the Iberian Peninsula would have known the plays of Gil Vicente or the poems of Camões (his *Lusiads* were translated into Spanish in 1580 and again in the 1590s, but there was no version in Latin till 1622 or in English till 1655). Virtually no one outside Poland would have been able to read the vernacular verses of Jan Kochanowski (figure 20), despite the poet's proud boast:

> About me Moscow will know and the Tartars,
> And Englishmen, inhabitants of diverse worlds.
> The German and the valiant Spaniard will be
> acquainted with me,
> And those who drink from the deep Tiber stream.

Monoglot readers were missing a great deal, since this period was a great age of vernacular literature in many European languages.

Why this should have been the case is not an easy question to answer. The translations of the Bible which followed the Reformation were obviously important in the development of the vernacular, but they do not explain why Spain, where vernacular Bibles were forbidden, was going through its literary 'golden age'. The rise of literature in other vernaculars was also a response to the challenge of Dante, Petrarch, Boccaccio, Ariosto and Tasso. A number of modern European writers were treated as vernacular classics, as the Italians had already treated Petrarch and Ariosto (see above, p. 104). Two commentaries on Ronsard's *Amours* were published in 1553 and 1560, for example, noting the poet's borrowings from Petrarch and explaining his allusions to ancient mythology and philosophy. The works of Ronsard were edited by his secretary in 1587, complete with a biography of the poet, just as the works of Virgil (for instance) were often prefaced with a biography. Before the end of the sixteenth century, nine editions of Ronsard's *Works* had been published in France. His admirers included Netherlanders (van der Noot), Englishmen (Daniel Rogers), Germans (Opitz), Poles (Kochanowski) and Italians (Speroni).[211]

In Spain, two critical editions of the poet Garcilaso de la Vega were published in 1574 and 1580, edited respectively by Francisco Sánchez (professor of rhetoric at the university of Salamanca) and the poet Fernando de Herrera. Sánchez tried to identify characters with classical names with people known to Garcilaso, and noted borrowings from the classics, such as Horace and Ovid, as well as from the Italians, notably Petrarch. For his part, Herrera tried to apply Bembo's critical terminology to Garcilaso's poetry. In Portugal, Manoel Correa edited and commented on the *Lusiads* (1613). In England, the schoolmaster Thomas Speght edited the works of Geoffrey Chaucer in 1598, with summaries of the texts and explanations of archaic or difficult words, made necessary by the changes in the English language in the previous 200 years.

A Variety of Genres

In European literature, this was an age of vernacular classics in a variety of genres: epic, lyric, comedy, tragedy, satire, romance and, not least, in non-fiction – histories, dialogues, essays. For instance, the gap was bridged at last between vernacular chronicles in the medieval tradition, which were vivid but loosely structured (Giovanni Villani in Florence, Jean Froissart in France, Fernão Lopes in Portugal, etc.), and humanist histories written in Latin, which were organized more formally but often lacked the immediacy of their predecessors.

Francesco Guicciardini's *History of Italy* (which was translated into French, English, Spanish and Dutch), is a famous example of this trend.[212] Guicciardini's battle-scenes, his character-sketches of major protagonists such as Alexander VI and Lodovico Sforza, and the speeches he puts into the mouths of leading actors all followed classical models. His emphasis on the way in which events have results not only different but sometimes directly contrary to the intentions of the main actors is reminiscent of the tragic ironies of Greek drama. His concern with analysis and explanation, often expressed in the form of pithy maxims, recalls not only Thucydides and Tacitus but also his Florentine predecessor Leonardo Bruni. However, Guicciardini's portraits of individuals such as Alexander VI or Julius II are more colourful than Bruni's, while his narratives are enlivened with vivid details in the style of Villani. At the battle of Fornovo, for example, the horses are described as 'fighting with kicks, bites and blows no less than the men' (*combattendo co' calci co' morsi con gli urti i cavalli non meno che gli uomini*). This image would recur in Tasso's *Jerusalem Delivered* (Canto 28), 'every horse too makes ready for war' (*ogni cavallo in guera anco s'appresta*) and also in Sidney's *Arcadia* (Book 3, chapter 7) with its reference to 'The very horses angry in their masters' anger, with love and servitude brought forth the effects of hate and resistance.'

The works of Niccolò Machiavelli (published posthumously in 1532), were major contributions to literature in the vernacular as well as to political thought. Despite attempts to ban them, these works attracted considerable attention outside as well as inside Italy. Machiavelli's *Discourses* were translated into French in 1544; into Spanish in the 1550s; into Latin in 1588. *The Prince* was translated into French (twice in 1553 and again in 1571) and into Latin (1560); *The Art of War*, into English (1560) and Latin (1610). Following Machiavelli's example, vernacular works on politics became more common, presumably in order to appeal beyond the traditional academic audience. Fadrique Furió Ceriol's *Council and Councillors* (1559), first published in Spanish, and Jean Bodin's *Six Books on Politics* (1576), first published in French, soon reached audiences beyond their native countries. Bodin's work was discussed by critics in Italy, Spain and Germany, as well as being translated into Latin and English. Furió Ceriol was twice translated into Latin and once into Polish.

Another Spanish treatise in the vernacular which resonated well beyond the peninsula was the physician Juan Huarte's *Examination of Wits* (1575), which discussed different kinds of ability. By 1628 Huarte's book had been translated into Latin, French, English and twice into Italian. Like Robert Burton's *Anatomy of Melancholy* it was at once a work of literature and psychology. A few years later came Luis de León's *The Names of Christ* (1583), a study of Christian Kabbala in the tradition of Reuchlin and Giorgi (see above, p. 90). Unlike these earlier scholars, however, Luis de León did not write in Latin. He divulged the 'secrets' and 'mysteries' of Kabbala and Neoplatonism in his native Spanish. No wonder that his attempt to enrich Christianity by drawing on Jewish traditions attracted the attention of the Inquisition, all the more so because he was of Jewish origin.[213]

Non-fiction often took the form of a dialogue, a form well suited to reading aloud, which was still a common practice in this period. In Italy, it was a rare year in which a dialogue of some importance was not published, whether the topic was language, painting, music, philosophy or politics. Some of these Italian dialogues were translated into other languages, and in many parts of Europe new dialogues were written on a variety of topics. For example, the anonymous *Discourse of the Common Weal*, attributed to the English humanist Sir Thomas Smith, discusses the reasons for the 'decay' of the English economy and the rise in prices in the form of a conversation between a knight, a merchant, a doctor of theology, a cap-maker and a farmer or 'husbandman'. These dialogues followed a variety of ancient models, especially Cicero and Plato. In some, a teacher expounds his doctrine and the listeners do little more than ask a few questions. In others, serious differences of opinion are presented and the personalities of the speakers are vividly portrayed as well as their ideas. Castiglione's *Courtier*, for example, presented the dialogue as 'a portrait of the court of Urbino' in which leading figures of the court come to life, from

Gasparo Pallavicino, who loves to tease the ladies, to the enthusiastic Neoplatonist Pietro Bembo. The Portuguese humanist Francisco de Holanda's dialogue *On Ancient Painting* did more than expound Michelangelo's views on art; it evoked his personality and his rough, passionate way of speaking.[214]

Another way of making information on a variety of topics easier to assimilate for readers who were not scholars or students was to present it in the form of a miscellany or collection of discourses. Out of this classical tradition came Montaigne's 'essays', in the sense of experiments or speculations, though they came to diverge more and more from their original model.[215] Montaigne's book was translated into Italian and English, praised in Germany and Spain, and imitated by Francis Bacon, who published his first ten essays in the genre in 1597. Bacon's *Essays* were soon given a wider European circulation by their translation into Latin. Given such a variety of literary genres it will be necessary – as was the case for painting and sculpture – to be brutally selective. The following survey will focus in turn on three genres, the epic, the romance and the comedy, and it will privilege a few examples of each.

Epics

The epic was normally considered to be the most noble literary genre. The modern examples most celebrated in Europe were, once again, Italian. Ariosto's *Orlando Furioso* was published in French (1544), Spanish (1549) and English (1591). Tasso's *Jerusalem Delivered* had even more success. Versions appeared in Latin (1584, 1623); English (1594, 1600); French (two in 1595, and a third in 1626); and Polish (1618). Emulation was inevitable. Edmund Spenser, for instance, admitted to writing his *Faerie Queene* in order to surpass (or as he said, to 'overgo') Ariosto. In practice, epic poets followed a variety of models, Italian and classical, the classical including not only Virgil and Homer but also Lucan, whose *Pharsalia* told the story of the Roman civil war. Agrippa D'Aubigné's poem about the French civil war, *Les Tragiques*, naturally drew on Lucan. Biblical themes also had a wide appeal. The heroes and heroines of epic included Joseph, Judith and Esther, while the epic of the creation by Du Bartas (see above, p. 131) was warmly received in different parts of Europe, and was translated into Latin (three times), Italian, English and German.

Another common theme for epics was the national past. Trissino's *Italy Liberated from the Goths* (1547–8), set in the early Middle Ages, resembled Guicciardini's *History of Italy*, written at about the same time, in expressing a new consciousness of Italy as a whole, a consciousness encouraged by the foreign invasions of the period. Indeed, the poem may be read as an allegory of these invasions, despite its dedication to one of the leading invaders, the Emperor Charles V. The dedication encouraged Charles to liberate eastern Europe from the Turks, and so, perhaps, to leave Christian Italy alone.

Ronsard's *Franciade*, dedicated to King Charles IX, went back still further into the past than Trissino and told the story of the foundation of the French nation by Francion, the son of Hector of Troy. Like Virgil's hero in Book VI of the *Aeneid*, Francion descends into the underworld, where he has a prophetic vision of the long line of future kings of France. The poet made his political aim quite explicit in his preface. It was 'to honour the house of France' and in particular the reigning monarch, Charles IX and his 'heroic and divine virtues', which led the poet to hope that Charles's achievements would be no less than those of his ancestor Charlemagne. Ironically enough, Charles was to be remembered chiefly for his part in the massacre of French Protestants on the feast of St Bartholomew in 1572. Ronsard's poem was left unfinished.

It was also in 1572 that an equally great poet, the Portuguese Luis de Camões, published his *Lusiads*. The title of the epic derives from Lusus, the legendary founder of Portugal, but the poem itself is not concerned with the remote past. The story it tells comes from recent history, the exploits of Vasco da Gama. Camões defined his epic history by contrast to the 'fantastic deeds' (*façanhas fantásticas*) of the heroes of Ariosto, preferring to follow Virgil. He had the advantage of being able to keep close to his own experiences of soldiering in the East while at the same time following Virgil's model of the foundation of a 'new kingdom' (*Novo Reino*). He showed his inventiveness by diverging from the model in a number of respects. For example, Camões made references to Indian culture which were based on personal observation and ranged from the caste system to the images displayed in Hindu temples, which the poet compares to those of Roman and Egyptian gods.

All the same, Vasco da Gama is presented as a new Aeneas. The description of his banners, for example, which represent scenes from the history of Portugal, echoes Virgil's description of Aeneas's shield. As in the case of Virgil, prophecy plays an important part in the poem. Jupiter tells Venus that the Portuguese will be victorious from Malacca to China and from the Sea of Bengal to the Atlantic. At the end of the poem the sea-nymph Thetis shows Vasco da Gama a model of the universe (a geocentric model, despite the publication of Copernicus thirty years earlier) and tells him that the Portuguese will conquer Brazil. As in Virgil, there are references to destiny and empire and at the end of the poem Camões exhorts King Sebastian to undertake a heroic enterprise himself. Six years later, Sebastian did so. His expedition to North Africa to fight the Muslims led to his death in battle in 1578 at Alcazarkebir.

The example of Camões illustrates the well-known link between epics and frontiers. The reason for this link was explained by Sir Philip Sidney in his *Defence of Poetry* when he recalled his visit to the border country between the Habsburg and Ottoman empires. 'In Hungary I have seen it the manner at all feasts, and other such meetings, to have songs of their ancestors' valour, which that right soldierlike nation think one of the chief kindlers of brave courage.' Sidney's contemporary, the Hungarian Bálint Balassa, wrote a famous poem 'in praise of the frontier', as a place for brave young men armed with 'banner-bearing lances' and 'good sharp sabres' and mounted on 'good Arab horses' to risk their lives 'to win a good name and excellent fame' fighting the Turks.[216] On the frontiers of the Ottoman empire, the traditional military epic survived longer than in other parts of Europe. The Croat Brne Krnarutić wrote an epic on the defence of the fortress of Sziget against the Ottoman Sultan Suleiman the Magnificent. The Hungarian nobleman Miklós Zrinyi, great-grandson of the defender of Sziget, wrote an epic on the same subject in the 1640s. As late as 1670 the Pole Wacław Potocki published an epic of the same type, *The Chocim War*, dealing with an earlier seventeenth-century conflict with the Turks.

Another frontier zone was the New World. The epic on

Columbus, the *Columbeidos* (1585) by the Roman noble Giulio Cesare Stella, never became famous, while the exploits of Cortés and Pizzarro do not appear to have attracted poets. However, the Spanish nobleman Alonso de Ercilla set his *Araucana* (1569–90) in the remote part of the viceroyalty of Peru which we now call Chile, in which he had himself lived and fought. The *Araucana* describes the resistance to the Spaniards of the indigenous peoples, presented as 'untamed' barbarians, 'without God or law' (*sin Dios ni ley*), but all the same valiant, bold, honourable and disciplined. Their leader Caupolicán is presented as a statesman, while brave Araucanian women such as Guacolda and Tegualda are reminiscent of the heroines of Ariosto. The Spaniards, on the other hand, are condemned on occasion for two major failings, cowardice and greed. No wonder that the author's prologue tried to disarm possible criticism that he was 'somewhat inclined to the side of the Araucanians' (*algo inclinado a la parte de los araucanos*).[217]

Ercilla's epic was also criticized for its departure from the classical model, notably its lack of a hero. All the same, the author did have classical exemplars in mind. He compared the Araucans with the Trojans, made frequent references to ancient gods and to leading figures from Roman history (Julius Caesar, Pompey, Marius, Sulla, Augustus and so on) and imitated Lucan's *Pharsalia*. His description of the cave of Fiton, for example, imitates the description of the cave of Erictho in Lucan.[218] Ercilla was equally aware of Italian models, notably Ariosto, who is mentioned by name in the poem, and imitated on more than one occasion. However, where Ariosto was equally concerned with love and war, Ercilla confined himself to the latter, as he warns readers in the very first lines, which reverse the opening of the *Orlando Furioso*. 'I do not sing of ladies, love or the courteous behaviour of impassioned knights' (*No las damas, amor, no gentilezas/de cabaleros canto enamorados*).

The *Araucana* pleased the Spanish-reading public sufficiently to have had eighteen editions by 1632. A translation into Dutch was published in 1619, and a partial translation into English prose was made by Sir George Carew, who had served with the Earl of Essex against Spain. In these two cases, however, the appeal of the poem was not – or not only – its poetic merit but its sympathetic account of resistance to Spanish conquest.

Romances

As we have seen, romances of chivalry remained popular at the courts of Renaissance princes and princesses, despite the criticisms of leading humanists such as Erasmus and Vives (see above, p. 96). To meet these and other criticisms the genre was in need of transformation. One way of doing this was to modernize the romance, as in the case of the many continuations of *Amadis de Gaul*, which introduced references to new practices and values. A second means of transformation was to classicize the romance, as in the case of Ariosto, who wrote with Virgil in mind as well as the deeds of Roland and other paladins. Another method was to parody the romance, as in the cases of Rabelais and Cervantes. Rabelais, for example, deliberately contaminated this noble genre by making giants the heroes instead of the villains of his *Gargantua* and *Pantagruel* and replacing the quest for the Grail by the quest for the bottle. As for Cervantes, his *Don Quixote* seems to have begun as an anti-romance before it took on a life of its own. Ariosto, Rabelais and Cervantes were all familiar with the popular culture of their day. Sometimes they appropriated it for their own purposes, while on other occasions it seems to have inspired them. There was nothing surprising in this. In this period the elites were 'bicultural'. They learned what we call folksongs and folktales from their nurses, and differed from ordinary people not by rejecting this culture but by adding another, the classical tradition learned in the grammar schools.[219]

The defence of the genre in humanist circles was made easier by the discovery of the ancient romance, especially the *Aethiopica* of the Greek writer Heliodorus, describing storms, shipwrecks, and the tribulations of a pair of lovers before they are finally united. The *Aethiopica* was published in French translation in 1547, in Italian in 1556, and in Spanish and English in 1587. Thanks to Heliodorus, the romance came to be taken more seriously by the humanist critics. Indeed, it came to be viewed as a prose equivalent of epic, the genre it eventually replaced. New romances were written along more classical lines, drawing, for example, on the tradition of pastoral poetry. The eclogues of Virgil, describing the loves of shepherds and shepherdesses, were much admired and frequently imitated. The

Italian writer Jacopo Sannazzaro introduced the sighing Petrarchan lover into the pastoral and inserted poems into the narrative framework. His innovations received a warm reception. His romance *Arcadia* was reprinted about fifty times in sixteenth-century Italy and set – or expressed – a fashion for wild landscapes which may be related to the rise of the villa at this same time. The *Arcadia* also inspired plays, notably Tasso's *Aminta* and its rival *Il Pastor Fido*, the 'Faithful Shepherd' by Guarini. Guarini came to rival Petrarch, since his verses were set to music by leading composers of madrigals, notably Luca Marenzio, Giaches Wert and Claudio Monteverdi. Monteverdi's opera *Orfeo* (with lyrics by the poet Alessandro Striggio) was presented as a 'pastoral fable' (*favola pastorale*).

The enthusiasm for the pastoral spread beyond Italy. Guarini's play was translated not only into French and English, but also into Croat and Cretan. In Spain in particular a number of writers emulated Sannazzaro by writing pastoral romances. Jorge de Montemayor's *Diana* introduced discussions of Neoplatonic theories of love. Gil Polo's continuation, *Diana in Love*, combined the pastoral tradition with themes from Heliodorus. In England, Philip Sidney's *Arcadia* drew on Heliodorus, Sannazzaro and Montemayor as well as alluding to contemporary political problems. In Poland, Szymon Szymonowicz's *Idylls* created a local ecotype from classical pastoral by introducing scenes from rural life, including witchcraft, harvesting and a wedding.

The complementary opposite of the pastoral was what is now called the 'picaresque' romance because its hero or antihero was a rogue, in Spanish a *pícaro*. Spanish writers dominated this genre. The anonymous *Lazarillo de Tormes*, for example, presented in the form of an autobiography, was reprinted some twenty times in Spanish and translated into five languages. Mateo Alemán's romance *Guzmán de Alfarache*, which also took the form of an autobiography, enjoyed a similar success, with some twenty editions between 1599 and 1604, followed by translations into French, Italian, English and German. The new genre may be regarded a translation into fiction of a long tradition of moralizing descriptions of the tricks practised by beggars and thieves, though the shift to a first-person narrative or fictional autobiography was a significant one (see below,

p. 218), presenting events, at least intermittently, from the rogue's point of view.[220] Even here, however, the authors followed classical models, notably the *Golden Ass* of Apuleius and the *Satyricon* of Petronius. Petronius also inspired another international success of the period, the Latin romance *Argenis* by the Scotsman John Barclay, stuffed with allusions to the international politics of the early seventeenth century.

Comedies

The later sixteenth century was the moment of the rise of permanent theatres and secular plays, in several parts of Europe. In Paris, the Hôtel de Bourgogne was in use from 1548 onwards. In Madrid, the Corral de la Cruz and the Corral del Príncipe were converted into theatres, complete with changing-rooms for the actors and boxes for the wealthier members of the audience. The cities of Valencia, Seville, Valladolid and Barcelona soon followed the example of Madrid. In London, it was in 1576 that the first permanent theatre or 'playhouse' was erected. In Vicenza, as we have seen, Palladio designed the Teatro Olimpico (inaugurated in 1585 with a performance of Sophocles), the first permanent indoor theatre to be constructed in the Renaissance style. The second Globe theatre in London, constructed in 1614, was in similar style, with a classical façade at the back of the stage.

The dramatists who took advantage of these new opportunities included many leading figures besides Lope de Vega and Shakespeare. In France, the civil wars of the later sixteenth century inhibited the rise of permanent theatres but not the rise of gifted dramatists such as Robert Garnier. The Portuguese had Francisco Sá de Miranda, whose *The Foreigners* was the first comedy in classical style in the language; the Dutch Gerbrand Bredero, author of *The Spanish Brabanter*, and the Croats Marin Držić, best known for his comedy *Uncle Maroje*.[221] In Poland, Jan Kochanowski wrote a tragedy about the outbreak of the Trojan War, *The Dismissal of the Grecian Envoys*. In England, Shakespeare's contemporaries included major playwrights such as Christopher Marlowe, John Webster and Ben Jonson.

The plays written by this remarkable cluster of gifted dramatists drew their subjects from a variety of sources, dealing as they did with recent history (Marlowe's *Massacre of Paris*, for instance), with the Orient (his *Tamburlaine*) and with the Middle Ages (his *Edward II*). Tragic themes from Roman history were extremely common, and the genre followed Roman models rather than Greek ones, notably the model of Seneca, in whose plays parents kill their children, children their parents, and a number of characters (such as Jocasta and Phaedra) kill themselves, sometimes on stage. However, this Roman model was contaminated by an early modern interest in revenge and also by a fashionable view of Italy in which Italians were viewed as specialists in assassination, especially by poison (see below, p. 174).

Comedy too followed Roman models. The Suabian playwright Nicolas Frischlin was unusual in his attempt to revive the comedy of Aristophanes, which commented on public issues, rather than the politically anodyne Terence or Plautus. The comedies of Plautus were frequently played, and his cunning servants, suspicious fathers and lovesick youths were put on stage again and again. The twin brothers in the *Menaechmi*, for instance, inspired a host of adaptations and transformations from Ariosto's *Suppositi* to Shakespeare's *Comedy of Errors*. Plautus was often imitated via Ariosto and other Italian writers of comedy, as in the cases of Sá de Miranda in Portugal and Držić in Dalmatia. The plot of Terence's *Eunuch* was transposed to Amsterdam by Bredero in his *Little Moorish Girl*.

The character of the boastful soldier offers an unusually vivid example both of the uses of the classical tradition and the creation of new ecotypes. The original model was Pyrgopolinices in Plautus's *Miles Gloriosus*, a braggart who never tires of telling how brave he is and how many men he has killed. The very name Pyrgopolinices, 'burner of cities', like the stylized boasts of the character, inspired many imitations: Spezzaferro (break iron), Taillebras (cut arm), Matamoros (kill Moors), Roister Doister and so on.[222] The popularity of this comic character doubtless owed a good deal to the number of real soldiers who were marching the roads of Europe and sacking its cities at this time. At any rate, the playwrights introduced topical and local references. The revived Pyrgopolinices usually spoke at least a few words of Spanish, a reminder of the fear and hatred inspired by Spanish armies in Italy and elsewhere. In Venice, on the other hand, he spoke a few words of Greek, creating a local ecotype and satirizing the Greek-speaking soldiers in the service of the Republic. Together with Pantalone, the foolish father, and Gratiano, the pedantic professor, the figure of 'Capitano' became one of the stock figures of the *commedia dell'arte*, the improvised drama in which the actors wore masks, a genre which became visible (if it was not invented) in this period and which itinerant Italian actors took to France, Germany, Poland and elsewhere. It was not necessary to understand Italian in order to enjoy these plays, in which mime was even more important than usual. Capitano's rhetoric of gesture is not difficult to imagine.

The Reformations

The theatre was one of the main targets for religious reformers, Calvin on one side and San Carlo Borromeo on the other. Calvin did not approve of plays, even on religious subjects. For his part, San Carlo regarded them as the liturgy of the devil. The followers of these two uncompromising reformers did not always go so far. Some preferred a compromise, an edifying drama in which classical forms serve Christian ends.

For example, the play by Calvin's disciple Theodore Beza about Abraham's sacrifice of Isaac skilfully blended the Bible story with a classical model, the sacrifice of Iphigenia by her father Agamemnon, as told by Euripides. Another Calvinist, Jean de la Taille, wrote a play about the madness of Saul which drew on Seneca's tragedy on the madness of Hercules. In German and Dutch Protestant schools the pupils often acted in plays written by their teachers in which biblical subjects were treated in the style of Terence, who was preferred to Plautus because his plays were considered less offensive to morals and written in a purer Latin. On the Catholic side, the Jesuits were the pioneers of school drama, usually in Latin, on religious subjects. Messina, Vienna and Córdoba were among the first cities in which these performances, to which parents and local elites were invited, could be seen.

As the example of the drama suggests, the relation between humanism and the Reformations, Catholic and Protestant, was

Figure 15   Lukas Cranach the younger, *Portrait of Philipp Melanchthon*, Frankfurt. (Copyright © Ursula Edelmann, Städtisch Galerie in Städelschen Kunstinstitut, Frankfurt.) The book is Basil of Caesarea's treatise on education in a bilingual edition in Greek and Latin.

not as simple as was once thought by the historians who brought the Renaissance to an end around 1530. On one side, as we have seen (pp. 31–2), there had always been tension between Christian values and the attempt to revive a pagan antiquity. On the other side, we find that some of the leading participants in the Reformation approved of the Renaissance as a forerunner. Luther argued that God had caused Hebrew, Greek and Latin to be revived (via the Greek diaspora of 1453) for the sake of the Gospel, and encouraged his colleague Melanchthon to teach the humanities at the university of Wittenberg. Ulrich Hutten published Lorenzo Valla's treatise on the *Donation of Constantine* in 1517 as a weapon in the conflict between Luther and the pope. Both Zwingli and Calvin had had good humanist educations before turning Protestant. Calvin, for instance, began his intellectual career by writing a commentary on Seneca's treatise on clemency. A fierce critic of the Neoplatonism of the circle of Marguerite de Navarre, Calvin nevertheless cited Plato many times in his most important treatise, the *Institutes of the Christian Religion*. His follower Beza praised François I for the revival of Hebrew, Greek and Latin, 'the gateways of the temple of true religion' (*les portieres du temple de la vraie religion*).

The Italian Protestant diaspora played an important role not only in the diffusion of the Renaissance but also in its assimilation in northern Europe.[223] In Basel, for instance, Pietro Perna printed Renaissance classics. One of them was Guicciardini's *History of Italy*, in which Perna restored the criticisms of the papacy which had been deleted from the Italian editions. In Altdorf, a Protestant professor of law, Scipione Gentili, translated Tasso's *Jerusalem Delivered* into Latin. In London, John Florio, the son of an Italian Protestant refugee, made his living teaching Italian, although he is now best known as the translator of Montaigne's *Essays*.

It is true that criticisms of classical paganism became more frequent and more radical from the 1530s onwards. The shift in mood may be illustrated by the fate of Lucian. In the early phase of the Reformation, when the destruction of the claims of the Catholic Church was a high priority, Lucian's mockery was much imitated, as we have seen (p. 92). In the next phase, however, he was increasingly criticized by Catholics and

Protestants alike for his scepticism, blasphemy and even 'atheism' (a term used less precisely in the sixteenth century than today, to refer to mockery of religion rather than the denial of God's existence). Luther and Calvin were among the Protestants who condemned him. Some of his works were placed on the Catholic *Index of Prohibited Books* in the 1550s and all of them in 1590.

Examples of religious attacks on secular literature are easy to find. Beza repented having written Latin epigrams in his youth and criticized the lies of the poets. The Calvinist printer Henri Estienne criticized Ronsard for paganism. Calvin had *Amadis* banned from Geneva, while an Italian was arrested there in 1576, charged with referring to his copy of *Orlando Furioso* as his 'New Testament'. Rabelais, who had criticized Calvin, became a special target of the Calvinists. Calvin included Rabelais among the 'filthy dogs' who mocked religion. One English Puritan, Joseph Hall, denounced 'wicked Rabelais' drunken revellings', and another, Everard Guilpin, his 'dirty mouth'.

Despite these attacks, humanist values were not so much rejected at this time as combined with Protestant or Counter-Reformation attitudes. The forces of compromise, or hybridization, were stronger than the forces of purism. Melanchthon, for example, appealed like his Italian predecessors to the example of Fathers of the Church such as Basil of Caesarea, and a portrait of the reformer (figure 15), shows him holding the text which Salutati had once used in his defence of pagan literature (see above, p. 32). Poetry was defended by the Protestant humanist Philip Sidney by citing the precedent of the Psalms, which he and his sister Mary translated into English verse. In similar fashion versified paraphrases of the Psalms were made in French by Theodore Beza and in Latin by George Buchanan. Major writers of the Renaissance were viewed through Protestant spectacles. Petrarch's criticism of the papal court at Avignon and Valla's undermining of the pope's claim to the States of the Church were read as evidence that their authors were proto-Protestants. The French poets Du Bartas and D'Aubigné revealed both their humanism and their Protestantism in their epics, which dealt respectively with the creation of the universe and the wars of religion in France. An unusually explicit example of the process of harmonization at work is that of the Englishman Arthur Golding, who translated both Calvin and Ovid. To his translation of Ovid's *Metamorphoses* he prefixed some verses arguing that by the golden age, Ovid had meant the period before the Fall.

Protestant humanists formed an international network. For an illustration of their personal ties one has only to look at the *Friends' Album* kept by Abraham Ortelius of Antwerp, which includes not only his fellow-Netherlanders but also Italians (such as Pietro Bizzari, who wandered through Europe after leaving Italy for religious reasons), Englishmen (the historian William Camden and the magician John Dee), Frenchmen (Hubert Languet, a friend of Philip Sidney) and East-Central Europeans (the Silesian Johannes Crato and the Hungarian Andreas Dudith).

The correspondence of Lipsius, who had lived in Calvinist Leiden and Counter-Reformation Leuven, ranged across the Catholic and Protestant worlds from Lisbon to L'viv. On the Catholic side, we find Lipsius in touch with the Jesuit scholars Martin Delrio and Antonio Possevino, the French magistrate Jacques-Auguste de Thou, the Polish nobleman Jan Zamojski and the Spanish poet Francisco de Quevedo. Among the Protestants, his correspondents included the Danish nobleman Henrik Rantzau, the German professor Nathan Chytraeus, the French scholar Isaac Casaubon and the Hungarian writer János Rimay. The correspondence of Lipsius illustrates the strength of the humanist commonwealth of letters even more vividly than the correspondence of Erasmus.

The Catholic reformers, like the Protestants, were both attracted to and repelled by Renaissance culture. What repelled them was loose morals and the borrowings from a 'pagan' antiquity, down to the details of a classicizing vocabulary. For example, Castiglione and Montaigne were both criticized for using the pagan term 'fortune' rather than its Christian equivalent 'providence'. A number of Renaissance texts were placed on the various *Indexes of Prohibited Books*. *Gargantua* and *Pantagruel* were condemned by the Sorbonne (that is, the Faculty of Theology of the University of Paris) in 1544. The Spanish Index of 1559 included the *Decameron* of Boccaccio, the *Colloquies* and the *Praise of Folly* of Erasmus, and the dialogue *Mercurio y Charón.* A later version of the Spanish Index included Montaigne's *Essays* as well. Among the books condemned by the Portuguese Index of 1581 were *Utopia* and the *Orlando Furioso.* On the other hand, the Italian Jesuit Roberto Bellarmino defended the great Florentine trio of Dante, Petrarch and Boccaccio as good Catholics, while no less a figure than the Grand Inquisitor himself (Michele Ghislieri, later Pope Pius V) came to the defence of Ariosto's *Orlando Furioso.*

As a case-study in ambivalence we may take the picaresque novel *Lazarillo de Tormes.* Banned in 1559, five years after its publication, the romance reappeared in expurgated form as *Lazarillo castigado* (1573). This was the version used for the Italian translation of 1622, which removed the anticlerical references, transforming the hero from a canon into a physician. Yet the story was republished in its original form in two Catholic countries, Italy (1587, 1597) and the southern Netherlands (1595, 1602).

A similar ambivalence can be seen in the relations between Catholic reformers and the visual arts. On the negative side, San Carlo Borromeo's *Instructions for Architects* (1577) criticized circular churches because they resembled 'the temples of idols'. In 1582, Bartolommeo Ammannati, the sculptor who had made the Neptune fountain in Florence, confessed his errors in a letter to his colleagues, asking pardon for offending God and arousing bad thoughts in the beholder by 'making many of my figures completely nude and uncovered' (*facendo molte mie figure del tutto ignude e scoperte*). On the positive side, the churches designed by Palladio in Venice and by Pellegrino Tibaldi (who worked for Borromeo) in Milan combined the classical tradition with reforming ideals. Palladio had visited the Council of Trent with his patron Daniele Barbaro, and his ecclesiastical buildings, especially San Giorgio Maggiore and the Redentore, with their dazzling white interiors, appear to symbolize the purification of the Church. Again, Philip II's great palace-mausoleum of the Escorial is a fine example of Counter-Reformation architecture, as austere and grave as San Carlo could have wished and consistent with, if not inspired by, the aesthetics of St Augustine, but also making use of classical forms.

In similar fashion, a synthesis between humanism and Counter-Reformation values, or at any rate a mixture of the two, was created with the help of the Christian antiquity of the Fathers of the Church. This synthesis may be illustrated by the example of Jesuit colleges after 1550.[224] It used to be said that the Jesuits simply used the forms of the Renaissance while ignoring or rejecting their content. Now that the age of Bruni and Valla is viewed as one of Christian rather than pagan humanism, this contrast has lost most of its validity. Ignatius Loyola was not the first to recommend, in a letter of 1555, treating pagan antiquity as the people of Israel treated 'these spoils of Egypt' (*questi spogli de Egipto*: see above, p. 33). In practice, however, the head of an order which had founded no fewer than 444 colleges by 1626 had a much wider European influence than Salutati (say) or Ficino. Cicero and Quintilian, Virgil and – in expurgated form – Ovid figured largely on the curriculum of these colleges, which were explicitly concerned with the *studia humanitatis*.[225]

The role of the Jesuits in the spread of Renaissance architecture as well as humanism was of special importance on the periphery, in cities such as Braunsberg (Braniewo), Vilnius (Wilno), Kolozsvár (Cluj) or L'viv (Lwów), in all of which they established colleges in this period. The church of St Casimir in Vilnius, for instance, was modelled on the Gesù in Rome. As a religious leader, Ignatius Loyola has sometimes been compared to Calvin. Whatever the merits of that parallel, the importance of the Jesuits in the reception of the Renaissance may reasonably be compared with that of Italian Protestants.

The Aristocratization of the Arts

The conscious adaptation of classical or Italianate ideas and forms to new contexts is particularly clear in the cases of the Reformation and Counter-Reformation. Less visible but equally relevant to the history of the Renaissance are the effects of social changes in this period. Princes continued to play a significant role. Civic patronage did not completely disappear, as we have seen. However, noblemen, and to an increasing extent noblewomen, were particularly important in this period, not only as patrons but also as writers. For this reason we may speak of the 'aristocratization' of the Renaissance. As in earlier chapters, it may be useful to discuss the social basis of the movement in terms of locales, in this case the court, the city and the country house.

The Habsburg courts remained important in this period. Philip II, for instance, not only commissioned El Escorial but took an interest in painters as diverse as Titian and Hieronymus Bosch, although the work of El Greco was not to his taste.[226] The Emperor Rudolf II is best known for his fascination with natural and occult philosophy, but his intellectual interests were wider. Himself active as a goldsmith, the emperor ennobled artists and appointed a number of poets laureate. Like François I, he exploited his position to request gifts for his collection. Rudolf presided over a cosmopolitan court in Prague, which included Italian artists such as Giuseppe Arcimboldo, Germans such as Bartholomaeus Spranger, and Netherlanders such as the sculptor Adriaen de Vries and the landscape painter Roelant Savery, as well as the Hungarian humanist Johannes Sambucus, the Czech poet Simon Lomnický, the Czech composer Kryštof Harant, and the Slovene composer Jacobus Gallus. The different members of this circle seem to have stimulated one another. Thanks to Rudolf's patronage, Prague became one of the leading artistic centres of Europe, at least for a few years.[227]

By this time, however, courts on the periphery of Europe were acquiring a new importance. João III of Portugal, for example, who had received a humanist education, invited humanists to his court and appointed João de Barros official historian of the Portuguese empire in the Indies. As we have seen, he also sent the artist Francisco de Holanda to Rome to study. In Poland, Zygmunt II August was the patron of Łukasz Górnicki, who dedicated his *Polish Courtier* to the king, and also of the musician Valentin Bakfark, though not (as the poet had hoped), of Jan Kochanowski. In Scandinavia, Frederick II and Christian IV of Denmark, and Erik XIV and Johan III of Sweden were all interested in the new Italianate culture. Christian IV, for example, was an enthusiast for architecture, and Inigo Jones worked for him before his employment by the Stuarts. Christian was also the patron of a number of musicians, including the English composer John Dowland, who was unable to obtain a post at the English court.[228]

In the case of cities, the most striking development in this period was the rise of the commercial theatre. The rise of secular drama in many parts of Europe has already been discussed. It was linked to the rise of playhouses, which allowed actors to settle down instead of spending their lives wandering from place to place. Underlying these developments was the growth of the population and the movement of migration from the country-side to the city. After a certain critical threshold had been passed (perhaps 100,000 people, perhaps a little less), it became pos-sible for companies of actors to make a living from presenting the same plays, at least for a few days, to different audiences in the same city.

Civic buildings continued to be commissioned, as we have seen (p. 116). Civic patronage for humanist schools remained import-ant, a famous example being Sturm's academy at Strasbourg (1538), which was a model for many later foundations.[229] On the other hand, civic humanism seems to have been declining. In Italy, the restoration of the Florentine republic in 1527 did not last for long. In Germany, the so-called 'free' cities such as Augsburg and Nuremberg were diminishing in political and cul-tural importance, although the Fuggers of Augsburg remained active as private patrons. Calvin's Geneva was an independent city-state, but as we have seen, Calvin was no friend of human-ists. Antwerp's independence was crushed when Spanish forces recaptured it in 1585. Apart from Venice, it was only in the new Dutch Republic, established in the course of the revolt against Philip II, that the ideals of civic humanism survived, expressed in architecture, painting, tapestry and even the decoration of ships as well as in texts. Stevin's treatise *Civic Life* (1590) virtu-ally identified political life, urban life and civilized life, his central concept being 'civility' (*Burgerlicheyt*). Samuel Ampzing's *Praise of Haarlem* (1628) was the Dutch equivalent of Bruni's panegyric on Florence some two centuries earlier.[230]

However, the position of the towns and townsmen so important in earlier phases of the Renaissance was threatened at this time by a social process discernible in many parts of Europe from Spain to Poland and sometimes described as 'refeudal-ization', the return to dominance of the landed aristocracy in the economic, political and cultural domains.[231] The term used here will be 'aristocratization', chosen to avoid the implication that increased aristocratic participation in the Renaissance movement was essentially the result of economic and political changes.

The case for this aristocratization is a double one. Nobles were not only active as patrons but also as writers, more especially as poets. Despite the example offered by the Emperor Rudolf II, many of them considered manual work like painting or sculpture beneath their dignity. To publish a book might be as much a source of social stigma as of social cachet, since publication was associated with profit. On the other hand, circulating poems in manuscript to select readers was an activity compatible with aristocratic values. As we have seen, noble poets, especially soldier-poets, were numerous in this period. In Spain there was Garcilaso de la Vega, who was killed at Nice during the war between France and Spain, and Alfonso Ercilla, who fought in Chile. In Portugal there was Luis de Camões, who served in the Far East. In Hungary there was Bálint Balassa, who fought against the Turks and was killed by a cannon ball at the siege of Esztergom. In England there was Sir Philip Sidney, who met his death at Zutphen fighting for the rebel Netherlanders against Philip of Spain.

Ronsard and Kochanowski did not take up arms, but they lived the life of country gentlemen, Kochanowski retiring to his estate of Czarnolas ('Blackwood') after his hopes of court patronage were disappointed. In France, England, Poland and elsewhere the life of studious leisure or *otium* became associated not only with the countryside, as in the villas of the Veneto, but also with the rejection or even the critique of the court. The international enthusiasm for pastoral, in which nobles play the role of shepherds, becomes more intelligible if it is replaced in this context.

Of these examples, some are of gentry rather than of aristocrats in the strict sense, but the contrast with earlier centuries remains striking. In France, for example, the social status of the poets of the Pléiade was considerably higher than that of the poets who preceded them, the so-called *rhétoriqueurs*.[232] To the example of the poets one might add that of the essayists Michel de Montaigne and Francis Bacon.

As for aristocratic patronage, it is visible in many parts of Europe, displacing our attention from the court and the city to the great house at the centre of a country estate. The following examples could easily be multiplied. In France some of the most important noble families, such as the Guises and Montmorencys, were active patrons of art and architecture in the new style. In Scandinavia, Henrik Rantzau, governor of Holstein, built or rebuilt no fewer than twenty-five houses and collected more than 6,000 books, including works by Vitruvius, Serlio and Du Cerceau which are testimonies to his interest in the classical style of architecture. A friend of Tycho Brahe (who stayed in his house at Wandsbek) and a correspondent of Lipsius, Rantzau himself wrote Latin poetry and books on history, genealogy, travel, health, dreams and astrology, while his patronage has been compared to that of Lorenzo de' Medici.[233] By his time, however, there were many more Lorenzos active than there had been in the later fifteenth century.

In the Czech renaissance, for instance, another friend of Tycho's, Peter Vok of Rožmberk, together with his brother Vilém, played an important role. The brothers were great collectors of books, patrons of musicians and alchemists, and the owners of a palace in Prague and a number of country houses in the south of Bohemia, such as Kratochvile and Třeboň.[234] In the case of Poland, an obvious example to choose is chancellor Jan Zamojski. The chancellor, who had studied at the university of Padua, was the patron of the musician Valentin Bakfark and the poets Klonowic, Szymonowic and Kochanowski, the last of whom wrote *The Dismissal of the Grecian Envoys* for Zamojski's wedding to Krystina Radziwiłł. Zamojski was also the founder of the town of Zamość, designed for him by an Italian architect, Bernardo Morando, for 3,000 inhabitants complete with church, three squares, three gates and a house for the meetings of Zamojski's academy.

Zamość presents an extreme case of aristocratic control, in a region where great estates and private towns were normal features of the landscape, but in Western Europe this was also an age of aristocratic patrons. In Spain, for instance, there was Don Diego Hurtado de Mendoza, who had lived in Italy in the 1520s. In the summer Don Diego was a soldier, but in the winter, when the campaigning season was over, he was a student at the universities of Rome and Siena. When he was Spanish ambassador in Venice, he studied Greek in his spare time, as well as having his portrait painted by Titian and building up a fine library of Renaissance books. His protégés included Vasari and the architect Jacopo Sansovino.[235] In England, Robert Dudley, Earl of Leicester was a major literary patron, as the hundreds of books dedicated to him attest. It was he who supported Edmund Spenser, for example, as well as the translators John Florio and Thomas Blundeville, who dedicated to the earl his versions of Italian texts on the arts of riding and history. The earl's library included works by Erasmus, Machiavelli and the Neoplatonist Leone Ebreo. Dudley was also interested in Italian art, which he is known to have discussed with an Italian diplomat.[236]

One might have expected ecclesiastical patrons to be a declining species in the age of the Counter-Reformation, but two spectacular examples survived into this period, Cardinals Farnese and Granvelle. Alessandro Farnese outlived by forty years the pope who had appointed him (his grandfather Paul III), surviving into the reign of Sixtus V when the cultural climate was very different. According to some scholars he was the most important patron of the arts of his time, although Michelangelo claimed (according to Francisco de Holanda) that the cardinal had 'no idea of painting'. At any rate he had good advisers, including the historian Paolo Giovio, who persuaded him to employ Vasari to decorate the hall of audience in his palace. It was in this palace, at a conversation after dinner, that Vasari was encouraged to write his *Lives*. Farnese was also a collector of books, manuscripts, marbles and medals. The Farnese Cup (Tazza Farnese), an antique, and the Farnese Hours, a manuscript illuminated by the Croat painter Giulio Clovio, have taken their names from their former owner, while his name in Roman capitals across the façade of the church of the Gesù in Rome proclaims his patronage of that famous building.[237]

Cardinal Granvelle was almost in the same class as Farnese. A leading minister of Philip II, Granvelle employed the humanist Justus Lipsius as his secretary and took him to Italy. He encouraged Plantin to print books by Italian scholars. He loved fine bindings and was painted by Titian with one of them in his hand. Granvelle's enthusiasm for collecting may be gauged from his letter to Primaticcio about a classical statue of Antinoüs which he wanted 'whatever it costs' (*quoy qu'il couste*). He commissioned works from both Italian and northern artists, including Titian, Antonis Mor, who painted the cardinal's portrait (figure 16) and the sculptor Giambologna. He also constructed an Italianate palace in Brussels, one of the first in the Netherlands. The engraver Hieronymus Cock dedicated a volume to this 'maecenas of all the good arts'.

Granvelle's letters give the impression that, although he came from a newly-ennobled family, he turned to the arts not so much in the pursuit of status as for pleasure and relief from the cares of a statesman. In art as in politics, he knew what he wanted. Asking Titian for a portrait of Christ, he wrote that 'Above all I should like the face to be beautiful, sweet and delicate as you know how to make it' (*sopra tutto vorrei che avesse la faccia bella, dolce e delicata tanto quanto la sapete fare*).[238]

Another leading minister of the period, the Englishman William Cecil, raised to the peerage as Lord Burghley for services to Queen Elizabeth, was also a patron of architecture and learning, and for similar reasons to Granvelle's (he seems to have been less interested in painting). His house at Theobalds may well have been the first in England to follow an Italian model. A marble fountain in the courtyard was ornamented with figures of Venus and Cupid, and the chimney-piece in the Great Chamber with a bronze Vulcan and Venus. Cecil's interest in the details of building emerges clearly from his correspondence – with his mason, who asked him for drawings; with the financier Thomas Gresham about obtaining a stone loggia from the Netherlands; and with the English ambassador to France, interrupting political instructions to ask for 'a book concerning achitecture . . . which I saw at Sir Thomas Smith's'.[239]

According to a contemporary biography, Cecil 'entirely loved learning and learned men', while 'his recreation was chiefly in his books.' He gave money to schools. He was said to carry Cicero's *Offices* about with him. Cecil was particularly interested in history, geography and astrology. He was the patron of the historian William Camden, while Arthur Golding dedicated to him his translation of a text by Leonardo Bruni on the invasion of Italy by the Goths. He ordered maps from France and had views of European cities painted in the hall at Theobalds. The ceiling in the Great Chamber was painted with the signs of the zodiac and the same signs were sometimes used as a code

Figure 16   Antonis Mor, *Portrait of Cardinal Anton Perrenot de Granvelle*. (Copyright © Kunsthistorisches Museum, Vienna.)

(the Duke of Parma was Aries, Maurice of Nassau was Gemini and so on).

The aristocratization of the Renaissance included women. The rise of the vernacular reduced the obstacles in the way of women writers, in Italy, France, the Netherlands, England and perhaps elsewhere. An outpouring of poetry in particular followed, so much so that it may not be misleading to speak of the 'feminization' of the Renaissance at this time as well as its aristocratization, especially if we consider the role of women in the domestication of the movement (see below, p. 182). The place of women in the Renaissance became less peripheral than before. Two mid-sixteenth-century Italian anthologies from the Venetian publishing house of Giolito were devoted entirely to the literary works of women. The first was the *Letters of Many Worthy Ladies* (1548), 181 of them altogether, though doubts have been expressed about the authenticity of some of these letters. The second anthology, *Various Verses of some Noble and Talented Women* (1559), included fifty-three contributors.[240] The majority of these women were nobles. Among the best-known women writers of this period, the poet Vittoria Colonna was a marchioness, while her correspondent Marguerite de Navarre, who wrote plays, poems and a collection of stories, the *Heptameron*, was the sister of King François I.

As we have seen (above, p. 79), aristocratic ladies had been active as patrons in earlier phases of the Renaissance. This tradition continued. In Poitiers in the later sixteenth century Madeleine Des Roches and her daughter Catherine organized a salon where poems were read and platonic love was discussed, as in the Urbino of Elisabetta Gonzaga and Baldassare Castiglione.[241] Two well-known English examples of female patronage are Bess of Hardwick and Mary Sidney. Elizabeth Talbot, the widowed Countess of Shrewsbury, is better known as Bess of Hardwick because she had Hardwick Hall constructed (with her initials, ES, on the battlements, in the style of Cardinal Farnese). It has been suggested that the innovations in the design were facilitated by the fact that a woman was not expected to provide hospitality on the traditional lavish scale.[242]

Philip Sidney's sister Mary became the Countess of Pembroke and presided over another great house at Wilton in Wiltshire. She translated Petrarch's *Triumph of Death*, Robert Garnier's tragedy *Mark Antony*, the *Discourse* of the French humanist Philippe Mornay and, with her brother, the *Psalms*, as well as editing Philip Sidney's *Arcadia* for publication. The Garnier and Mornay translations were published in 1592, translation being considered a more respectable activity for a woman than independent publication. Mary, known in her time as 'a second Minerva', took over from her late brother the patronage of the poets Edmund Spenser and Samuel Daniel, and also encouraged Nicholas Breton, who compared her to the Duchess of Urbino at the time of Castiglione and his *Courtier*.[243]

In Spain, France and England, aristocratic ladies encouraged the translation of Castiglione's book. The Spanish translation by Joan Boscán was made at the 'command', so he said, of Gerónima Palova de Almogáver. The existence of a manuscript translation into French of Book III of the *Courtier*, in which the court lady is the main subject of discussion, suggests a female initiative, perhaps that of Marguerite de Navarre. In England, Sir Thomas Hoby's translation was made at the request of the Marchioness of Northampton, Elizabeth Parr.[244]

The humanist interests of a number of ladies from this period are well documented. These interests were not completely new, but they appear to have been becoming more acceptable to men – in the fifteenth century, Isotta Nogarola and Cassandra Fedele had been snubbed by Guarino and Poliziano respectively when they tried to join in the exchange of letters normal among humanists.[245] The French noblewoman Marie de Gournay, on the other hand, received a warmer response from both Montaigne and Lipsius when she wrote to them. The daughters of humanists were particularly well educated. Antonio Nebrija's daughter taught rhetoric at the university of Alcalà. Bembo, for example, directed the studies of his daughter Elena, while Thomas More taught his daughter Margaret, later Margaret Roper. The scholar-printer Christophe Plantin's daughter Magdalene read proofs for him in Latin, Greek, Hebrew, Chaldean and Syriac.

A second group of women with access to a humanist education was the nobility, from princesses to gentlewomen. Before she became queen, Elizabeth I received a good humanist education from Roger Ascham. A few more English examples will show humanism spreading among noblewomen. Lady Jane Grey, whose royal blood cost her her life, was observed reading Plato's *Phaedo* in the original Greek. Mildred Cooke, the second wife of William Cecil, was compared by Ascham to Lady Jane and described as the most learned woman in England. In fact, four of the Cooke sisters shared these interests. Mildred translated the Greek preacher St John Chrysostom. Anne, the wife of Sir Nicholas Bacon (and the mother of Francis), translated the Italian Protestant Bernardo Ochino. The younger sisters, Elizabeth and Katharine, composed epitaphs, one of the genres (like lyric poetry, letters and translations) in which men most easily accepted female authors.[246]

It is usually difficult to reconstruct the interests of women through libraries, since the books would carry the husband's name. Henrik Rantzau was unusual in including the name of his wife Christina von Halle on his book-plates.[247] The evidence of a few libraries registered in the name of women supports this picture of an increasing number of aristocratic ladies outside Italy who took literature and ideas seriously. Maria of Hungary, for instance, had a number of what we might describe as major Renaissance texts in her library, not only Italian texts such as Castiglione, Machiavelli and Serlio, but the works of Erasmus in Latin and a number of works on history.[248] Catherine de' Medici had a good library which reveals her interest in geography. The library of Mary Queen of Scots, who knew Latin and some Greek as well as four modern languages, and wrote poems in French, reflected a mixture of interests in humanism (Biondo, Erasmus, Vives) and vernacular literature (not only the usual Ariosto and Bembo, but also Du Bellay, Rabelais and Ronsard).

For this period there is also substantial evidence of female interest in other arts and also of the involvement of non-aristocratic women in Renaissance culture. Mary Queen of Scots drew, sang and played the lute. A group of female singers, the *concerto delle dame*, was active at Ferrara in 1580, including the noblewoman Tarquinia Molza. Actresses included Isabella Andreini, of the Compagnia dei Gelosi, who performed at the courts of Florence and France. Laura Terracina was perhaps the first female literary critic. Dürer bought the work of a female illuminator and commented that 'it is a great miracle that a mere female should do so well.'[249] Despite his disparagement a few female painters were well-known at this time, notably

Figure 17   Catherine van Hemessen, *Self-portrait*, 1548. (Copyright ©
Öffentliche Kunstsammlung Basel, Kunstmuseum; photo Martin Buhler.)

Catherine van Hemessen (figure 17) in the Netherlands, Levina
Teerlinc in England and Sofonisba Anguissola and Lavinia
Fontana in Italy. Catherine became a gentlewoman at the court
of Maria of Hungary, Levina (the daughter of an illuminator
from Flanders) a gentlewoman at the court of Queen Elizabeth,

while Sofonisba became lady in waiting to the Queen of Spain. Lavinia, on the other hand, made a living from her portraits and religious paintings, her husband acting as her agent. Still more unusual was Anna Coxcie, the daughter of a Flemish sculptor who followed her father's profession.

Two Venetian courtesans were famous for their poetry, Gaspara Stampa, known as 'the new Sappho', and Veronica Franco, who engaged in poetic duels with men. Stampa was also a singer, like her sister Cassandra.[250] In Rome, Tullia d'Aragona occupied a similar position. In Lyons, female poets included the merchant's daughter Louise Labé, whose verses were addressed to the ladies of her city. Anna Bijns, a schoolmistress in Antwerp, was able to enter one of the literary clubs or 'chambers of rhetoric' (*Rederijkerkamers*) in which poems and plays were produced. In the same city there was a school for girls, the 'Bay Tree', with a humanist in charge.

A few women used their literary talents to criticize the society which limited their opportunities. When Louise Labé, for instance, dedicated her works to Mademoiselle Clemence de Bourges, she criticized men for the wrong they had done women by denying them access to education and remarked that at last 'the severe laws of men no longer prevent women from applying themselves to learning' (*les sévères lois des hommes n'empêchent plus les femmes de s'appliquer aux sciences et disciplines*). In Venice, two women wrote on this subject. Lucrezia Marinella's *Nobility and Excellence of Women* was published in 1591 and Modesta Pozzo's *Merit of Ladies* (a fine example of a Renaissance dialogue) in 1600. In France, Marie de Gournay's *Equality of Men and Women* dates from 1622.[251]

The freedom of women to write and more especially to publish must not be exaggerated. The works of some female writers who are now famous – Gaspara Stampa and Pernette Du Guillet, for example – were published only after their death. All the same, the publication of a number of books by women in their lifetime marks a significant change in this period. In Italy, apart from the anthologies discussed above (p. 164), Vittoria Colonna published her poems in 1538; Tullia d'Aragona published her poems and also a dialogue in 1547; Laura Terracina published poems in 1548 and her discourse on Ariosto in 1550, both with Giolito of Venice; Laura Battiferri published her poems in 1560;

Veronica Franco published her poems in 1576 and her letters in 1580; Isabella Andreini published her pastoral *Mirtillo* in 1594; and Lucrezia Marinella published her defence of women in 1591. Outside Italy examples are not so easy to find, but Anna Bijns published her poems in three volumes in 1528, 1548 and 1567; Louise Labé published her works in 1555; and Mary Sidney published two translations in 1592.

In short, the later Renaissance was the period in which the movement was most widely accepted socially as well as geographically. A great variety of groups appropriated and adapted ideas and forms which had previously appealed to relatively few. This was also the period in which the movement penetrated most deeply into social life. This process of the domestication of the Renaissance is the subject of the following chapter.

5

The Domestication of
the Renaissance

'Renaissance' is a powerful but also an ambiguous term. For some historians it signifies an event, for others a period, and for a third group a movement. The difficulties in describing a trend lasting centuries as an event were described above (p. 102). To use the term to describe a period, as Burckhardt did in the case of Italy, is virtually impossible when writing about the whole of Europe. In the effort to describe contrasting and conflicting trends the term would become as vague as to be useless. The sharper definition of the Renaissance as a self-conscious movement, favoured by Gombrich and others, is much more useful, and it has generally been followed in this book.

However, this concept too has its disadvantages. What began as a movement of a tiny group of Italians in the fourteenth century changed in the course of spreading to other countries and other social groups. What had once been conscious innovation gradually became part of everyday practice and habits of thought, affecting mentalities, material culture and even the body, as we shall see (pp. 200ff.). The focus of this chapter will be on unexamined assumptions and changing lifestyles.

Whose assumptions and lifestyles were affected by the Renaissance in this period is not an easy question to answer. With a few exceptions, outside the cities of Florence and Venice there is little evidence of the movement's effect on other social groups apart from certain types of craftsman, such as masons and carpenters. One of the most remarkable of these exceptions is the record in the judicial archives of a play performed in the village of Aspra near Rome during the Carnival of 1574, 'an old play in print', as a witness described it, a pastoral with nymphs and shepherds acted by a cobbler, a potter and some peasants who could read and write, they said, 'but not much'.[252] Juxtaposed with this document, Shakespeare's vignette in *A Midsummer Night's Dream* of Bottom, the weaver playing the lover Pyramus, and Flute, the bellows-mender playing Thisbe, no longer seems as fanciful as it once did. All the same, such pieces of evidence are rare. The following pages will therefore concentrate on the nobility and clergy but make some reference to the world of lawyers, physicians, merchants and their wives. If the group to be studied is socially restricted, it is geographically extended. We return to a recurrent theme of this book, the Europeanization of Europe.

The idea of the history of everyday life, *Alltagsgeschichte* as the Germans call it, is no novelty, but it has attracted increasing interest in the last generation or so as part of the movement to write history from below. It has often been pursued more or less independently of other kinds of history. In what follows, however, the emphasis will fall on the interaction between a movement of cultural renewal and the structures of everyday life in different parts of Europe. This interaction may be described and analysed in terms of reception, resistance, hybridization, and what the title of this chapter calls 'domestication', not in the sense of 'taming' the Renaissance' but of its entry into the house and everyday life. The most appropriate word is a German one, *Veralltäglichung*, a term which might be rendered in English as 'domestication', 'quotidianization', or 'routinization', three words which privilege different aspects of this complex process, all of which are relevant to the chapter.

It will be impossible to avoid the term 'fashion', in the sense of interests which did not last more than a few years or at the most a few decades. However, the long-term consequences of the combined enthusiasm for antiquity and Italy are even more important. The Dutch historian Johan Huizinga has written a famous essay on historical ideals of life.[253] This chapter will study the process of translating one such ideal, that of the

'Renaissance man' or woman, into everyday practice. At least some of the participants in some of the practices to be described here were self-consciously implementing this cultural ideal.

Most of the examples which follow will come from the late Renaissance, the phase in which the new ideas and forms not only spread most widely geographically and socially, as described in the previous chapter, but also penetrated more domains of activity than ever before. Even the idea of the Renaissance changed at this time. By the middle of the sixteenth century contemporaries who claimed they were living in a new age were likely to be thinking not only of the revival of antiquity but also of the invention of printing and gunpowder and the discovery of the New World. Examples include the French physician Jean Fernel, whose treatise on hidden causes appeared in 1548, and the German humanist Christophorus Mylaeus, who published a book about the writing of history in 1551. Fernel described 'this age of ours' as notable for the revival of eloquence, philosophy, music, geometry, painting, architecture, sculpture, the invention of cannon and printing, and the voyages of discovery especially in the New World. For his part Mylaeus singled out the revival of Greek, the invention of cannon and the printing-press 'in Germany', the discovery of America, and the work of painters such as Michelangelo and Dürer.

Italophilia and Italophobia

In many parts of Europe, as we have seen, Italian culture became fashionable in court circles. In Poland, for example, the trend seems to have been launched by the arrival of Queen Bona Sforza in 1518. Piotr Tomicki, Bishop of Cracow, was nicknamed 'the Italian' because of what a member of his circle described as his 'tremendous nostalgia' for Italy. Polish enthusiasm for Italy seems to have been at its height in the middle years of the sixteenth century. There was a similar enthusiasm in Transylvania a generation later, when Isabella (the daughter of Bona) was Queen Mother. The Italianization of the court seems to have reached its peak at about the same time in France as in Poland, in other words, in the later sixteenth century, the age of Catherine de' Medici, Henri of Anjou (who was briefly King of Poland before becoming Henri III of France) and Stefan Bathory.[254] In England, to judge from the debate on the subject, the trend seems to have peaked a little later, towards the end of the reign of Queen Elizabeth.

Italy was viewed as a model of both art and life. A Welshman who knew Italy well, William Thomas, declared in 1549 that 'the Italian nation . . . seemeth to flourish in civility most of all other at this day.' In similar fashion, the Italian cleric Beccadelli told a friend in Ragusa (now Dubrovnik) to send his son 'to polish himself in Italy (*per affinarsi in Italia*)'.[255] It would be easy to multiply examples of this kind of Italophilia but it would also be otiose, as the attitude has been illustrated in almost every chapter of this book.

However, the very success abroad of Italian manners and fashions led to an anti-Italian backlash in the late sixteenth century, visible from England and France to Hungary and Poland. Italophobia coexisted and interacted with Italophilia in the sixteenth century, just as the love and hatred of American culture have coexisted and interacted – sometimes within the same individuals – in Europe and other parts of the world in the second half of the twentieth century.

A certain hostility to Italy on the part of other Europeans was traditional, a reaction against papal taxation, Lombard bankers or Roman law. The rise of Protestantism increased suspicion of Italy as the home of the Papacy. Hostility and suspicion were increased still further in this period in response to what might be described as the 'cultural imperialism' of the Italians, in other words, the invasion of their artefacts, practices and ideas, not to mention their claim that other Europeans were mere barbarians. This rejection of Italy was not so much nationalist (though it encouraged national consciousness in the long run) as a reaction to a sense of cultural inferiority. These hostile reactions should also be linked to the revaluation of the Middle Ages discussed above (p. 127).

Thus the Swedish humanist Olaus Magnus was critical of the 'soft' southerners. A Hungarian chronicle attacked Sigismund of Transylvania for his 'adulation' of Italians. The Polish writer Marcin Bielski described visits to Italy as a cause of effeminacy and luxury. In Łukasz Górnicki's adaptation of Castiglione's *Courtier*, transposing it to a Polish setting, one of the characters was given the role of the defender of local traditions and the opponent of everything Italian. In Germany, the humanist Conrad Celtis claimed that 'Italian luxury is corrupting us' (*Nos italicus luxus corrupit*). The phrase 'An Italianate German is a devil incarnate' (*Tedesco Italianato, Diabolo incarnato*) became proverbial in Germany.

A similar phrase, 'Inglese italianato, diavolo incarnato', became proverbial in England. In his book *The Schoolmaster*, the Protestant humanist Roger Ascham criticized 'italianated' Englishmen who preferred Petrarch, Boccaccio and Cicero to the Bible. In a book with the arresting title of *The English Ape* (1588) the author associated Italy with flattery, cunning, and vanity and denounced the corruption of Englishmen who 'italianate' themselves. The Duke of York in Shakespeare's *Richard II* denounced 'proud Italy', 'Whose manners still our tardy apish nation / Limps after in base imitation' (Act 2, Scene i). The sentiment expressed here is ambivalent; resentment of the foreign is combined with contempt for the self.

In France the criticism of Italy and above all of the Italianate Frenchman, the *françois ytaliqué*, was particularly strong.[256] The proverb *dissimuler comme un Italien*, 'to dissimulate like an Italian', was current at this time. Joachim Du Bellay satirized the kind of Frenchman who returned from his visit abroad Italianized in his gestures, clothes and language (*De gestes et d'habits, de port et de langage*). In one poem he denounced a phenomenon still well-known today, the admiration for the exotic and the contempt for one's own culture: 'To praise the foreigners and despise the French' (*Louer les étrangers, les Français mépriser*). The Calvinist printer Henri Estienne especially disliked what he called the 'italianization' of the French language, for which he blamed the Italian wars and the court with its special 'jargon'.

The fear of Italy was sometimes expressed through the metaphor of poison, employed by two Protestant gentlemen, François de La Noue, who wrote of the 'sweet poisons' (*douces poisons*) of Italy, and Agrippa d'Aubigné, who referred to the 'Florentine venom' (*venin florentin*). Spenser's friend Gabriel Harvey, himself regarded by some Englishmen as too Italian by half, denounced Machiavelli as 'a poisonous politician', Aretino as 'a poisonous ribald' and Pomponazzi as 'a poisonous philosopher'. Some foreigners viewed Italy as the home of poison in the literal sense, thanks in part to the story told in Guicciardini's history of Italy about Pope Alexander VI accidentally drinking a cup of poison he had intended for one of his cardinals. It is tempting to treat the image as symbolic and to think of Italophobia as a movement of purification, a reaction against an overdose of foreign culture.

Out of these conflicts over Italian and also over classical culture (see above, p. 150), there emerged a synthesis or at any rate a compromise or mixture, which affected daily life as well as the arts. In examining different domains of everyday life in more detail it may be useful to distinguish three broad areas: material culture, practices and mentalities.

Material Culture

To begin with the material aspects of what might be called 'Renaissance chic', with the embedding of objects in new styles of life, the study of domestication may appropriately begin with the house and its furnishings. Building was a conspicuous example of conspicuous consumption, which sometimes led to the financial ruin of the patron, but it was also an investment, both a symbol of and a means to status and power.[257] At the same time, to build a house in the new manner was a symbol of participation in the revival of antiquity. A style of building was a metaphor for a style of life.

For this reason, by the later sixteenth century if not before, architecture had become too serious a business to leave to architects, and still less to master masons. Tycho Brahe and William Cecil have already been mentioned as examples of noblemen who took a strong personal interest in the construction of their houses (see pp. 116, 162). Such amateur builders, copies of Serlio or some other architectural treatise in their hands, were not uncommon in the period. For example, Sir John Thynne played an important role in the design of his huge house at Longleat in Wiltshire, and Francis Bacon in the design of his house at Verulam. Sir Thomas Smith, an Elizabethan architectural enthusiast, owned no fewer than six editions of Vitruvius. The illustrations to Vitruvius, Serlio and other treatises may well have been more important for many readers than the text, since they offered a range of gateways, doors, windows, fireplaces and ceilings to potential clients (figure 22).

Many European nobilities, French, English, German, Bohemian, Polish or Scandinavian, lived in castles or manor houses in the countryside. Where their Italian equivalents lived in the city and retired to their villas only in the summer, these nobles did the opposite. In the later sixteenth century, the decline in many parts of the need to fortify these manors coincided with the discovery of classical forms and led to the development of the distinctively Renaissance country house. It was only to be expected that local ecotypes would be developed according to the local building material and the social needs of the owner. Rural nobilities in different parts of Europe needed different kinds of accommodation from the patricians of Italy because their everyday lives were different. The social distance of the nobles from the farm workers varied, like the spatial distance between the country house and the village. In some places, including Britain, the great hall was still a necessity in the late sixteenth century, to provide meals for retainers or clients. When the noble families gradually withdrew from the hall to the 'drawing-room', their action expressed a need for privacy which was greater or at any rate more visible in England than it was in Italy.[258]

The glamour of Italy is revealed by the determination to adopt an Italian style despite a northern climate (ironically enough, ignoring the advice of Vitruvius on the need to adapt buildings to local conditions). A spectacular example is the fashion for open loggias in English country houses of the late sixteenth century. Used for dining, walking and the display of statues, Italianate loggias were constructed for William Cecil (Theobalds and Burghley House), for his friend Sir Thomas Smith (Hill Hall, Essex), for Bess of Hardwick and for Cecil's son Robert (Hatfield House).[259] Francis Bacon's essay 'Of Building' recommended the construction of 'an open gallery upon pillars to take the prospect and freshness of the garden'.

Later generations objected to this fashion. In his *Elements of Architecture* (1624) Sir Henry Wotton noted that 'the natural hospitality of England' made the buttery and kitchen more important than in Italy. A generation later, in his treatise *Of*

Building, Roger North criticized Inigo Jones, remarking that 'It hath been the use of the Italians, and ill imitated in England by some fond surveyors [foolish architects], to set the portico into the house, as we find at Greenwich, the Queen's House . . . In Italy this is proper and useful, because it abates heat and averts the force of the sun's light, which is offensive . . . We have, generally speaking, too much air and too little heat, and therefore need not spoil an order of rooms to obtain the one and abate the other.' In the eighteenth century, the poet Alexander Pope was still mocking those enthusiasts who were 'proud to catch cold at a Venetian door'. Other critics singled out new forms of decoration. According to an anonymous French discussion of the recent rise in prices, the *Discourse on Dearness* (*Discours sur les causes de l'extresme cherté*, 1586), one of the causes of inflation was the new 'excessive and proud style of building' (*cette excessive et superbe façon de bastir*), in other words, building in the classical style with its galleries, porticos, balustrades, friezes, cornices, capitals and so on.

All the same, the Italianate style spread not only from palace to palace and from country house to country house but also to relatively modest houses in town. Among the models for the latter were the houses of Italian artists such as Mantegna, Raphael, Giulio Romano, Vasari and Zuccaro. Vasari, for example, painted his house at Arezzo with illustrations of stories about artists, while his house in Florence was decorated with allegories of the arts and portrait medallions of famous artists.

In Nuremberg, the patrician Sebald Schreyer, a friend of the humanist Konrad Celtis, had his house in the Burgstrasse decorated with images of Orpheus, Apollo and the Muses. In Amsterdam, the Frisian banker Pompejus Occo had a house on the Kalverstraat with interior decoration and furnishings so rich that the house was known as 'Paradise'. In Antwerp, the merchant Niclaes Jongelinck commissioned the artist Frans Floris to decorate his house with a painting of the Labours of Hercules. Floris's own house advertised his trade with a painted façade imitating statues in their niches which represented allegorical figures such as 'skill', 'knowledge of poetry' and 'knowledge of architecture'. On occasion, the novelty of the town house was little more than a façade or even less. In the Netherlands and Central Europe, a house with traditional

On the image:

Les
OEVVRES
DE PIERRE
DE RONSARD
GENTILHOMME
VANDOSMOIS PRIN-
CE DES POETES
FRANÇOIS.

Reueues et augmentées
et Illustrees de Commentai-
res et remarques.

A PARIS,
Chez NICOLAS BVON
rüe St Iacques à l'enfei-
gne S. Claude et de
l'Homme fauuage.

Auec priuilege du Roy.
M. DC. XXIII.

I. Gaultier sculp.

Figure 18   Léonard Gaultier, woodcut portrait of Ronsard from his
Oeuvres (Paris, 1623). (Photographie Giraudon, Paris.) Compare the bust
of Ronsard with that of Ariosto (figure 5).

stepped gables could be given a Renaissance façade by fitting it out with pilasters, balustrades, statues and obelisks.

The rapid spread of classical or at least classicizing forms was made possible by printed pattern-books, beginning in the 1520s and including those of Serlio (Book 4), Jacques Androuet Du Cerceau and Hans Vredeman de Vries, who published no fewer than twenty-seven volumes of designs in Antwerp between 1555 and 1587, including orders of architecture, caryatids, fountains and gardens. The pattern-books offered a whole new system of signs to replace the Gothic system, which had itself extended from cathedrals to cutlery. Classical architectural and sculptural forms such as columns, capitals, caryatids, pediments, friezes, garlands and cherubs proved themselves marvellously adaptable and inspired the decoration of beds and bindings, cups and clocks, textiles, tombs and title-pages, the last of which often imitated triumphal arches or doorways with columns, so symbolizing the reader's entry into the world of the book (figure 18).

However, the new system was not purely classical or even italianate. As we have seen (p. 74), grotesques, however unclassical or even anti-classical (*senza alcuna regola*, 'without any rule', as Vasari described them), had appealed to ancient Romans and were revived in Italy at the end of the fifteenth century. Pattern-books from the Netherlands (Vredeman), France (Du Cerceau) and Germany (Jamnitzer) spread the knowledge of this wealth of fantastic and monstrous forms. The books codified the rules of disorder. Grotesques were often hybrids of humans and animals (satyrs, centaurs, harpies and so on). It was only appropriate that they should have promoted hybridization. In this genre, as an Englishman wrote in 1612, 'the greater variety you show in your invention the more you please.'[260] Through this breach in the walls of the classical rules a variety of other forms were able to enter.

For example, a new type of decoration created in the Netherlands at this time and widespread in northern Europe from Cambridge to Koenigsberg is known as 'strap-work' because the forms look as if they had been cut from leather (figure 19). It was used to ornament houses, tombs, fountains, books and so on. The abstract forms known as 'arabesques', a striking example of the influence of Islamic culture on the West,

Figure 19   Patterns from Hans Vredeman de Vries, *Architectura* (1577),
f. 21. (By permission of the syndics of Cambridge University Library.)

had long been familiar in Spain, but in the sixteenth century they invaded Italy, France and other parts of Europe. Du Cerceau published a pattern-book of *Grandes arabesques* (1582). In the midst of this riot of forms it is possible to identify Gothic elements too, whether they should be described as survivals or as recuperation, the return of the repressed. A Renaissance satyr is not always easy to distinguish from a medieval gargoyle.

The pattern-books answered a need because in this period there were more and more objects available for or requiring ornament. The sixteenth century has been called the age of the 'discovery of things' because the houses of the wealthy began to fill up with material objects at this time. Moral criticism of these luxuries or 'superfluities' was common. Konrad Celtis and Marcin Bielski have already been quoted to this effect, while the *Discourse on Dearness* noted that in the good old days before the middle of the sixteenth century, 'people did not buy so much rich and precious furniture' (*on n'achetoit point tant de riches et precieux meubles*). All the same, the criticism of these *braveries* (a term which might perhaps be translated as 'objects designed to impress') was not strong enough to halt the process of accumulation and display. Many of these luxury objects embodied Renaissance ideals and may therefore be read by historians as evidence of the allegiances of their owners, of their attempts to construct or reconstruct their identities in the new style.[261]

The concern with identity is particularly clear in the case of two genres, the tomb and the portrait. A family chapel in a local church might be regarded as an extension of the great house and the tomb as part of the furniture. Tombs were constructed in a classicizing style as filtered first through the perceptions of Italian sculptors and then of the Netherlanders spread through Europe (see above, p. 106). They frequently included the family coat of arms, epitaphs praising the virtues of the deceased and representations of husband, wife, and not infrequently of the children as well, boys on one side and girls on the other, arranged in rows from tallest to smallest. Whether or not the sculptors attempted true likenesses (figure 20), the tomb represented the family in the community as the gallery of portraits did inside the house (see below, p. 223).[262]

The interiors as well as the façades of houses were transformed

Figure 20   Jan Kochanowski monument at Zwolén, *c*.1610, in Samuel
Fiszman (ed.), *The Polish Renaissance in its European Context* (1988).
(Reproduced by courtesy of Indiana University Press, Bloomington.) This
style of funeral monument could be found from England to Poland.

in this period, the ceilings, doorways and staircases no less than
the furniture.[263] That the interior of the house was the realm of
women, at least originally, is suggested by the fact that among
the earliest items of splendidly decorated furnishings were
cassoni and *deschi di parto*. *Cassoni* were chests in which brides
kept their trousseau, often painted with images illustrating

Homer or Virgil, Petrarch or Boccaccio, and representing famous women such as Helen of Troy, Dido of Carthage, Lucretia or Griselda. *Deschi di parto* or 'birth trays', used to bring refreshments to the mother after childbirth, were decorated in similar fashion.[264] *Cassoni* declined in the sixteenth century, to be replaced by cabinets, which impressed some foreign visitors, the Englishman Fynes Moryson for example, by the skill demonstrated in their carving and inlay.[265]

What the English did have, in compensation, were carved four-poster beds, which were sometimes decorated with grotesques and caryatids following the patterns provided by Du Cerceau and Vredeman.[266] Tables too were redesigned in the new style. In Italy, they were sometimes inlaid with coloured marble. In the Hôtel Montmorency in Paris, the Constable displayed an ebony table decorated with bronze medallions of twelve Roman emperors. Octagonal stone tables carved with classical gods and goddesses could be found in an English country house of the mid-sixteenth century, Lacock Abbey in Wiltshire. Chairs were decorated in the new style, including the light chairs now coming into use, such as the Italian *sgabello* (in French *escabelle*), little more than a stool with a back. Musical instruments such as the virginals were for display as well as for use, with elaborate painted decorations.

The famous salt-cellar which Benvenuto Cellini designed for King François I, with its statuettes of the goddess Earth (symbolizing salt) and Neptune (symbolizing pepper), was hardly an everyday object, but it may function as a reminder of the importance of new forms of tableware in this period. The Jamnitzer family of Nuremberg were renowned in this domain and worked for emperors, but less famous craftsmen working for less distinguished clients produced large numbers of jugs, ewers, tankards and standing cups which might be surmounted or supported by statuettes or take the form of a fruit – apple, pear or pine cone – as well as being covered with decoration.

Armour and weapons were intended for display as well as for use and symbolized the identity of the owners as warriors. Whether their purpose was ceremonial or for use in battle, the joust, the duel or the hunt, swords, guns and other weapons were made into works of art. Among the main centres of production were Milan and Augsburg. Swords might be inlaid with

Figure 21   Majolica dish showing the *Judgement of Paris*, after Raphael.
(Reproduction by permission of the syndics of the Fitzwilliam Museum,
Cambridge.) The non-mechanical reproduction of the work of art.

gold, a process known as 'damascening' and a speciality of
Spanish craftsmen. Their hilts might be decorated with strap-
work, foliage or masks. The stocks and butts of guns were
frequently inlaid with staghorn and ornamented with hunting-
scenes or scenes of battle according to their intended use.[267]

Cheaper products included terracotta and maiolica. Some of
the painted terracotta images produced in Florence by the Della
Robbia family workshop were magnificent objects intended for
churches or for rulers such as René of Anjou, but the workshop
also produced small images for wayside shrines or private indi-

Figure 22   Sebastiano Serlio, design for a fireplace from *Five Books of Architecture* (London, 1611), Book 4, chapter 7, f. 43. (Reprinted by Dover Publications, New York, 1982).

viduals. It might be an exaggeration to speak of 'mass production' at this point, but signs of hasty work have been noticed and
images of popular subjects such as the Adoration of the Magi or
the Madonna and child have survived in multiple copies which
are virtually identical.[268]

Many of the maiolica plates, dishes and jugs produced by
workshops in Faenza, Urbino, Deruta and elsewhere in
Italy were extremely magnificent and they were probably
extremely expensive as well. These ceramics were not despised
by Isabella d'Este, a lady who was as difficult to please as she
was interested in acquiring works of art. A dinner-service of
painted maiolica was fit for a prince, and one, designed by a
well-known painter, Taddeo Zuccaro, was presented to Philip
II of Spain by the Duke of Urbino. However, maiolica also came
in cheaper forms, such as the series of plates painted with images
of pretty girls, labelled 'Laura Bella', 'Jerolima Bella' and so on,
which still survive in many museums.[269]

Maiolica frequently reproduced famous paintings. Plates and
dishes from Urbino, for example, imitate paintings by the local
hero Raphael (figure 21). It can be shown that the painters knew
Raphael's work at second hand via prints by Raimondi (see
above, p. 74). A similar situation obtained in France, where the
tableware decorated in enamel by the craftsmen of Limoges
imitated works by Raphael, Primaticcio and Dürer. By this
means some of the most famous images of Renaissance art
became part of the everyday life of a group of consumers,
although what they looked at every day was the reproduction of
a reproduction.

The fireplace or chimney-piece offers another striking example of the entry of new forms into daily life. In the fifteenth
century, the marble fireplace was already an important part of
Italian interior decoration, for example, in the palace of Urbino.
Serlio's treatise on architecture offered alternative patterns of
fireplaces (figure 22), rich with classical details, models which
were followed with variations at Fontainebleau, for example, in
Burghley House, in Hardwick Hall and so on.[270] Later treatises
on architecture offered a variety of models, sometimes classified
as Doric, Ionic, Corinthian and so on. The *Discourse on
Dearness* complained that in the old days 'one knew nothing of
putting marble or porphyry on fireplaces' (*on ne savait que*

c'était mettre du marbre ni du porphyre aux cheminées), but there was no turning back.

The increasing popularity of images of emperors in the decoration of houses made the history of ancient Rome part of everyday life. Château Gaillon, built for Cardinal Georges d'Amboise, was decorated with marble roundels containing 'heads of Roman emperors'. Emulating Château Gaillon, Cardinal Wolsey's Hampton Court was ornamented with eight terracotta roundels of Roman emperors by Giovanni da Maiano (figure 6). It was common to display a set of the 'twelve Caesars' whose biographies were written by the Roman historian Suetonius, thus making them canonical: Julius, Augustus, Tiberius, Caligula, Claudius, Nero, Galba, Otho, Vitellius, Vespasian, Titus and Domitian. For example, a French official, Florimond Robertet, decorated his house at Blois with medallions of the twelve Caesars. Titian painted portraits of the Caesars for Federigo Gonzaga of Mantua. To own the set of twelve marble busts became a fashion. Cardinal Farnese had one, the cardinal of Lorraine another, the duke of Mantua a third, the duke of Bavaria a fourth.[271] William Cecil ordered a set from Venice and displayed them at Theobalds. The scholar Sir Robert Cotton used his set (together with busts of Cleopatra and Faustina) to mark the subject categories into which his famous library was divided.

Discussions of images at this time generally emphasized their moral purpose, to offer concrete examples of virtue. Erasmus, for example, in his *Education of a Christian Prince*, declared that moral exempla should be 'carved on rings, painted in pictures', in order to be impressed on the minds of viewers. A favourite example, from paintings to plates, was the ancient Roman Mucius Scaevola placing his hand in the fire. All the same, the popularity among European elites of sets of the twelve Caesars, in which 'good' rulers like Julius or Augustus were juxtaposed with 'bad' ones like Nero and Caligula, suggest that the aim of the owners was not so much to encourage virtue as to identify themselves with the culture of ancient Rome.

Within the house, the chief symbol of humanist values was the study or, as Italians called it, the *studiolo*: the secular version of a monk's cell, a room (or at least a corner of a room) dedicated to the *vita contemplativa*, to thinking, reading and writing

Figure 23   Peter Vischer the younger, inkpot, *c*.1516. (Reproduced by courtesy of the Trustees of the Ashmolean Museum, Oxford.) An appropriate furnishing for a humanist's study.

(another name for this space was 'writing-room', *scrittoio*). Maxims might be painted on the walls, as they were in Ficino's study in his villa at Careggi outside Florence, in order to encourage the right kind of thoughts. In a letter to his friend Vettori, Machiavelli described himself as putting on his best clothes before entering his *scrittoio* in order to converse with the ancients. As we have seen (pp. 43, 79), humanists such as Salutati and Poggio and princes and princesses such as Federigo of Urbino and Isabella d'Este were proud of their studies and took the trouble to decorate them appropriately, not only with desks and inkwells but also with paintings of illustrious men, statues and (as an adviser recommended Cardinal Farnese) 'all your small objects, such as medals, cameos, inkstands and clocks'. Paintings of St Jerome or St Augustine writing or meditating provide more or less accurate representations of studies of this kind. Before the end of the sixteenth century, this fashion had spread beyond humanists and princes. In 1569 the *studiolo* of a Venetian courtesan, Julia Lombarda, included 'a bronze figure holding a bow' (*una figura de bronzo con un arco in man*) (presumably Cupid), a portrait of Dante, the *Triumphs* of Petrarch, four maiolica jugs and some books.[272]

Outside Italy, it is also possible to follow the progress of the fashion for the 'study' or *étude* by examining surviving furnishings. Silver inkwells are one example, together with boxes for writing instruments, including some made by leading German goldsmiths such as Peter Vischer the younger (figure 23) and Wenzel Jamnitzer. A writing box made at Nuremberg in 1562 was surmounted by a figure of a woman representing philosophy and holding a tablet inscribed with the essentially Renaissance message that learning 'revives what is dying' (*rebus caducis suscitat vitam*), while the arts 'bring back to light what had fallen into shadow' (*revocant ad auras lapsa sub umbras*). Desks are another illustration of the increasing importance of the study. Different parts of Europe developed their own ecotypes, such as the Spanish *escritorio*, often inlaid with mother-of-pearl and decorated with arabesques, or the German *Schreibtisch* or *Kunstschrank*, which might take the form of the façade of a church or temple, ornamented with statuettes, an appropriate place (as one German writer declared in 1619) for 'beautiful meditations and contemplations' (*schöne meditationes et contemplationes*).[273] Nuremberg was an important centre for the production and export of such desks and cabinets.[274]

To these surviving objects may be added the evidence from inventories. Jacques Perdrier, a royal secretary who died in 1578, had a room with books, with two desks, a statuette of Jupiter, an astrolabe and a collection of medals. Juan Bautista de Monegro, a Spanish architect who died in 1623, kept his books in a room which also contained a clock, astrolabes, quadrants, and terrestrial and celestial globes. The teachers and students of sixteenth-century Cambridge furnished their studies with hour-glasses, globes and lutes. Inventories tell us nothing about the painted decoration of these rooms, but Montaigne's famous study in the tower of his country house had and still has inscriptions on the beams, twenty-five Greek quotations and thirty-two Latin ones.

In the course of the period there was a gradual displacement of interest, at least among the owners of grand houses, from the study to the museum.[275] The term 'museum' (literally a place dedicated to the Muses) was put into circulation by Paolo Giovio, the humanist bishop who assembled a collection of portraits of the famous men of his day (and a few women) in his house near Como, built (so he claimed) on the ruins of Pliny's villa and decorated with paintings of the nine Muses.[276] A space for the display of statues and other objects was also known as a *galleria*, in other words, a space through which to move. An early example of a purpose-built museum was the room added to Palazzo Grimani in Venice in 1568 to display classical sculptures. Part of the Uffizi was dedicated in the 1570s to the public display of the Medici collection by Grand Duke Francesco I, who had previously displayed his treasures in his private *scrittoio*.

By this time some Germans were also collecting and displaying antiques. Raimund Fugger of Augsburg owned an important collection which was described by the humanist Beatus Rhenanus in 1531. The idea of a museum or gallery soon attracted these collectors. An Italian correspondent of Raimund Fugger's son Johan Jakob wrote him a letter about the new museum in Palazzo Grimani as if he would want to follow this model. A number of German rulers displayed their collections in what was called a *Kunstkammer* (a term first recorded in the 1550s). The Elector August of Saxony founded a museum of this kind in Dresden (1560), soon followed by the Emperor Ferdinand I in Vienna, Archduke Ferdinand II of Tyrol at Ambras and Duke Albrecht V of Bavaria in Munich, where the museum was known as the *Antiquarium*.[277]

The garden of a house often functioned as an open-air sculpture gallery. The humanist Poggio wrote with excitement to his friend Niccoli that he had found in Rome 'a marble bust of a woman, wholly undamaged, which I like very much' and intended to erect in 'my little garden at Terra Nova, which I shall decorate with antiquities'. In his dialogue *On Nobility*, Poggio described his dream of filling his garden with the remains of classical statues, while Lorenzo Valla ridiculed his devotion to 'these little broken bits of marble'. Lorenzo de' Medici achieved Poggio's ambition in his garden behind Piazza San Marco in Florence. The magnificent gardens at Pratolino for the Medici family, or at Tivoli for the Este, attempted to recreate the ancient Roman gardens described by Cicero and Pliny.[278]

This Italian model was being followed elsewhere by the beginning of the sixteenth century. It was, for example, in his garden that Florimond Robertet chose to place the bronze copy of Michelangelo's David that he had acquired in Italy, or that the Count of Benavente displayed his collection of statues in Seville. The garden, with its flower-beds and terraces, pavilions and galleries, fountains and grottoes, and artificial lakes and mountains, was often a work of art in itself. Designs for gardens had a prominent place in Serlio and also in Vredeman, who offered readers the choice between Doric, Ionic and Corinthian styles. Curiously enough, the sixteenth century was the age of the rise of the garden as an aesthetic object and an item of conspicuous consumption in China as well as in Europe. One of the few people in a position to make a comparison, the Jesuit Matteo Ricci, visited a garden in Nanjing in 1598 and praised its terraces, pavilions and towers as if it had been Italian.[279]

As in architecture, the major exemplars were Italian: the Medici gardens in Pratolino and Florence (the Boboli) and the gardens of the Este villa outside Rome at Tivoli. The Emperor Maximilian II, for example, asked his ambassador in Rome to send him designs of Italian gardens and in 1571 he received a drawing of the garden at Tivoli. Laurentius Scholz, a physician from Breslau who had studied in Padua and Bologna, laid out a garden on the Italian model combining specimens of medicinal herbs and exotic plants with fountains, grottoes, a pavilion and a *Kunstkammer*.[280] On the other hand, the Englishman Sir Henry Wotton, despite the many years he spent in Italy, distanced himself from Italian formality and declared that 'gardens should be irregular or at least cast into a very wild regularity.' In France, the ever-critical *Discourse on Dearness* found room to complain of the new fashion for flower-beds, alleys, canals and fountains. The uses of gardens as places to walk, meditate, converse or dine are made very clear in literary descriptions such as Erasmus's dialogue 'The godly feast' (*convivium religiosum*) or the description of Kalander's garden and 'house of pleasure' in Sidney's *Arcadia*.

Towns were less easy to modify than gardens but town planning was another way in which Renaissance ideals affected the everyday life of considerable numbers of people. The completely symmetrical city was a rarity outside treatises on architecture such as the one in which Filarete described his ideal city of 'Sforzinda', octagonal in form. One of the few was Valletta in Malta, rebuilt after it had been besieged by the Turks in 1565. Another was Palmanova in Friuli, a Venetian fortress in the shape of a nine-pointed star. Northern examples include Frederikstad in Norway, Freudenstadt in Württemberg, Glückstadt in Holstein and Christianstad in Skåne, the last two built for Christian IV of Denmark, who took a personal interest in the towns. In the case of the Spanish cities in the New World, two traditions of planning met. A law of 1571, codifying earlier practice, required the new settlements in which many of the Indians were compelled to live to be constructed on a grid plan expressing what has been called 'the geometric mentality of the Renaissance'. However, building straight streets and central places were indigenous practices in both Mexico and Peru. In Mexico City, for instance, the streets and squares followed the lines of the Aztec city of Tenochtitlán, on the ruins of which it was built.[281]

It was not so much the symmetrical city which was part of everyday experience as the symmetrical square. More or less regular squares with arcades as described by Vitruvius and

Alberti became increasingly common. In Venice, Piazza San Marco was reshaped in the sixteenth century to make it more regular. On Piazza del Campidoglio (the Capitol) in Rome and Piazza SS Annunziata in Florence, new buildings were constructed to make the square symmetrical.[282] In the 1590s, the new town of Livorno in Tuscany was given a Piazza Grande, lined by loggias. By the end of the century, this Italian example was being imitated in other parts of Europe. Paris, for example, had its Place Royale (now Place des Vosges) on the Livorno model, begun in 1605. Madrid had its Plaza Mayor, begun in 1617. London had to wait till 1630 for Covent Garden. In the case of squares the periphery led rather than following, for a central feature of the new towns of the New World was the Plaza de Armas, with the cathedral on one side and the town hall on the other. As the law of 1571 put it, 'The main plaza should be in the centre of the town and of an oblong shape, its length being equal to at least one and a half times its width, as this proportion is the best for festivals in which horses are used and any other celebrations which have to be held.'[283]

Practices

From the perspective of the history of everyday life, the history of the Renaissance movement can be viewed as a set of cultural practices. In the arts, for example, the practice of studying, measuring and copying classical statues and buildings became increasingly common. So did the study of anatomy and the naked human model, the 'life class', an institution which originated in Italy in the later sixteenth century and was imitated in the Netherlands and elsewhere. Humanism too might be viewed as a sub-set of such practices, including textual criticism, imitation, and reading, writing and speaking in particular ways which were formally taught in school.

The Latin school was one of the most important locales for the quotidianization of the Renaissance. A few of these schools, staffed by humanists, became models for the rest. St Paul's School, founded by John Colet in order to drive out 'barbarism', was a pattern for the school at Ipswich founded by Cardinal Wolsey and for Merchant Taylors' school in London.

Strasbourg Academy, founded by Johan Sturm in 1538, attracted students from many parts of Europe, while schools in Basel and Geneva and the academy at Zamość followed the pattern.[284] The numbers of pupils at some of these schools deserves emphasis. The Strasbourg Academy was attended by over 600 pupils in 1546. Some Jesuit colleges were even larger. Munich, for example, had 900 students in 1597. The Jesuit college in Paris had 1300 students in 1580, and the college at Billom had 1500 students in 1582. These schools trained pupils in the practices of speaking and writing classical Latin, both prose and verse. Latin plays performed by the students (see above, p. 150) helped familiarize them with the language. This was how the Scottish humanist George Buchanan came to write his Latin plays while teaching at the Collège de Guyenne in Bordeaux, where the pupils included Montaigne, who acted in some of these productions. The plays also reinforced everyday training in rhetoric, which included elocution, gesture and the art of memory, as well as the technique of persuading or dissuading an audience or attacking or defending a proposition.

Treatises on rhetoric multiplied at this time, among the most famous being those written by Erasmus, Melanchthon, Sturm and Cipriano Soarez, whose textbook was officially adopted by the Jesuits.[285] Their popularity should not surprise the modern reader, since rhetoric had many practical uses in this period. Formal orations marked special occasions such as funerals or royal visits to cities, while for lawyers, preachers and diplomats they formed part of everyday working life. A practice encouraged in schools from the 1530s onwards was the keeping of 'commonplace books', in other words, notes on reading intended to furnish the student with a treasury of ready-made phrases and examples which could be employed in orations or letters on different occasions.[286] Montaigne's early essays developed out of a commonplace book of this kind, before the author found his personal style. So did the treatise on politics by Lipsius (see above, p. 7), essentially an anthology of comments on politics by ancient writers and so much appreciated in the period that by 1604 it had been translated into seven European languages.

Informal practices were also important in the penetration of humanism into daily life. There was even a distinctively humanist style of friendship, following the recommendations of Cicero and Seneca and making reference to eternal love, altars of friendship and the example of antiquity, notably that of Pylades and Orestes. This humanist style, following what were called the 'laws' of friendship, was marked by inscriptions in books that they were the property of the owner 'and his friends' (*et amicorum*); by gifts, especially books and portraits, such as the paired portraits of Erasmus and Peter Gillis which the sitters presented to their common friend Thomas More; and by the 'album of friends' (*album amicorum*), which might contain autographs, coats of arms, pictures, verses and mottoes. More than 1,500 examples of these albums have survived from the sixteenth century. The custom seems to have begun in the circle of the patricians of Augsburg and Nuremberg, especially among students at foreign universities, spreading to Switzerland, the Netherlands, Denmark, Poland and Scotland. By the 1550s there was so much interest that blank albums were printed with titles like 'A Treasury of Friends' (*Thesaurus Amicorum*).[287]

Collecting objects associated with classical antiquity was another practice through which Renaissance values became part of everyday life. The bookseller Vespasiano da Bisticci wrote of the Florentine patrician Niccolò Niccoli that those who wished to court his favour would send him marble statues, or antique vases or inscriptions. In the next generation, Lorenzo de'Medici was a famous collector of gems, cameos, statues, vases and medals. Pietro Bembo was another enthusiast; witness a letter he wrote to Cardinal Bibbiena in 1516 that 'since Raphael of Urbino was unable to find a place in your new bathroom for the little marble Venus that Signor Giangiorgio Cesarino gave you . . . be so good as to give it to me. I will cherish her and put her in my study (*camerino*), between Jupiter and Mercury her father and her brother.'

By Bembo's time such interests were no longer remarkable. They were shared by an international network of connoisseurs. By the 1560s the artist Hubert Goltzius claimed to know of nearly a thousand collections in different parts of Europe. The objects collected were also diversified. Giovio's gallery of historical portraits was emulated by many collectors and surpassed by Archduke Ferdinand II of the Tyrol, who owned over a thousand examples. The Antwerp patrician Cornelius van de Gheest collected fifteenth-century Flemish paintings. The famous collection of the Emperor Rudolf II included objects from the Ottoman Empire, Persia, India, China and the New world. The marvellous works of nature were also of interest to collectors: shells, or dried or stuffed specimens of exotic animals, birds, fish or plants.[288]

Linguistic practices were another sign of the domestication of the Renaissance, naming practices, for example. Personal names were a sign of allegiance to humanist values, a link to the cult of antiquity. In the Anguissola family, for instance, Sofonisba and Asdrubale were the children of Amilcare; in the Aldrovandi family of Bologna, Ulisse the famous naturalist and his brother Achille were the sons of Teseo. Scholars often Latinized their surnames, especially if these names were German or Dutch, as in the examples of Agricola (originally Bauer or Huusman), Melanchthon (Schwarzstein), Mercator (Kramer), Sapidus (Witz) and Vulcanius (Smet). Identification with antiquity may also be illustrated by the practice of giving classical titles to modern institutions. Milan, Wittenberg and Coimbra were all described as a 'new Athens'. Venice, Antwerp and Seville were new Romes. The pope was called by the title of his pagan predecessor, *pontifex maximus*. The French infantry were described as 'legions'. The Parlement of Paris and the town councils of many cities were given the title of 'senates'.

Borrowings from Greek, Latin and Italian illustrate both the enthusiasm for classical and Italian culture and the need for a new vocabulary to discuss new concerns. Discussions of poetry introduced words such as 'elegy', 'epigram', 'hexameter' and 'sonnet' into several European languages. In music, technical terms for songs (*madrigale, strambotta, villanella*) or dances (*pavana, alla gagliarda*) passed into French, English and even German (*Paduanen, Gagliarden*). It would have been difficult to discuss the classical style of architecture without terms like 'architrave', 'cornice', 'frieze', 'gallery', 'pilaster', 'piazza' or 'portico', whether the words were borrowed from Italian (as tended to happen in French, English and Spanish) or neologisms invented for the purpose (as in German).

Montaigne condemned what he called the 'jargon' of architecture, which was probably used, as jargons so often are, to impress the uninitiated. In similar fashion the Breton nobleman Noël Du Fail's *Stories of Eutrapel* mocked the people who 'had no other words in their mouth but frontispieces, pedestals, obelisks and columns' (*n'avaient autres mots en bouche que frontispieces, piedestals, obelisques, colonnes*). Henri Estienne, as we have seen, saw nothing but absurdity in the 'italianization' of French. However, the long-term consequences of this fashion were significant. An international language of art was coming into existence, with words not only for techniques such as fresco or damascening but also for styles – rustic, grotesque, arabesque and above all classical (*all'antica, à l'antique, a lo romano, nach antiquischer manier* and so on). Since language affects perception, it is likely that this cluster of terms sharpened the consciousness of differences between styles. Looking back at the year around 1500, when all these words had not yet passed into currency, it is difficult to imagine how non-Italians could have spoken or even thought about new trends in architecture, painting or music.

Writing was another practice which came to follow the models of antiquity and Italy. Italian humanists revived the style of handwriting practised by scribes in the time of Charlemagne, thinking it the style of the ancient Romans, while Poggio and Niccoli introduced the style now known as 'italic'. Classical inscriptions influenced Italian calligraphy, especially the capital letters. Students learned to write in this way (figure 2), and Italian chanceries, writing-masters and printed treatises all helped to spread the new ideals.[289] For many, the italic hand was a sign of allegiance to the humanist movement (though some people with humanist interests, such as Rabelais, did not adopt it). Dürer changed to this style of handwriting after visiting Italy.[290] So did Inigo Jones a century later. Typography followed the same model, though at different rates in different countries and also in books on different subjects. Devotional books, romances of chivalry and books on law were still being printed in Gothic type after italic had become the norm for lyrics and dialogues.

Another social practice through which the Renaissance entered everyday life was writing verses, especially sonnets about love in the manner of Petrarch, a practice described half-mockingly at the time as 'petrarchizing' (*petrarcheggiare, pétrarquiser*). Celia, Delia, Julia, Helen, Stella and many others joined Petrarch's Laura as the object of such poetic tributes. In Italy, this practice was not confined to young nobles but extended to artists such as Raphael and Michelangelo and to courtesans. A Venetian courtesan under investigation by the Inquisition declared that she had read Petrarch and 'composed many sonnets' (she seems to have taken Veronica Franco as her role model). The praises of the lady in terms of roses, lilies, coral and alabaster, and the paradoxes of the beloved as 'dear enemy', the lover's 'sweet torment' (*dolce tormento*) and the 'icy fire' all passed into the language of love.[291] Dictionaries of the vocabulary of Petrarch were compiled, editions of Petrarch indexed his adjectives, and one Italian critic condemned a poet for using words which were not in Petrarch, a critique reminiscent of the debate over the imitation of Cicero (see above, p. 99). To speak or write in this way was a kind of game. Conversely, a parlour game current in Italy in the sixteenth century required players to associate parts of the body with lines from Petrarch.

The writing of letters, especially love-letters, was another practice which owed much to classical and Italian models. Like sonnets, letters were supposed to be an elegant expression of commonplaces, a new permutation or combination of items already familiar. Treatises on the art of letter-writing multiplied. Model letters were much in demand – letters of recommendations, letters of thanks, letters of excuse, letters of consolation and so on. The letters of Cicero, Petrarch, Aretino and other masters of the genre were available in print. Anthologies of letters by different hands were also published, like the *Letters of Many Worthy Women* discussed above (p. 164). Montaigne claimed to own a hundred collections of letters, purchased on his visit to Italy.

Model love-letters formed a genre of their own, which inspired an early epistolary novel, Alvise Pasqualigo's *Love Letters* (1569). Recurrent themes include the sending of a present, the complaint about the cruelty or 'harshness' of the beloved, the tortures of jealousy, and so on. The charms of the loved one were described in a formulaic manner – *la vostra angelica bellezza, l'incredibile bellezza vostra, quella bellezza estrema* and so on. The language is that of the Petrarchan lover, sighing and weeping, or the 'poor and humble little shepherd' (*umile e povero pastorello*) of the pastoral tradition.

Readers may be wondering whether real people ever wrote in this way. That some of them really followed the models and practised the recommendations of the treatises may be illustrated by a case from the tribunal of the Governor of Rome in 1595, a sodomy trial in which a priest from Subiaco was accused of making advances to a boy, apparently his organist. Key documents in the case were the unsigned love-letters in the boy's possession, written in a vaguely Petrarchan style, calling him 'my only hope' (*unica mia speranza*), referring to 'my most faithful service' (*mio fidelissimo servire*), complaining of his abandonment, 'evil fortune', 'great pain', 'heart torn open' (*sviscerato core*) and describing himself as 'he who has loved you more than himself' (*quel che vi ha amate più che se stesso*). What would Petrarch have thought of this appropriation of his language?

Another practice which reveals enthusiasm for antiquity and Italy was travel, or what we may call 'tourism', in other words, visits for the purpose of viewing places with certain cultural associations.[292] Petrarch not only meditated on the ruins of Rome but also visited the grave of Virgil at Capri and the tomb of Livy at Padua. Practices of this kind became increasingly common. Alfonso of Aragon, for instance, visited what he took to be Ovid's house and Cicero's tomb. Virgil's grave at Capri was visited by Erasmus and by King Charles VIII of France. In 1598, a Polish visitor carved his name there.[293]

Italophilia was also expressed and encouraged by tourism. This practice can be documented from the fifteenth century, when the municipality of Arezzo declared Petrarch's house there to be a public monument. The Florentine humanist Traversari visited Petrarch's tomb at Arquà, while the French humanist Fichet went to see what he thought was Petrarch's tomb at Avignon. It was only in the sixteenth century, however, that tourism became common, thanks in particular to the growing cult of Petrarch and his beloved Laura. In 1533 the poet Maurice Scève, then a student at Avignon, discovered what he believed to be Laura's tomb.[294] In the following year the Spanish poet Garcilaso de la Vega visited the tomb. The English traveller Fynes Moryson visited Arquà in 1594 and saw not only Petrarch's tomb but also his house, where the owner 'showed us some household stuff belonging to him, and the very skin of a cat he loved, which they have dried, and still keep'.

The sites of cultural pilgrimage included Ariosto's tomb at Ferrara, Boccaccio's tomb at Certaldo, Sannazzaro's tomb at Mergellina, Castiglione's tomb at Mantua, and the tombs of Giotto, Ficino and Michelangelo in Florence. From 1620 onwards, Michelangelo's house was open to visitors. The itineraries of travellers to Italy also included works of art and living artists and scholars. The future magistrate Jacques-Auguste de Thou visited the *studiolo* of Isabella d'Este at Mantua and met Vasari in Florence. The Medici Chapel was frequently mentioned by foreign visitors to Florence around the year 1600. The practice of the Grand Tour, in which young noblemen from England, France, the Netherlands, Germany, Denmark, Poland and elsewhere visited Italy and to a lesser extent other countries, was established by the late sixteenth century. Treatises by Justus Lipsius, Henrik Rantzau, the Swiss humanist Theodor Zwinger and others codified the practice, teaching what they called the 'art' or 'method' of travel, what to do and what to see – antiquities, churches, fountains, gardens, inscriptions, libraries, squares, statues and so on.[295]

Warfare is not often viewed as part of the Renaissance, but in this domain too European practices increasingly followed the joint models of antiquity and Italy. Italian military terms such as *bastione* and *cannone* entered French, Spanish, English and other languages (the Germans resisted the word *cannone* as they resisted *pilastro* and other Italian contributions to the language of architecture). Italian treatises on warfare were studied and translated, among them Machiavelli's *Art of War*, with its stress on the military virtues of ancient Rome. Ancient writers on warfare such as Julius Caesar, Polybius and Aelian were taken seriously by the commanders of the period.

Maurice of Nassau, for example, a former pupil of Lipsius and one of the leading generals of his age, followed ancient models in his military practice, replacing squares by linear formations and emphasizing drill and the digging of fortified camps. Maurice was familiar with the commentary by Lipsius on Polybius's description of the Roman army. It would seem that a 'military renaissance' was essential to the 'military revolution' of the late sixteenth century.[296] There are several ironies here. In the first place, the successful invasion of Italy by the 'barbarians' in 1494 did not prevent the Italians being taken as military models. In the second place, the epoch of gunpowder, sometimes celebrated as part of the 'new age', coexisted with a return to the example of antiquity. In the third place, hard-headed, pragmatic and successful generals such as Maurice of Nassau learned something useful from academics such as Lipsius. As in the case of music, handwriting and architecture, humanists contributed to the transformation of cultural practices.

Other everyday practices such as dancing, riding and fencing also followed Italian models. The majority of the treatises on these subjects, which proliferated in the sixteenth century, were written by Italians, and their technical terms entered other languages, like the vocabulary of architecture and war. Italian dancing-masters, riding-masters and fencing-masters were in demand abroad, at court and in the academies in which young nobles learned the style of behaviour considered appropriate to their class. These practices may seem rather remote from what is generally known as the Renaissance, but the example of Castiglione's *Courtier* may be sufficient to show the connections. The *Courtier* discusses dancing, walking, gesture and posture as ways of demonstrating grace (*grazia*) or an elegant negligence (*sprezzatura*), concepts derived from Cicero and other ancient writers which were gradually 'incorporated' into everyday life.

Italian books on carving and other elements of the ritual of the table, such as the art of folding napkins, also attracted interest elsewhere. It was from Italy that the use of the fork spread to other parts of Europe, though resistance remained strong and the practice cannot be said to have been widespread even among the upper classes until the seventeenth century. An Italophil in many respects, King Matthias of Hungary is said to have refused to use the forks given to him by the ruler of Ferrara.[297] However, Hungary was not particularly backward in this respect. In England, as late as 1608 the traveller Thomas Coryate had to explain to his countrymen what a fork was, with an illustration to make his description of this exotic object more intelligible.

Figure 24   Gateway of Honour, Caius College, Cambridge. (Reproduced by permission of the Master and Fellows of Caius College, Cambridge; photo Wim Swaan.)

Attitudes and Values

It is time to examine the principles underlying the practices, in other words, changes in everyday thought, unspoken assumptions, mental habits or sensibility. For example, architectural forms sometimes expressed complex ideas. When Gonville and Caius College Cambridge was rebuilt in Renaissance style during the 1560s and 1570s, three gateways were constructed: the simple Gate of Humility, at the entrance; the more elaborate Gate of Virtue; and finally the highly ornate Gate of Honour, complete with obelisks, at the exit to the place where degrees were conferred (figure 24). To walk through these gateways was to imitate the student's passage through the university. It was to enact a ritual of initiation, a kind of rebirth or Renaissance, the gateway representing the womb. The symbolism – and the reference to virtues – is reminiscent of the Renaissance emblem (see below, p. 205). The Gate of Honour, like the portico of the University of Alcalá (figure 10) represents an academic variation on the triumphal arch, fame as the spur to study.

Again, the museums or 'cabinets of curiosities' of the Renaissance may be viewed as materializations of the contemporary interest in the marvellous, in prodigies or sports of nature.[298] Their rise is related to a new and more positive valuation of curiosity, an attitude long condemned by Christian thinkers from Augustine to Calvin.[299] They have also been analysed as embodiments of an encyclopaedic ideal, attempts to construct a microcosm of the universe which would include animals, vegetables and minerals alongside the products of human skill from different parts of the world. Attempts have been made to reconstruct the system of categories underlying the arrangement of such museums, with the aid of treatises such as the physician Samuel Quiccheberg's *Inscriptions* (1565), which told its readers how to arrange and classify their collections.[300]

Again, the ideas formally expounded by Machiavelli in his *Prince* and his *Discourses* have been compared with political thought at the everyday level of memoranda from councillors to princes, debates in assemblies or the reports of ambassadors. It was not simply a matter of high theory influencing ordinary practice. Everyday political ideas were changing in Florence in

Machiavelli's time, especially after the crisis following the French invasion of 1494. The political debates among the members of the ruling class in Florence reveal less confidence in reason than there had been before the crisis, and more concern with force. Machiavelli's writings at once reflected, articulated and influenced these assumptions.[301] Some of his ideas passed into the common currency of the innumerable treatises on 'reason of state', including the ones which explicitly attacked him, including Giovanni Botero, whose treatise *Ragione di Stato* (1589) was translated into French, German, Spanish and Latin before the end of the century and had reached its sixth Italian edition by 1606.

Another example of changes in unspoken assumptions is what might be called the 'sense of the past'. The movement to revive classical antiquity depended on two conflicting if not contra-dictory assumptions. The first was that of cultural distance, the assumption that the ancients did things in a different way from the moderns. The second was that it was not only desirable but also possible to annihilate this cultural distance, to bring back the language of Cicero, for example. Material culture sometimes reveals unspoken assumptions more clearly than texts do. Building in the classical style and representing moderns in the costume of the ancients were so many attempts to annihilate cultural distance. On the other hand, the sense of distance is revealed by what might be called 'the Roman soldier test'. Where medieval artists had represented Roman soldiers (sleeping at the tomb of Christ, for example) in the armour of their own time, Mantegna studied Roman sculpture in order to represent ancient armour and weapons accurately. In similar fashion, the stage directions to a play by Cervantes, *The Siege of Numancia*, describe the Roman soldiers as 'armed in the ancient manner, without arquebuses'.

Ultimately, the sense of distance became so sharp as to under-mine the will to imitate antiquity. As we have seen (p. 99), Erasmus attacked Ciceronianism, on the grounds that Cicero spoke and wrote in the language of his own time, not an earlier one. A character in Castiglione's *Courtier* declared that if we imitate the ancients we actually diverge from them because the ancients did not imitate others. The French scholar François Hotman's studies of Roman law led him to conclude, in his *Anti-*

Tribonian (1567), that these studies were useless for a modern Frenchman because 'the Roman republican system is very different from that of France' (*l'état de la république romaine est fort différent de celui de France*).[302]

To follow the process of the formation of mental habits, it is obviously necessary to pay attention to changes in education. Commonplace books helped to structure commonplace thoughts, encouraging students to view the world in terms of moral qualities arranged in hierarchical order and also to see it in terms of binary oppositions – between the profession of arms and the profession of letters, between *otium* and *negotium*, between vices and virtues, and so on.[303] Encyclopaedias such as Zwinger's *Theatre of Human Life* (1586), which was also organized for the most part by moral qualities, reinforced the message. So did collections of moral maxims, like the best-selling *Adagia* of Erasmus. So did the *gnomologiae*, the indexes of maxims provided by the publishers of books such as Guicciardini's *History of Italy* and Lipsius's *Letters*, and a useful guide to the way in which these books were read at the time. One reason for the enthusiasm for Tacitus in the late sixteenth and early seventeenth centuries, besides his relevance to the debate on 'reason of state', was the Roman writer's love of maxims. Botero cited him no fewer than seventy-three times.

The view of the world in terms of moral qualities was also supported by the fashionable genre of the emblem-book, launched by the humanist lawyer Andrea Alciati in the 1530s. The emblem was an image with a moral, deliberately cryptic but combined with a motto and an epigram which were supposed to allow the viewer to decode it. The emblem was both a development from and a popularization of the *impresa*, the personalized device with a motto which humanists and others used on medals and elsewhere. For example, the device of the Emperor Charles V, invented for the emperor by an Italian humanist, consisted of two columns and the motto 'Beyond' (*plus oultre*), signifying that Charles's empire extended beyond the Pillars of Hercules, once considered by Europeans to be the boundary of the known world.[304]

Hundreds of emblem-books were published in the sixteenth century in Italy, France, Spain, the Netherlands, Central Europe and elsewhere. The moralized world of nature, as described in Pliny's *Natural History* and in medieval bestiaries, was one of the richest sources for emblems. Some of the mottoes entered everyday language (if they did not come from it in the first place) and have survived to this day. To saw off the branch on which one is sitting, for example; to weep crocodile tears; or to kill with kindness (with an image of an ape smothering its offspring by hugging them too tightly).[305]

The philosophy of Plato and the stoics also penetrated or at least coloured the everyday life of some groups, including artists such as Michelangelo and El Greco. That the Neoplatonic theory of love, based on Ficino's commentary on Plato's *Symposium*, became a fashionable topic of conversation in mixed company of a certain status in sixteenth-century Italy is suggested by the proliferation of dialogues on the topic, which seem, as the art historian Erwin Panofsky once put it, 'to have played a role in Cinquecento society not unlike that of semi-popular books on psychoanalysis in our own day'. As one humanist drily remarked, 'finally the courtiers thought it an indispensable part of their job to know how many and what kinds of love there were' – physical, intellectual, spiritual and so on.[306] Whether or not they realized that Plato was concerned with love between men, the participants in these debates concentrated on relations between men and women. Women contributed to the debates, sometimes by writing dialogues such as *The Infinity of Love*, by the courtesan Tullia d'Aragona. One might even say that platonism was 'feminized'.

The most influential of the dialogues on love, with the possible exception of the speech on the subject pronounced by Bembo at the end of Castiglione's *Courtier*, was published in Rome in 1535 by Leone Ebreo, otherwise known as Judah Abravanel, a Jewish physician from Lisbon. After the expulsion of the Jews from Portugal in 1492, his family settled in Italy. Leone's exposition of the definition, origins, varieties and effects of love took the form of a dialogue between a master and a pupil with whom he is in love, Philo and Sophia. 'Sophia' of course means 'wisdom' and the two names combined form the word 'philosophy'. Of all the contemporary treatises on love, this was the one with the greatest success: fourteen Italian editions by 1607, together with one translation into Latin, two into French and three into Spanish. Montaigne and Cervantes both mention Leone's dialogues, while the ideas expounded in them recur in the poetry of the Pléiade as in Montemayor's pastoral romance *Diana* (see above, p. 147), especially in the discussion of love in Book IV.

The strength of interest in the topic is confirmed by the attention devoted to Platonic doctrines of love in Italian 'academies', discussion groups or clubs some of which, like the Dubbiosi of Venice or the Incogniti of Naples, admitted women. The increasing currency of the idea of 'Idea', is a pointer in the same direction. The term played a central role in the theory of art from Michelangelo to Giovanni Paolo Lomazzo, who published his treatise *Idea* in 1590, and Vincenzo Scamozzi, whose *Idea of Universal Architecture* appeared in 1615.[307] It was also employed in a variety of other contexts. For example, a certain Bartolomeo Zucchi entitled his guide to letter-writing *L'idea del segretario* (1606).

Enthusiasm for the ideas of Plato and his followers spread beyond Italy and probably reached its height in the second half of the sixteenth century. In 1548, a student of Magdalen College, Oxford, bought a Latin Plato and wrote on the title-page 'Deus Philosophorum Plato'. Many of Plato's dialogues were translated into French in the 1540s and 1550s. The imagery of the poets of the Pléiade and their contemporaries, from Edmund Spenser in England to Sá de Miranda in Portugal, drew on Neoplatonism. What attracted the poets was not only the analysis of the varieties of love but also the parallels between the ecstasy, madness or inspiration of lovers, poets and prophets. Through the poets, these ideas reached even wider groups.

If Neoplatonism was feminized as it was adapted to a new milieu, the complex of ideas described as 'neostoicism' and expounded by the Roman philosopher Seneca in his letters and elsewhere had a resolutely masculine image. The penetration of these ideas into everyday life was assisted by Antonio Guevara's idealized biography of Marcus Aurelius (1528), which was translated into French, English, Italian, Latin and German, and the dialogue *On Constancy* (1584) by Justus Lipsius, which went through twenty-four Latin editions in the author's lifetime as well as being translated into French, Dutch, English, German, Spanish, Italian and Polish. Lipsius's many published letters often returned to the subject and abounded with moral maxims.

The central idea of stoicism, at least in its Renaissance version, was that of 'apathy', 'constancy', or 'tranquillity of mind'. A favourite image was that of a man confronting disaster as calmly as a tree or a rock in a storm. Guicciardini's personal medal, for example, showed a rock in the sea. In his tragedy about St John the Baptist, George Buchanan compared his hero to an oak-tree standing firm in a storm, or a rock amid the waves. In his romance *Arcadia*, Sidney described his heroine Pamela as 'like a rock amidst the sea, beaten both with the winds and with the waves, yet itself immovable' (Book 3, chapter 30). An anonymous biography of the period presented William Cecil as 'never moved with passion . . . neither joyful at the best [news] nor daunted at the worst'.

It was not difficult to make stoicism compatible with Christianity, with the help of the Fathers of the Church. The discussions of *adiaphora*, things 'indifferent' or 'external' over which it was folly to dispute, were so many practical applications of stoicism by Melanchthon and others to the problems of the Reformation. Catholics and Protestants alike applauded the constancy of Job, like that of their respective martyrs. Jacques-Auguste de Thou, for example, made a Latin verse paraphrase of the book of Job (1587), with the subtitle 'on constancy', echoing the title of the dialogue by Lipsius published three years earlier. The appeal of the idea of constancy at a time of civil wars is clear. Its relevance to the problems of the later sixteenth century was stressed by Lipsius and also by his follower, the French magistrate Guillaume Du Vair, whose dialogue on constancy in times of public calamities (*De la constance et consolation ès calamités publiques*) was set in Paris during a siege.[308]

The uses of this virile virtue in a military context are even more obvious. It is no accident that Lipsius should have been attracted to the study of both stoicism and the Roman army. The self-discipline recommended by Seneca and Lipsius was transformed into military discipline in the age of drill. Neostoicism even affected the fashion for gardens. Lipsius set his dialogue in the garden of his house at Liège, and turned the garden into a symbol of the moral qualities he was recommending. The first part of Du Vair's dialogue also takes place in a garden.[309]

Even the stoic recommendation of suicide was taken seriously at this time, despite its incompatibility with Christianity. The Florentine patrician Filippo Strozzi killed himself in 1538 after the defeat of his republican aspirations at the battle of Montemurlo, leaving a letter referring to the example of Cato of Utica in a similar situation. The practice of suicide on the classical model of Cato, Lucretia or Seneca (who cut his veins in his bath) may never have become fashionable, but the theory of suicide attracted increasing attention in this period. Guicciardini, Lipsius, Montaigne and John Donne all discussed the ethics of suicide. Lipsius even commissioned a painting on the subject.[310] The topic recurred in the poems, plays and romances of the later sixteenth century. The Croat Dominko Ranjina wrote poems about the suicides of Cato, Sophonisba and Cleopatra. George Chapman's *Caesar and Pompey* represented Cato's suicide on the stage, Garnier's *Porcie* that of Cato's daughter. Shakespeare showed Brutus and Cleopatra in the act of committing noble suicides (although earlier in the play Brutus had condemned suicide as 'cowardly and vile'). Sidney's *Arcadia* described Pyrocles and Philoclea trying to decide whether or not to kill themselves in order to avoid disgrace.

The Discovery of the World

It is time to return to the Burckhardtian ideas of 'individualism' and of the discovery of the world and of man (see above, p. 18). However, the following pages will diverge from Burckhardt in some important respects. It will not be assumed that individualism was completely absent from the Middle Ages or that an inexplicable change in the 'spirit of the age' took place in the time of Petrarch.[311] Instead the stress will fall on a circular process or chain reaction in which changing perceptions created a demand for new kinds of text and image, including travel writing, landscapes, biographies and portraits, but these new texts and images in their turn affected perceptions of the world. People learned to see nature as 'picturesque' or their own life as a story.

The idea of discovery has long been associated with the idea of Renaissance, as we have seen (above, p. 18). The word itself came into use in the fifteenth century in a geographical context. For example, Poggio used the term 'discovery' in a letter to the Portuguese prince Henry the Navigator on the grounds that the places in Africa where the Portuguese had recently landed had been unknown to the ancients. Fifty years later, and about three years before Columbus made his famous landfall, Poliziano wrote to the king of Portugal about the 'discoveries of new lands, new seas, new worlds'. The discovery of the Americas was part of a larger movement of European expansion.

As in the case of the manuscripts of classical writers, Italians played an important role in the process of discovery and also in spreading the news. Columbus was a Genoese, in touch with the Florentine humanist geographer Paolo Toscanelli. The Florentine Amerigo Vespucci, whose name was applied to 'America', visited Patagonia in 1501–2. Lodovico di Varthema visited Egypt, Persia and India between 1500 and 1508. Antonio Pigafetta, from Vicenza, went with Magellan (Fernão de Magalhaes) in his voyage round the world in 1519, and wrote about what he saw. The humanist Pietro Martire, from Anghiera in Lombardy, remained in Europe but wrote an influential book about the New World, perceiving its inhabitants through classical spectacles and describing them as living in a golden age of the kind described in the poems of Ovid, without property. Gianbattista Ramusio, a Venetian civil servant in the circle of Bembo and Navagero, collected earlier travel accounts and published them in three large volumes of *Navigations* in 1550–9.[312]

An awareness of the world beyond Europe can also be detected in the histories written by Bembo, Guicciardini and especially by Giovio. Giovio wrote the history of his own time, concentrating on Europe but mentioning other parts of the world 'from Cathay to Tenochtitlan' as he once put it. He was the first European writer to point out that printing originated in China. Giovio was a man of omnivorous curiosity. All the same, his curiosity, and that of his readers, was not completely disinterested. He wrote a book about the Ottoman empire, for instance, to encourage a crusade against the Turks. The 'discovery of the world' by Europeans did not take place in a political vacuum.[313]

Once made, however, the discoveries affected the imagination of many Europeans, including their sense of their position in space and time. As we have seen, Columbus, sometimes described as 'the second Neptune', and Magellan were incorporated into the definitions of the 'new age'. A Venetian senator told Ramusio that Columbus deserved a bronze statue, an idea taken up by a late sixteenth-century Genoese patrician, Andrea Spinola, who recommended the erection of a marble statue of Columbus outside the town hall. Francis Bacon described the image of Columbus displayed in his imagined research institute, Solomon's House, among 'the statues of all principal inventors'. Lope de Vega wrote a play about Columbus, while Giulio Cesare Stella made him the hero of an epic. The more famous epics of Ercilla and Camões (see above, pp. 143–5) also described the world beyond Europe.

Printed matter obviously helped to widen the horizons of those who stayed at home. Many first-hand accounts of travel outside Europe were published in the sixteenth century, including such classics as the letters of the Flemish diplomat Ogier Ghiselin de Busbecq describing the Ottoman empire, and the accounts of the Tupinamba of Brazil by the German mercenary Hans Staden and the French Protestant missionary Jean de Léry. Following the example of Ramusio, collections of travels were published by the clergyman Richard Hakluyt in London and the engraver-publisher Theodor de Bry in Frankfurt.[314] The two men were acquainted. Hakluyt also knew André Thevet, the French cosmographer royal, and the humanist geographers Gerard Mercator and Abraham Ortelius, who encouraged the Englishman to publish.

By the second half of the sixteenth century, histories of the world outside Europe were proliferating. João de Barros told the story of the exploits of the Portuguese in Asia (see above, p. 157). For the sections on India and Persia he consulted returned soldiers, merchants and administrators. For China he used Chinese sources, including maps, having bought a Chinese slave 'for the interpretation of these things'.[315] González de Mendoza wrote about China. Lopez de Gómara, who had been chaplain to Hernán Cortés, and the Jesuit José de Acosta described the Americas from the point of view of conquerors and missionaries. The history written by Girolamo Benzoni, a Milanese who had spent fourteen years in the New World, condemned the cruelties of the Spaniards, while Garcilaso (see above, p. 108) celebrated the achievements of his ancestors, the Incas.[316] Some at least of these histories were an international publishing success. Lopez de Gómara, for instance, appeared in Italian, French and English. Benzoni's book was published in French and Latin versions in Geneva and also translated into German and Dutch because its anti-Spanish attitudes appealed to the Protestant world. González de Mendoza had an even better international reception, translated into six languages (Italian, French, English, German, Latin and Dutch) within ten years of its original publication.[317]

One of the most remarkable sixteenth-century accounts of the world beyond Europe was the *Description of Africa* published in Italian in 1550 by 'Leo Africanus', who was soon hailed as a second Columbus.[318] It was the work of a man who knew Europe from both inside and outside. Hasan al-Wazzân, to give him his Islamic name, was born in Granada. After the expulsion of the Muslims in 1492, his family moved to Fez, where he had a distinguished career as an envoy in the service of the ruler. Captured by Sicilian corsairs in 1518, Hasan was taken to Rome and presented to Pope Leo X. Converted to Christianity and baptized by the pope himself, Hasan became Giovanni Leo. Probably composed in Arabic, and translated into Italian by the author, his historical geography of Africa was first published in Ramusio's collection of voyages. It was also translated into Latin, French, Spanish and (by a friend of Hakluyt's) into English. Jean Bodin praised the author as 'the only one who after a thousand years discovered Africa . . . and revealed it to everyone'. What he revealed, it should be added, was essentially North Africa. Only the rather brief seventh book of the description deals with Africa south of the Sahara.

By the later sixteenth century, visual images were making exotic countries and their peoples more familiar to many Europeans. The Spanish historian Oviedo once expressed the regret that Leonardo da Vinci and Mantegna had not painted America. However, many items from the Americas, natural or man-made, including armadillos, alligators, feather-work and mosaic masks could be found in European cabinets of curiosities.[319] Engravings, such as the illustrations in Theodor de Bry's multi-volume collection *America*, made some images of the New

World widely known. Painted and printed maps helped their viewers to place what they knew about different regions. The painted maps in the Vatican *Galleria delle carte* are a spectacular example of information combined with decoration. Inventories reveal the growing importance of globes as part of the furniture of studies, and presumably of the minds of their owners as well. Travel books, such as Sigismund von Herberstein's account of Muscovy, were increasingly illustrated with maps. World maps and complete atlases, like the *Theatre of the World* compiled by the Netherlander Abraham Ortelius, gave the viewer a sense of the whole.[320] This volume, first published in Latin in 1570, had been translated into six languages by 1608, a sign of its appeal beyond the humanist community in which it originated. Detailed information about political systems and religions was provided in the *Descriptions of the World* (*Relationi Universali*) compiled by the Piedmontese writer Giovanni Botero in the 1590s. The interest awakened by this work, modelled on the reports which ambassadors and missionaries sent home, but extended to the globe, is shown by the many subsequent editions, as well as translations into German, Latin, English, Spanish and Polish.[321]

Images of the world beyond Europe were often stereotyped. These stereotypes were not infrequently classical ones. For instance, the idea of the so-called 'monstrous races', whether one-legged (the Sciopods), one-breasted (the Amazons), dog-headed (the Cynocephali) or lacking heads altogether (the Blemmyae), inhabiting faraway places such as India or Ethiopia, was an ancient Greek one, transmitted to posterity by Pliny's *Natural History*. After 1492 these peoples were relocated in the imagined New World. Printed images made their appearance more vivid as well as better known, as in the case of the cannibals, who were especially though not exclusively associated with Brazil. Images of the New World as a survival of the golden age (as in Pietro Martire) or as populated by noble savages (as in Jean de Léry) were no less stereotyped than the hostile ones. Montaigne's originality was not so much in offering a sympathetic portrait of the inhabitants of the New World as in turning a conventional argument on its head and arguing that it was the Europeans who were the true barbarians.[322]

Asia too was viewed in stereotyped ways. The Muslim

empires of the Ottomans and the Mughals were not infrequently described (as the ancient Greeks had already described the Persian state) in terms of oriental despotism. In his *Republic* (1576) Jean Bodin described the Ottoman empire as a *monarchie seigneuriale* in which the prince was the owner of all property. Venetian diplomats in Istanbul made similar observations in their reports. Christopher Marlowe's tragedy *Tamburlaine* (*c*.1587), offered audiences an unforgettable image of what would later be known in the West as 'oriental despotism', presenting the Ottoman sultan Bajazet, first in triumph, surrounded by his janissaries and pashas, and then in defeat, brought on stage in a cage and used by Tamburlaine as his footstool. In similar fashion an English ambassador to India, Sir Thomas Roe, described the Mughal form of government as 'uncertain, without written law, without policy' (using 'policy' in the sense of a constitution limiting the ruler's power).

Encounters with the outside world appear to have had a significant influence on European perceptions of humanity and also of Europe itself. The encounter with the indigenous inhabitants of the Americas led to a debate about human nature in which some participants applied Aristotle's concept of 'slaves by nature' to the Indians, while others rejected it.[323] Reflection on what it meant to be European also took place on the borders. The threat of invasion by the Turks, especially in the 1450s and 1520s, encouraged European solidarity. When he heard of the fall of Constantinople, Pius II commented that 'now we have really been struck in Europe, that is at home.' It is somewhat ironic that a pope should have been a pioneer in the replacement of the term 'Christendom' by 'Europe', but Pius (previously Enea Silvio Piccolomini) was a humanist with a strong interest in geography. The first history of Europe to bear such a title, the *Storia dell'Europa*, was written by another humanist, the Florentine Pierfrancesco Giambullari, and published in 1566, at a time of intense Western concern with the Ottoman empire. The invasion of the New World by Europeans was as important as the invasion of Europe by the Turks in stimulating consciousness of a European identity. The cosmographer André Thevet, for example, contrasted the way of life of the Indians of Brazil with that of 'nostre Europe'.[324]

Whether or not their interest was stimulated by awareness of contrasts with other parts of the world, a number of humanists produced 'chorographies' or historical topographies of different parts of Europe, following a classical model, that of the Greek geographer Strabo, and an Italian example, that of Flavio Biondo's *Italy Illustrated* (see above, pp. 39, 78). When written by outsiders, these chorographies often included the description of the manners and customs of different peoples in the style of Herodotus on the Persians and Tacitus on the Germans. Well-known contributions to the genre included *The Two Sarmatias* (1517) by Matthias of Michow, rector of the University of Cracow; the *Commentary on Muscovite Affairs* (1549) by the imperial ambassador to the tsar, Sigismund von Herberstein; the *Description of the Netherlands* (1567) by Lodovico Guicciardini, nephew of the historian; the *Description of Britain* (1572) by the Welsh scholar Humphry Lluyd; and the *Britannia* (1586) by the English historian William Camden.[325] It should be added that the publication of the books by both Lluyd and Camden, like the collection edited by Hakluyt, owed something to the encouragement of the Netherlander Ortelius. At a micro-level the chorographical model was followed in the series of histories of the counties of England which began with William Lambarde's *Perambulation of Kent* (1576) and led one scholar to speak of the 'Elizabethan discovery of England'.[326] Painted images of Europe and the world beyond were also changing in this period. The work of Venetian painters such as Vittore Carpaccio or Gentile Bellini was remarkable for its 'factual' or 'eyewitness' style and its relative freedom from stereotypes, especially stereotypes of Islam.[327]

Some sixteenth-century artists and scholars also concerned themselves as never before with the details of the appearance of animals and plants, stimulated, perhaps, by the flow of information about exotic flora and fauna, including the giraffe which the sultan gave Lorenzo de' Medici and the elephant and the rhinoceros which King Manoel I of Portugal acquired from India and sent to the pope in 1514 and 1515. Raphael painted the elephant, while Dürer made a woodcut of the rhinoceros, after seeing a sketch made when it arrived in Lisbon.[328] Some scholars, notably the Frenchman Pierre Belon and the German

Leonhard Rauwolf, visited the Middle East specifically to study its plants and animals. A Portuguese physician, García d'Orta, wrote a book about the plants and drugs of India (1563), while a Spanish colleague, Nicolás Monardes, published a similar study for the Americas (1565). The encyclopaedia of animals published by the Swiss humanist Konrad Gessner from 1551 onwards included 1,200 woodcut illustrations. Illustrations were also crucial in other sixteenth-century classics of natural history, such as the book on fish by the French physician Guillaume Rondelet (a friend of Rabelais), and the studies of fish and birds by Pierre Belon. The pictures of animals and plants made for the naturalist Ulisse Aldrovandi of Bologna are yet another example of the links between what we now distinguish as 'artistic' and 'scientific' observation.[329]

In a famous passage of his book on unbelief in the age of Rabelais, Lucien Febvre remarked on the lack of interest in the visual: 'there was no Hotel Fairview in the sixteenth century, nor any Prospect Hotel. They were not to appear until the age of Romanticism.'[330] He was forgetting the Villa Belriguardo near Ferrara, not to mention the Belvedere in the Vatican and the fortress of the same name in Florence. Petrarch, who climbed Mont Ventoux in 1336 and admired 'the unusually open and wide view', was sensitive to the aesthetic qualities of landscape, as Burckhardt knew very well.[331]

The history of literature tells a similar story. The descriptions of the 'beauty spot' (*locus amoenus*) to be found in Homer, Virgil and other classical writers were often imitated by Renaissance poets and they influenced perceptions of hills, groves and other features of the landscape. Sannazzaro's *Arcadia* reveals an acute sense of the beauty of wild scenery. In short, literary evidence supports what the existence of landscape paintings and the choice of sites for villas suggests, that an appreciation of views was not uncommon among fifteenth- and sixteenth-century Italians.[332]

By the sixteenth century, if not before, this form of sensibility can be found in other parts of Europe. Landscape painting was becoming an independent genre at this time in the Germany of Albrecht Altdorfer and the 'Danube school', as well as in the Netherlands of Joachim Patinir. It was around 1520 that the German word *Landschaft*, like the Italian word *paese*, was first used to refer to paintings of nature rather than to the land itself. The Swiss humanist Joachim Vadianus climbed the Gnepfstein near Luzern with his friends in 1518 in order to view the lake, as it had been described by the ancient geographer Pomponius Mela, on whom he gave a course of lectures.

The new interest in nature is most easy to document in the case of Italy, the Netherlands and Central Europe, though examples can be found from other regions, notably El Greco's famous view of Toledo. This interest was often an aesthetic one. The poetic vocabulary for the description of the beauties of nature was increasing, and individual poets, such as Ronsard, described rivers and forests, spring and autumn, dawn and dusk with increasing interest and precision.[333] Writers on the art of travel, such as the German Hilarius Pyrckmair, told their readers to look out for 'mountains, woods, valleys, rivers' (*montes, sylvae, valles, flumina*). For others, however, the interest in nature was more 'scientific'. Roelandt Savery was sent into the Tyrol by his employer, the Emperor Rudolf II, in order to portray the marvels of nature for the imperial collections. Poems describing travel, a revival of the classical genre of the *hodoeporicon*, were the literary equivalent of landscape paintings and diversified into local ecotypes. Two Polish examples reveal an ethnographic as well as an aesthetic interest in the region. Sebastian Klonowić, for example, described the countryside of Ruthenia and the customs of its inhabitants in his Latin poem *Roxolania* (1584), while his Polish poem *The Raftsman* (1595) described the river Vistula. His contemporary Szymon Szymonowić portrayed Polish landscapes and local customs in his *Idylls*.

The Discovery of the Self

The human body, like those of animals, was 'discovered' in the late Renaissance in the sense of being dissected, studied and illustrated more precisely, notably in the study of anatomy by Vesalius (see above, p. 132). All the same, this section will concentrate on the human personality. In the case of the discovery of the self as in that of the world, representations of discovery encouraged further exploration. As Burckhardt noted, portraits and self-portraits, biographies and autobiographies

Figure 25   Huntley Gallery façade, Strathbogie, Gordon.
(Photograph © Historic Scotland; Crown copyright reserved.) An
example of self-advertisement, Renaissance style.

became more frequent in Italy in the fifteenth and sixteenth centuries and often followed classical models, from Caesar's *Commentaries* to Augustine's *Confessions*. In this domain as in so many others, the Italian example was followed a little later in other parts of Europe. For example, the 'moment of self-portraiture' in Germany came in the age of Dürer.[334] The moment of autobiography came a little later, after 1550. In the case of Italy, one thinks of Benvenuto Cellini and the Milanese physician Girolamo Cardano. In the case of France, one thinks of Montaigne or the soldier Blaise de Monluc. In the German-speaking world, one thinks of Bartholomaeus Sastrow and Thomas Platter; in the Netherlands, of Justus Lipsius; in England, of the musician Thomas Whythorne. In Spain, St Teresa, St Ignatius, Capitain Alonso Contreras, and a number of others wrote their autobiographies. It is unlikely to be coincidence that these Spanish texts coincided with the emergence of the first-person picaresque novel (discussed above, p. 147), whether 'fact' influenced 'fiction' or the reverse.[335]

It cannot be claimed that this trend is uniquely Western or modern. Portraits and biographies, including autobiographies or 'ego-documents' (a deliberately vague term which begs fewer questions), can be found in other cultures such as China, Japan and the Islamic world. Indeed, the 'golden age' of Chinese autobiography has been described as beginning around 1566, at virtually the same moment as in Europe, a coincidence which – like the rise of the aesthetic garden, noted above – should give food for thought.[336] Biographies and a few ego-documents can be found in Europe in the twelfth century, and portraits, in the sense of recognizable likenesses, in the fourteenth. On the other side, despite Burckhardt, there is no lack of evidence in Renaissance Italy of the continuing identification of individuals with their families, guilds, factions or cities. The *ricordanze* or 'memoranda' so common in Florence are not individual autobiographies, despite their personal details, but a mixture of account-books, family diaries and local chronicles.[337]

It is probably more illuminating to consider Renaissance conceptions of the individual than to speak as Burckhardt did of 'the development of the individual' at this time. It might be better still to think in terms of changes in the category of the person or in views of the self, or in styles and methods for the presentation of self or self-fashioning.[338] Castiglione's *Courtier* may be viewed as a guide to self-presentation, and so may the many manuals of letter-writing of the period. Awareness of the importance of epistolary self-presentation is revealed by the concern of Petrarch, Erasmus and Lipsius, among others, for the collecting and editing of their letters.[339] Again, many forms of material culture discussed earlier in this chapter – houses and their furnishings, to say nothing of clothes – may be regarded as so many aids to self-presentation. This point is particularly clear in the cases in which patrons had their names inscribed on the buildings they commissioned. Marco Antonio Barbaro's name appears on the façade of the church next to his villa at Maser, that of Cardinal Farnese on the church of the Gesù in Rome, Bess of Hardwick's initials on the parapets of Hardwick Hall. In 1602, the gallery at the Scottish castle of Strathbogie was inscribed in Roman capitals, 'GEORGE GORDOUN FIRST MARQUIS OF HUNTLIE' (figure 25).

Medals, which normally carried a portrait on one side and a personalized device on the reverse, were another example of self-presentation. The fashion for medals, mainly Italian in the fifteenth century (see above, p. 43) spread through Europe in the sixteenth century, not only among rulers, who used them for propaganda purposes, but also among humanists: Erasmus, for example, whose medal was designed by the artist Quentin Matsys; Willibald Pirckheimer; Sir John Cheke, whose medal was made in Padua; and the astronomer Tycho Brahe.

Biographies

As in other domains, Petrarch is a necessary point of departure, in this case with his collection of lives of famous Romans and others. Fifteenth-century collections included Bartolomeo Fazio's *Illustrious Men*, Platina's *Lives of the Popes*, Vespasiano da Bisticci's memoirs of famous men he had known, and the Augustinian hermit Jacopo Filippo Foresti's lives of famous women, following the model of Boccaccio (see above, p. 25) but including the humanists Isotta Nogarola and Cassandra Fedele. Turning to individual biographies: Boccaccio wrote about Dante and Petrarch, Leonardo Bruni wrote about Aristotle, Cicero, Dante and Petrarch, Guarino of Verona wrote about Plato and Giannozzo Manetti about Socrates and Seneca. Among the contemporaries honoured in this way were Nicholas V, Alfonso of Aragon, Filippo Maria Visconti, Cosimo de' Medici, the architect Brunelleschi, the humanist Pomponio Leto and the *condottiere* Braccio da Montone.[340]

In sixteenth-century Italy, biography became a still more important part of the cultural landscape. If we think first of Vasari's lives of artists, contemporaries probably thought of Giovio's biographies of soldiers and sultans, followed by Giuseppe Betussi's lives of ladies, which brought Boccaccio up to date by adding (among others) Isabella d'Este and Marguerite de Navarre. Individual lives included Corsi's Ficino, Machiavelli's Castruccio Castracani, Condivi's Michelangelo and Pigna's Ariosto.

Before 1500 there is little to report beyond the Alps. Rudolf Agricola wrote about Petrarch, and Hernando Pulgar about the 'famous men of Castile'. The life of Henry V of England was written not by an Englishman but by an expatriate Italian, Tito Livio Frulovisi (a pupil of Guarino da Verona), just as the life of the Polish bishop Gregory of Sanok was written by another Italian humanist, Filippo Buonaccorsi 'Callimaco'. After 1500, however, the situation changed. The life of Jerome by Erasmus, published in 1516, was at once a symptom of a new interest and a stimulus to it. A life of Erasmus was written in 1540 by the humanist Beatus Rhenanus, while Beatus himself was to become the hero of a biography eleven years later.

In England, Sir Thomas Elyot wrote a biography of the Roman emperor Alexander Severus. William Roper and Nicholas Harpsfield wrote lives of Thomas More and George Cavendish that of Cardinal Wolsey. A life of Philip Sidney was written by his friend Fulke Greville. In the French-speaking world there were biographies of Guillaume Budé, Jean Calvin, Catherine de' Medici, Petrus Ramus and Pierre Ronsard, as well as Brantôme's collected lives of 'Great Captains'. The poets Eoban Hessus and Jan Kochanowski, the artists Albrecht Dürer and Lambert Lombard, the composer Josquin des Prez, the reformer Philip Melanchthon and the humanist Justus Lipsius all had their biographers.

In some of these cases the Italian model is obvious enough. Karel van Mander's *Schilderboek* or 'Book of Painters' (1604) was an emulation of Vasari, just as Brantôme emulated Giovio. The Italians too followed models. Petrarch was probably inspired by Jerome's *De viris illustribus*, itself modelled on Suetonius on Roman writers. Giovio admitted imitating Plutarch. His lives of soldiers followed Cornelius Nepos, while Vasari adapted to artists the model of the lives of the philosophers by Diogenes Laertius. Even Brantôme, a soldier not a scholar, studied Plutarch and Suetonius in French translations and sometimes saw his heroes and heroines through their eyes.

Biographies were produced for various purposes and in various contexts. Lives of the saints, which were still being written, proposed models for readers to imitate. Vasari wrote about artists, so he tells us, for similar reasons, a point which helps explain the fact that he tells the same anecdote about different artists, just as certain stories about the saints turn up in one piece of hagiography after another. Other biographies originated as funeral orations.[341]

One context of biography is particularly revealing of general changes in attitude or mentality. From the later fifteenth century onwards, the lives of authors were frequently written and published as prefaces to their works. For example, lives of the ancient Roman poets by the humanist Pietro Crinito, originally published as a collection in 1508, were later used to introduce editions of these poets. Erasmus's biography of Jerome was prefixed to an edition of Jerome's works published by the Basel printer Froben in 1516. In similar fashion, the Erasmus biography by Beatus Rhenanus was commissioned by Froben as a preface to a new edition of the works of Erasmus. Pigna's biography of Ariosto was quickly added to editions of the *Orlando Furioso*. The editions of Ronsard, Chaucer and Francisco de Sá published in 1586, 1598 and 1614 respectively were also prefaced by biographies. This new convention illustrates the rise of the idea of the individuality of authorship, in other words, the idea (or assumption) that information about the personal lives of writers helps readers understand their works.

Portraits

Portraits and self-portraits offer obvious parallels to biographies and autobiographies, and the genres developed at much the same time and in much the same places, especially Italy, Germany and the Netherlands. Jean Fouquet's self-portrait is an early example (figure 3). Among the best-known Italian examples are the self-portraits of Titian, Parmigianino and Vasari, while as many as twelve by Sofonisba Anguissola have survived. In the case of Germany, one thinks of the series of self-portraits by Dürer; in the Netherlands, of Maarten van Heemskerck and of Catherine van Hemessen (figure 16).

Biographies and portraits were combined, following the model of the ancient Roman scholar Varro, in the books by Giovio and Vasari (144 historical portraits were included in the second edition of his *Lives*, published in 1568). Portraits of illustrious men, and more rarely women, were becoming an increasingly important part of the furnishings of great houses or public buildings, especially libraries. Those people who shared the interest in these historical figures but could not afford to commission oil paintings could acquire a 'paper museum', in other words, books of printed portraits of popes, rulers, scholars, heretics and so on, scores of which were published in the sixteenth century.[342]

Editions of famous writers were accompanied not only by their biographies but also by their portraits, usually in the form of frontispieces, as in the cases of Dante (1521), Ariosto (1532: figure 5), Erasmus (1533), Petrarch (1536), Ronsard (1552), Tasso (1593) and Shakespeare (1623). Verses below the portrait sometimes explain the reason. Under Ronsard's portrait was written 'Ici le corps, et l'esprit dans ses vers'; under Shakespeare's, Ben Jonson's famous verses about the artist:

> O could he but have drawn his wit
> As well in brass, as he has hit
> His face: the print would then surpass
> All that was ever writ in brass:
> But since he cannot, reader, look
> Not on his picture but his book.

Scores of minor jurists, physicians and others joined the trend. By 1600 at least eighty Italians, including two or three women (Isabella Andreini, Modesta Pozzo and possibly Veronica Franco), had been protrayed in the frontispieces to their books.[343] For the rest of Europe a systematic investigation is lacking, but I have found fifty examples, all but eight after 1550.

How can we account for the rise of the portrait in Europe at this time? The temptation to frame an answer to this question in terms of 'individualism' – Western individualism in general, and Renaissance individualism in particular – is a strong one. It is no surprise to find that Jacob Burckhardt, who placed such stress on the 'development of the individual' in the Italian Renaissance, should also have devoted an essay to the history of the portrait. This argument certainly has something to be said for it. The existence of 'halls of illustrious men', celebrating the achievement of outstanding individuals (see above, pp. 23, 43, suggests connections between the rise of the portrait and what Burckhardt called 'the modern sense of fame'. So does Giovio's museum of historical portraits and other collections of this type. The idea of the unique individual fits well with increasing demands for verisimilitude, for a 'likeness'. Margareta of Austria sent Jan Vermeyen to Augsburg to portray Charles V 'as closely to life as possible' (*au plus pres du vif que possible luy seroit*). The instructions for the funeral of Philip II included the order to portray him 'as naturally as possible' (*el más al natural que fuere posible*).[344] At about the same time, English men and women who commissioned tombs for themselves or their families began to ask for actual portraits of the deceased.[345] When Montaigne visited Ariosto's tomb at Ferrara, he remarked that the effigy was 'a little fuller in the face than he is in his books' (*un peu plus plein de visage qu'il n'est en ses livres*), in other words, in the frontispiece to *Orlando Furioso*. It is therefore likely that the effigy of Jan Kochanowski on his tomb (figure 20) is a portrait.

All the same, the thesis that the rise of the portrait is an expression of the rise of individualism raises awkward problems. An examination of the uses of the portrait in the Renaissance shows that most of these objects were originally hung in groups, including members of a particular family or holders of particular offices (bishops, doges and so on). The portrait usually represented social roles rather than individuals. Important people in particular are weighed down by their cultural baggage, surrounded by such accessories as robes, crowns, sceptres, swords, columns, curtains. These practices suggest that the identities supported by the paintings were collective or institutional rather than individual, with the exception of portraits of the owner's friends (a type of portrait which accounts for only a small proportion of the genre).

An even more serious difficulty is raised by the persistence of what is sometimes known as the 'generic portrait', representing a knight or a lady rather than a particular individual. In the late fifteenth century, the 1493 world chronicle of the Nuremberg humanist Hartman Schedel used the same woodcut to portray Homer, the prophet Isaiah, Hippocrates, Terence, the medieval lawyer Accursius and the Renaissance philosopher Francesco Filelfo. In the 1550s, the anonymous illustrations to a collection of biographies by the Swiss scholar Heinrich Panteleon used the same woodcut to portray the German humanist Johan Reuchlin and Einhard, the ninth-century biographer of Charlemagne. In similar fashion, the Netherlands humanist Gemma Frisius was conflated with Albrecht Dürer – Dürer of all people, a man whose many self-portraits suggest his obsessive concern with his appearance.

In short, there is an apparent contradiction between two types of explanation of the significance of the portrait – two perspectives. A broad, comparative view reveals an uneven distribution of portraits over time which demands explanation and which runs parallel to the uneven distribution of biographies. On the other hand, in close-up, the picture looks quite different. The uses of the portrait were more often institutional than individualistic. There was a similar tension between the styles and functions of biography. The more 'individualist' biography coexisted with the exemplary, generic or typical biography, which stressed the role rather than the individual and offered a model for readers to imitate.

Renaissance and Middle Ages

The coexistence between an individual-centred mentality and a type-centred mentality revealed by biographies and portraits is both an example and a symbol of a wider split in the culture of the period discussed in this book. The conflict between Burckhardtian and anti-Burckhardtian historians, debating whether to describe the Renaissance in terms of realism or symbolism, may be unnecessary, like the choice between individual and collective identity. Groups and even individuals may have switched from one to the other according to the occasion and the context. The coexistence of contrasting attitudes and the tension between them were important structural features of Renaissance culture.

The Emperor Charles V's taste for the traditional culture of the court of Burgundy is well known, including the romance of chivalry *Le chevalier délibéré*. François I combined the Renaissance interests described above (pp. 80–1) with enthusiasm for other romances of chivalry such as *Amadis*. In the case of the later sixteenth century, historians of Elizabethan England speak not of survival but of 'chivalric revival'. This revival included jousts in which Renaissance courtiers such as Sidney took part and also a return to Gothic forms of architecture, now combined with elements of the classical tradition.[346] Such a return of the repressed, already discussed in the case of decoration (p. 179), can also be found in other parts of Europe and has been linked to the process of 'refeudalization' or 'aristocratization' described above (p. 158).

By this time, however, the situation was the inverse of the one described in chapter 2: medieval elements in Renaissance culture rather than Renaissance elements in medieval culture. Objects and attitudes which had once seemed strange had been familiarized or domesticated. New practices which had once expressed a rejection of tradition had turned into traditions or routines, against which later generations would in turn rebel, as the following chapter will argue.

Coda

The Renaissance after
the Renaissance

When the Renaissance ended is a question as controversial as when the movement began. The answer given – with some qualifications – in the pages which follow is that the disintegration of the cultural complex came in the early seventeenth century, with the scientific revolution and the rise of the baroque, though in certain domains, from grammar schools to academies of art, Renaissance practices persisted much longer.

With hindsight it might be argued that a vague awareness of these changes could already be found in the late sixteenth century, expressed in the form of a sense of chaos or decline, to be found, for example, in the French humanists Etienne Pasquier, Louis Le Roy and Montaigne. 'All things are in continual movement, change and variation,' wrote Montaigne in his *Essays* (Book 2, chapter 12). Or again (Book 3, chapter 2) 'The world is in perpetual motion' (*le monde n'est qu'une branloire perenne*).[347] Whether we call them 'late Renaissance', 'metaphysical' or 'baroque', the poets of the period – D'Aubigné, Quevedo, Donne, Sęp-Szarzyński – communicate an acute and often an anguished sense of the flux or inconstancy of human affairs. In the cases of the last two poets, their sense of instability was accentuated by their conversions, from Protestant to Catholic in the case of the Pole, from Catholic to Protestant in the case of the Englishman. No wonder that the

Dutch Catholic poet Vondel called Donne a 'dark sun' (*duistre zon*).[348]

Such an attitude helps explain the popularity of Ovid's *Metamorphoses* (a favourite book of Montaigne's) as a source for poets, artists and composers of this period: Actaeon turning into a stag, Daphne into a laurel, and so on. As we have seen (p. 129), the story of Daphne inspired one of the first operas in 1598. Gianlorenzo Bernini's Apollo and Daphne, generally regarded as one of the first great works of baroque sculpture, dates from 1622–4.

The philosopher Tommaso Campanella, writing to Galileo in 1632, claimed to see a 'new age' announced by 'new worlds, new stars, new systems, new nations'. He did not say anything about rebirth or the example of antiquity. On the contrary, he asserted that his contemporaries were the true ancients, because the world was older in their day than in the time of the ancient Greeks and Romans. This argument was not infrequently employed in the seventeenth century, the time when a group of self-conscious 'moderns' argued that they had more achievements to their credit than their ancient predecessors. Galileo and Descartes offer particularly clear-cut examples of a deliberate break with tradition, notably with the natural philosophy of Aristotle. Galileo rejected the idea that the heavens were perfect, while Descartes tried to make a completely fresh start in philosophy. The party of the 'moderns' used the example of the 'new philosophy' of Galileo and Descartes to support their rejection of what had been a central assumption for Renaissance humanists, that of the primacy of the ancients.

The increasing respectability of innovation was reflected in the titles of books such as Kepler's *New Astronomy* (1609), Bacon's *New Organon* (1620) and Galileo's *Discourses on Two New Sciences* (1638).[349] The world-picture of the European elites had been relatively stable since the reception of Aristotle in the thirteenth century. Aristotle's views were often criticized and sometimes modified, but the intellectual system associated with Aristotle was not replaced. Humanist attitudes to the dignity of man, for example, may have been new in their emphasis, but they did not disturb the traditional image of the cosmos.[350]

However, this image was modified in many important respects between 1600 and 1700, as the Copernican hypothesis that earth was not the centre of the universe was more widely known and the cosmos was increasingly viewed not as animate but as mechanical, its workings subject to the laws of physics. Kepler, who had once believed that the planets were driven by souls or 'intelligences', was converted to the idea that planetary motion could be explained in mechanical terms. Descartes compared the workings of the bodies of humans and animals to those of machines.[351] Another major change was what has been called 'the breaking of the circle', in other words, the decline of the idea of objective 'correspondences', between the microcosm and the macrocosm, for instance, or between the human body and the 'body politic', with different social groups playing the role of the head, the hands, the stomach and so on. Poets and philosophers continued to draw 'analogies' of this kind, but they were increasingly viewed as no more than metaphors.[352] Reason, exemplified by mathematics, especially geometry, gained the intellectual prestige which the authority of antiquity was in the process of losing. In his *Leviathan* (1651), Thomas Hobbes discussed political theory in the language of the mechanical philosophy and tried to deduce his conclusions from general axioms. Spinoza claimed that the propositions in his *Ethics* were 'proved geometrically'. Attempts were even made to apply the geometrical method to historical writing.

It is for these reasons that the phrase 'scientific revolution' was coined and used to describe the period between the Renaissance and the Enlightenment. A British historian declared in the 1940s that this revolution was so important in world history that it reduced the Renaissance and the Reformation 'to the rank of mere episodes'. More recent studies have emphasized gradual change rather than sudden 'revolution', pointing out criticisms as well as celebrations of the geometrical method and noting that – as in the case of the Renaissance – the coherence of the movement has been exaggerated. All the same, few historians deny the historical importance of the seventeenth-century reform of natural knowledge.[353]

Whether the artistic styles now known as Classicism and Baroque mark an equally important break with those of the Renaissance is a matter for debate. Monteverdi, for example, has been claimed for the late Renaissance (see above, p. 129) as well as for the baroque.[354] A similar case might be made for

Rubens, given his membership of the humanist circle around Lipsius, his interest in antiquity, his visit to Italy in 1600, and the admiration for the age of emulation shown in his sketches after Michelangelo and Raphael and his copies of paintings by Titian.[355] The point, once again, is not to annex Rubens to the Renaissance, but to blur the lines between historians' periods by viewing them from more than one standpoint. Just as Petrarch and Giotto may be described as medieval as well as playing central roles in the Renaissance, so Rubens can be placed in more than one category.

A more obvious change is the gradual decline of Italian cultural hegemony. In the seventeenth century, the age of Descartes and Corneille, Racine and Molière, Boileau and Bossuet, there was a new *prépondérance française*, as there had been in the High Middle Ages (see above, p. 19). The hegemony of the classical tradition was also challenged. The rise in importance of genres such as the novel and the landscape, which had few classical precedents, increased the distance between seventeenth-century writers and painters and the example of antiquity. The 'battle of the books' between the supporters of the ancients and those of the 'moderns', in France and England in the late seventeenth century, dramatized an older conflict between the two worlds. These changes in ideas and practices imply that the end of the Renaissance as a coherent movement came around 1630, most obviously in Italy.[356] However, this generalization needs to be qualified in at least three respects.

In the first place, the decline of the movement was generally slow rather than sudden, a fading away or disintegration rather than an abrupt end. In contrast to the age of Petrarch, the forces of resistance and cultural reproduction now worked in favour of the Renaissance. As in the case of Gothic, it is not easy to distinguish survival from revival. After all, the process of appropriation and adaptation, whether conscious or unconscious, was active in both situations. In the second place, it cannot be assumed that all cultural domains shared a common chronology. They had their own continuities and discontinuities. In the third place, there were regional variations in the fate of the movement. Certain trends were discovered on the periphery of Europe at the very time that they were disappearing from the centre. In English provincial towns town halls began to be constructed in a classical style only in the late seventeenth century, as in Abingdon, for example, in 1678.[357] Russia, which had participated only marginally in the Renaissance in the fifteenth and sixteenth centuries (see above, pp. 62–4), discovered it at the end of the seventeenth century. Tsar Peter the Great, for instance, celebrated his triumph over the Tatars in 1696 with a triumphal entry in Renaissance style. His well-known enthusiasm for technology seems to have coexisted with an interest in the culture of humanism, including emblems (see above, p. 205). At any rate, a book of emblems was published for him in Amsterdam in 1705, and reprinted in Russia in 1719.[358]

Hence the story to be told in the remainder of this chapter is that of a series of survivals and revivals in both humanism and the arts.

The Survival of Humanism

Humanism survived the scientific revolution, even if its place in European culture was increasingly restricted. The curriculum of Latin schools remained more or less the same until the beginning of the nineteenth century. In the universities, the replacement of Aristotelianism by the mechanical philosophy began around the year 1650 but the process took over a century to complete. No wonder then that the thought of Galileo, Hobbes and Descartes was shaped in part by the concepts, methods and values of humanism. Indeed, Galileo has been described as 'a faithful heir of the humanist tradition'.[359]

In literature, the Rome of Urban VIII was the scene of a 'second Roman Renaissance' on the model of the age of Leo X.[360] More generally, continuities between the classicism of the seventeenth century and the High Renaissance are not difficult to detect. In the Netherlands, the literary Renaissance is normally considered to include the age of the playwright and poet Joost van den Vondel, in other words, to last until the 1660s. Boileau and Racine may be regarded as humanists in the sense that the high style in which they wrote, like their imitation of the ancients, is difficult to distinguish from the theory and practice of Pietro Bembo. The classical age of French literature was a return to the standards of the High Renaissance in reaction against late sixteenth-century rule-breaking.

In England too the end of humanism was almost imperceptible. Robert Burton began his *Anatomy of Melancholy* (1621) in true humanist style with the phrase 'Man, the most excellent and noble creature of the world'. In his *Religio Medici* (1642) the physician Thomas Browne wrote about 'the dignity of humanity'. If we include Browne in the humanist movement, then it is difficult to justify excluding the politician Edward Hyde, whose reflections on the respective merits of the active and contemplative life followed the tradition of Leonardo Bruni. If we include Hyde, it is difficult to justify excluding the so-called 'Cambridge Platonists', who continued the tradition of Ficino into the late seventeenth century. Elsewhere in Europe the encyclopaedic interests of scholars, such as the German Jesuit Athanasius Kircher or the Swede Olaus Rudbeck, are reminiscent of a number of earlier humanists. When the complete works of Erasmus were republished in Leiden between 1703 and 1706, in ten folio volumes edited by Jean Leclerc, it is difficult to know whether we should speak of survival or revival. For Leclerc, a Calvinist pastor of the more voluntarist or 'Arminian' persuasion, Erasmus's defence of free will was a legitimation of his own position. Leclerc suggested that there was a need for 'a new Erasmus' in his own day to combat new superstitions. For his contemporary and enemy Pierre Bayle, another Calvinist pastor living in the Dutch Republic, Erasmus was above all a giant figure in the Republic of Letters, a cause to which Bayle too devoted a good deal of effort. For Voltaire, on the other hand, he was most memorable as a critic of the monks.[361]

Even in the eighteenth century, the attitudes and values of some leading European intellectuals still had much in common with those of Bruni (say), Pico or Bembo. The philosopher Ernst Cassirer once described the Renaissance as 'the first Enlightenment'; it seems at least equally appropriate to call the Enlightenment a 'second Renaissance'. In Germany, Gotthold Ephraim Lessing and Johan Gottfried Herder were both concerned with what Herder called *Humanität*, an adaptation of the ideal of *humanitas*. There is a sense in which they may usefully be described as late humanists, although Herder's interest in popular culture might have shocked Bembo (say), while Lessing's *Laokoon* (1766) undermined the analogies between poetry and painting which had been so dear to Renaissance critics. The point of these comparisons, as in the case of Rubens, is not to deny change or to attempt to annex the eighteenth century to the territory of the Renaissance, but simply to note the power of tradition. Lessing and Herder may be said to have reconstructed humanism to adapt it to the needs of their time. However, the humanist tradition had always been under construction. Bruni diverged in some ways from Petrarch, Ficino from Bruni, Erasmus from Ficino and Lipsius from Erasmus.

In England, the circle of Samuel Johnson has been described in terms of 'Augustan humanism', thanks to its attempt to emulate the cultural achievements of the Rome of Bembo and Leo X as well as the Rome of Virgil and Augustus.[362] A movement of civic humanism has been discerned in eighteenth-century Britain (especially Scotland), and also in North America at the time of the Revolution: a concern with civic virtue, liberty, and the active life, following the example of Renaissance Florence and Venice as well as ancient Rome.[363] Eighteenth-century civic humanism was not confined to the English-speaking world. Herder combined a devotion to antiquity with a critique of courts and a sense of the responsibility of the citizen in France at the time of the Revolution, and so did the young Wilhelm von Humboldt.[364.] Thus the cult of antiquity survived until the American and French Revolutions, in both of which the Roman republicans were models of political conduct. Participants in the Romantic movement, a protest against imitation in the arts in the name of spontaneity and the 'true voice of feeling', may well have been right to note continuities between the Renaissance and the eighteenth century.

By the time of the Romantics, however, around the year 1800, two important changes had taken place. In the first place, Greece, especially Athens, was replacing Rome as a model, in literature and politics as in the visual arts. Humboldt, who was Minister of Education in Prussia and one of the founders of the university of Berlin, considered ancient Greece to be the ideal of the whole of humanity (*das Ideal alles Menschendaseins*). In this respect 'neoclassicism', as the movement of this period is often described, differed from the classicism which had preceded it. In the second place, devotees of the *studia humanitatis* (unlike their Renaissance predecessors), had come to see science as a threat. Around 1800, Germans were discussing whether or not to make a place in the curriculum for practical and useful subjects such as the natural sciences. It was at this point and in this context that the term *Humanismus* was coined (and contrasted with *Philanthropismus*) to describe the values which were under attack.[365] The classics ceased to be the staple diet of schoolboys, some of whom would now study modern subjects in the *Realgymnasien*, so-called because they were supposed to be closer to 'reality'. The supporters of *Humanismus* were conscious 'reactionaries' rather than unconscious conservatives, concerned with revival rather than survival. In this sense they were 'neo-humanists'. As a distinguished sinologist once put it, 'an audience which appreciates that Mozart is not Wagner will never hear the eighteenth-century *Don Giovanni*.'[366]

The case for the survival of humanism into the nineteenth century is a weaker one, but it may still be useful to make it with the aid of a few English examples. John Stuart Mill has been described as humanist on account of his classical education and his lifelong concern with ethics. Walter Pater has also been described as a humanist. Pater identified himself with what he viewed as the humanist reconciliation of paganism with Christianity, and more generally with the Renaissance as a movement for what he called 'the love of the things of the intellect and the imagination for their own sake, the desire for a more liberal and comely way of conceiving life'.[367] To these two Victorians we might add a third, Matthew Arnold, who combined the roles of poet, cultural critic and inspector of schools and was apparently the first person to use the term 'humanism' in English. Even Arnold may not have been the last of the humanists. The British historian Arnold Toynbee once remarked that 'My generation was almost the last in England to be given an education in the Greek and Latin languages and literature that remained faithful to the strictest fifteenth-century Italian standards.'[368] It is only relatively recently that the world of humanism has become alien territory.

The Arts

In the arts as in humanism, it is difficult to identify a precise moment when the Renaissance came to an end. The years around 1630 are often chosen on account of the rise of the style we now call 'baroque', but this style, like that of the Renaissance, used a classical vocabulary. The Gothic Revival of the nineteenth century was a much more profound break with the classical tradition. Compared to this rupture, baroque and neoclassicism are no more than cracks in a classical edifice.

In painting, the 'grand manner' of Nicholas Poussin, who lived in Rome, was as close to that of Raphael as Boileau's was to Bembo's. The traditional visits to Italy by foreign artists continued. Velázquez went in 1629, for example, Mengs in 1740, Reynolds in 1749 and Romney in 1773. They visited Italy in order to study antiquity, as Renaissance artists had done, and also to learn from Raphael, Titian and Michelangelo. Academies of art continued to train painters and sculptors to imitate the antique. Equestrian monuments in the manner of Donatello and Giambologna continued to populate the squares of Europe and the Americas. Poses which had been invented by Raphael or Titian became part of the traditions of portraiture in later centuries; the modern family photo still follows some of these conventions. It might therefore be claimed that the Renaissance survived – in attenuated form – until the beginning of the twentieth century, the age of revolt against perspective, representation and the tradition of 'academic' art. Ironically enough, the end of the influence of the Renaissance in the arts came, in Italy at least, with a movement which like the Renaissance aspired to *renovatio*. Marinetti hoped for the regeneration of the world through Futurism.

Revivals

In the eighteenth century Palladianism, or Neo-Palladianism, became an international movement of architectural revival. Palladio's *Four Books of Architecture* was published in German in 1698, in French in 1726, in English in 1715 and again in 1728. Illustrated books with titles like *Danske Vitruvius* and *Vitruvius*

Britannicus spread his ideals. His disciples included Ottavio Bertotti in Italy, Jacques-Germain Soufflot in France, and two famous amateur architects from the English-speaking world. The third Earl of Burlington collected drawings by Palladio, visited Italy in order to study his buildings and imitated his style. Burlington's Chiswick villa, for example, begun around 1725, follows the famous Villa Rotonda near Vicenza, like Mereworth Castle in Kent, built two or three years earlier. Thomas Jefferson knew Palladio's work only through the *Four Books*, but he too followed the model of the Villa Rotonda for his house at Monticello. In neither the English nor the American case was the choice of Palladio politically neutral. His association with the republic of Venice made him a more attractive model for Whigs in Britain and for republicans in the United States.[369]

Neo-Palladianism needs to be placed in a wider context: that of the eighteenth-century Renaissance of the Renaissance, especially the age of Leo X, when (as Alexander Pope wrote) 'a Raphael painted and a Vida sung'. Pope's poem *An Essay on Criticism* was itself modelled on Vida's *Art of Poetry*. As for Raphael, he was the inspiration for the neoclassicism of the Bohemian painter Anton Raphael Mengs. Gianbattista Tiepolo's frescoes for the Residenz at Würzburg in the 1750s, in which many figures wear sixteenth-century costume, evoke the paintings of Veronese and so the golden age of Venice. In Italy, this revival of the Renaissance was marked by new editions of Petrarch, Poggio, Castiglione and other humanists, and by the publication for the first time of a number of sixteenth-century texts, notably the autobiography of Benvenuto Cellini, which appeared in 1728.

The nineteenth century was also an age of Renaissance revivals for a number of different purposes. Two striking if paradoxical examples come from painting, the Nazarenes and the Pre-Raphaelites. The Nazarenes were a group of young German artists who lived in Rome from 1810 onwards. They were hostile to the neoclassicism of Mengs and to his idol, Raphael. In similar fashion, Dante Gabriel Rossetti and his friends wanted to return to the period before Raphael. Hence their name, the 'Pre-Raphaelite Brotherhood'. Alexis Rio in France, the author of a book about Christian poetry which discussed the 'spiritual' art of the Middle Ages, had similar aims.

All the same, these artists and writers helped to rehabilitate the art of what they called the 'Middle Ages', though we view it today as 'early Renaissance'. The Nazarenes, for instance, were admirers of Masaccio and Fra Angelico. Rio was an admirer of Giotto. It was at this time and in these circles that Botticelli (figure 1) was rediscovered. In other words, the standards formulated by Vasari according to which the third phase of the Renaissance, the age of Raphael and Michelangelo, was the best, were no longer accepted. The canon which had dominated European art from 1550 to 1850 was challenged and reconstructed.[370] The rise of Art Nouveau would boost the reputation of Botticelli still further, while Expressionism aided the rediscovery of the Mannerists. For example, in a lecture given in 1920, the art critic Max Dvořák noted the appeal of El Greco to 'a new, a spiritual and anti-materialist age' following the First World War.[371] The rise of Post-Impressionism and the interest in geometrical forms aided the revaluation of the early Renaissance painters in the same way. The painter Giorgio Morandi, for instance, was inspired not only by Cézanne but also by Giotto, Masaccio and Piero della Francesca.

Enthusiasm for the Renaissance sometimes went as far as the Renaissance enthusiasm for antiquity. Isabella Stewart Gardner of Boston, for instance, re-enacted the career of her 'patron saint' Isabella d'Este by collecting *objets d'art* of the Renaissance, especially if they had been associated with women, as well as having herself painted by John Singer Sargent. Her collection was housed in an italianate palace, Fenway Court, which was opened to the public in 1903.[372] The interest in the Renaissance as a model for the present spread to furniture, ceramics and jewellery, for example the so-called 'Medici brooches' made by jewellers in Paris. For a highly visible case-study of this Renaissance of the Renaissance, we may turn to architecture. In the age of Gothic Revival, a number of architects discovered the uses of the Renaissance as an alternative style for modern buildings such as town houses, villas, banks, clubs, libraries and town halls. The most famous secular buildings of Renaissance Florence, Rome and Venice were translated more or less freely into an idiom considered suitable for nineteenth-century Germany, France, England, Italy or the United States.[373] In Germany, for example, the princely

Residenz at Munich (1826) imitated the Palazzo Pitti in Florence. Gottfried Semper's Villa Rosa at Dresden (1839) imitated a Renaissance villa, and his Palais Oppenheim (1845) a Renaissance palazzo. In Paris, the most striking examples of the Renaissance revival include the Ecole des Beaux-Arts (1833) and the Bibliothèque Sainte-Geneviève (1842).

In London, Charles Barry, who had made measured drawings of Renaissance buildings in Rome in the 1820s, designed the Travellers' Club (1832) and the Reform Club (1841) in the Roman manner, while a bank in Bristol in the 1850s followed the model of Sansovino's Marciana Library in Venice. In Italy, the neo-Renaissance style arrived relatively late, shortly after the unification of the country in 1860, a good example being the bank in Bologna, the Palazzo della Cassa del Risparmio, designed by Giuseppe Mengoni (1868). In New York, Boston and Chicago, libraries and apartments were built in the form of Renaissance palaces, notably the Palazzo della Cancelleria in Rome. The style of the French Renaissance was also revived, and not only in France. Schloss Schwerin (1843) was built on the lines of a French château after the architect had been sent on a tour of the Loire valley. Holloway College, built near Egham in Surrey (1879), is an imitation of Chambord.

These examples are well known to architectural historians and have been discussed by them as examples of a search for a modern style which was neither Gothic nor exactly classical. It should be added that in some cases, at least, the style was probably chosen for its associations. Its choice for Sheffield Town Hall, for example, suggests a parallel between the Italian city-states and the new democratic municipalities. Banks traded on the associations between the Renaissance and the Medici, while the Italianate style added to the cultural capital of the Victoria and Albert Museum and the Newberry Library in Chicago. Charles Barry adopted the Roman Renaissance style for London clubs, but he designed Highclere Castle in the Elizabethan manner as if this was more appropriate for a country house.

As it receded into the past, the Renaissance was perceived more and more clearly as a collective entity. For Voltaire, in the 1750s, Italy in the age of the Medici and 'the rebirth of learning' (*la renaissance des lettres*) represented the third of the four most glorious periods in human history, following classical Greece and Rome and preceding the age of Louis XIV. In 1775 the Italian scholar Saverio Bettinelli published a history of the 'resurgence' of learning and the arts in Italy. Bettinelli used the term *risorgimento*, applied a generation later to the movement of national revival. History paintings began to represent the lives of the heroes of the Renaissance. Leonardo's death in the arms of François I, for instance (an event which never took place), was painted by François-Guillaume Ménageot (1781) by Jean-Auguste-Dominique Ingres (1818) and by Luigi Mussini (1828). The death of Raphael was painted by Nicolas-André Monsiau (1804), Pierre-Nolasque Bergeret (1806) and Rodolfo Morgari (1880).

In the nineteenth century Jules Michelet, Jacob Burckhardt and other historians began to write about the Renaissance as a great event which had made a major contribution to the culture of europe, inserting it into the Grand Narrative of Western Civilization (see above, p. 3). The Renaissance with a capital R, one might say. Michelet and Burckhardt agreed that the discovery of the world and of man occurred at the Renaissance. Ernest Renan, in his *Averroès et l'averroïsme* (1852), and Burckhardt agreed that Petrarch was the first modern man. Italian historians, notably Francesco De Sanctis in his *History of Italian Literature* (1870–1) and Pasquale Villari in his *Machiavelli and his Times* (1877–82), recontextualized the Renaissance by describing it as an expression of the Italian spirit and emphasizing its contribution to the sense of national identity. Walter Pater described the 'Renascence' (as he preferred to spell it) as 'a general excitement and enlightening of the human mind'. Whether they viewed the Renaissance as an age when the human spirit awoke, or an age of paganism, or the corruption of morals, or all of these things, poets, playwrights, composers and novelists made their publics familiar with Lucrezia Borgia (Victor Hugo, 1833), Cola di Rienzo (Richard Wagner, 1842), Savonarola (George Eliot's *Romola*, 1863) and other leading figures of the period.[374]

To the work of historians and other writers, we should add the contributions made by museums, tourism and photographs to the nineteenth- and twentieth-century images of the Renaissance. From the late eighteenth century onwards, there was a general European movement to open royal, aristocratic and ecclesiastical galleries and libraries, to make their treasures more available to 'the public'. The Uffizi opened its doors to the public in 1769. The Louvre opened as a museum in 1793, the Prado opened in 1818. To illustrate the triumph of the arts and the transmission of the great tradition, museums were often decorated with images of great artists, many of them from the Renaissance. For example, the South Court of the Victoria and Albert Museum in Kensington was decorated with mosaic portraits of Giotto, Raphael, Michelangelo, Holbein and the ceramic artist Bernard Palissy. Hence the nickname of the 'Kensington Valhalla'. The idea was similar to that of Renaissance halls of illustrious men, with a significant difference. Artists were now the heroes rather than rulers or philosophers.

From visiting museums it was a natural step to view Renaissance art in its original settings, and the rise of organized tourism and the European railway system made such viewing easier than before. Thomas Cook in Britain and the Baedeker family in Germany were organizing tours to Italy by the middle of the nineteenth century. Burckhardt's *Cicerone*, a tourist guide to the treasures of Italian art, was published in 1855, five years before his famous essay on the Renaissance. Baedeker's guide to northern Italy, published in 1862, also emphasized the art and architecture of the Renaissance, and so did Cook's handbook for travellers to Italy.

The rise of photographic reproduction allowed tourists to bring back souvenirs of the Renaissance, and armchair travellers to have some sense of what they were missing. The Alinari family opened their photographic establishment in Florence in 1854 and concentrated on reproductions of Florentine art. The Medici Society was founded in 1908 to make the work of the 'old masters' more familiar through photographic reproduction, using the new technology of the 'collotype'. Today the camera has made some of the masterpieces of the Renaissance familiar as never before. In 1500 or even 1600 few individuals even knew of the existence of Botticelli's *Primavera*, and Vasari had to describe it from memory, inaccurately, because the painting was not easily accessible. Today millions of people have seen it directly, if only for a moment, and millions more are able to recognize the image from photographs.

Today the products of the Renaissance are no longer Europe's private property. An early example of this process of globalization was a monograph on Botticelli published in 1925 (by the Medici Society) and written by a professor of the history of art at the Imperial Academy of Tokyo, Yukio Yashiro. Yashiro was drawn to Botticelli by the affinity he perceived between that artist and Japanese traditions, from picture scrolls to the woodcuts of Utamaro, by what he called 'the spontaneous confluence in his genius of the Oriental and the Occidental ideals'.[375]

The acquisition of paintings such as Leonardo's *Ginevra de' Benci* by galleries outside Europe (in this case the National Gallery in Washington) illustrates the process by which the art of the Renaissance has become part of a global 'heritage'. Exhibitions, like photographs, assist the process of decontextualization. Objects are removed from their original settings and viewed in new ways, for example, as 'works of art' rather than devotional images. Renaissance literature is read in new ways. The plays of the period are produced in new ways in order to show that Shakespeare, for example, is in a sense our contemporary. The Renaissance continues to recede from us at an accelerating rate. However, as this book has tried to demonstrate, the double process of the appropriation and the domestication of the Renaissance is as old as the movement itself.

Chronology

Dates of books before 1450 are of composition or dedication; after 1450, of publication.

1336	Petrarch climbed Mont Ventoux
1337–	Petrarch, *De viris illustribus*
1345	Petrarch found Cicero's *Letters to Atticus*
1356	Petrarch in Prague
1368	Petrarch, *De ignorantia*
1375	Salutati appointed chancellor of Florence
1397	Chrysoloras arrived in Florence
1398	Metge, *Lo Somni*
1401	Ghiberti defeats Brunelleschi in Baptistery doors competition
1403	Bruni, *Laudatio florentinae urbis*
1415–	Bruni, *Historiae florentini populi*
1418	Competition for dome of Florence cathedral
1419–	Brunelleschi, Foundling Hospital, Florence
1427–54	Bruni chancellor of Florence
*c.*1427	Masaccio, *Tribute Money*
1435	Alberti, *Della pittura*
1444	Enea Silvio Piccolomini, *De duobus amantibus*
1444–6	Biondo, *Roma Instaurata*
*c.*1445–53,	Donatello, Gattamelata, Padua
1450	Gutenberg Bible, the first printed book
1453	The Ottomans captured Constantinople

1453	Poggio chancellor of Florence
1469	First book printed in Venice
1470	First book printed in Paris
1474	Ficino, *Platonic Theology*
1476	First book printed in Greek
c.1478	Botticelli, *Primavera*
1486	Pico, oration *De Dignitate Hominis* delivered
1487–91	Granovitaia Palata, Kremlin
1490	Isabella d'Este went to Mantua
1492	Nebrija, *Gramática castellana*
1494	French army invaded Italy
1496	Colet's lectures on St Paul
c.1497	Leonardo, *Ultima Cena*
1497	Sodalitas litteraria danubiana founded, Vienna
1499	Rojas, *Celestina*
1502	Celtis, *Amores*
1504	Pietro Martire, *Decades de orbe novo*, part 1
1506	Bramante, St Peter's begun
1506–	Esztergom, Bakócz Chapel
1508	Budé, *Annotationes in Pandectarum libros*
1508–12	Michelangelo frescoes, Sistine Chapel
1509–11	Raphael, Parnassus, School of Athens
1511,	Erasmus, *Moriae encomium.*
c.1513	Machiavelli, *Il principe* (written)
1515–17	*Epistolae Obscurorum Virorum*
1516	Ariosto, *Orlando Furioso*
1516	Erasmus, *Institutio Principis Christiani*
1516	More, *Utopia*
1516	Pomponazzi, *De immortalitate animae*
1519	Erasmus, *Colloquies*
1519	Michelangelo, tomb of Giuliano de'Medici begun
1520	Vives, *Contra pseudodialecticos*
1520	Hutten, *Inspicientes*
1524	Erasmus, *De libero arbitrio*
1525	Biblioteca Laurenziana begun
c.1525	Giulio Romano, Palazzo del Tè, Mantua, begun
1526	Palace of Granada begun
1527	Palace of Fontainebleau begun
1527	Vida, *Ars poetica*
1527	Sack of Rome by imperial troops

1528	Castiglione, *Cortegiano*
1528	Erasmus, *Ciceronianus*
1529	Altdorfer, Battle of the Issus
1529	Guevara, *Relox*
1529	Valdés, *Mercurio y Carón*
1530	François I established *lecteurs royaux* in Paris
1531	Alciati, *Emblemata*
1534	Rabelais, *Gargantua*
1537–45	Serlio, *Architettura*, Books 1–4
1537	Biblioteca Marciana begun
1537–41	Michelangelo, *Last Judgement*
1538	Strasbourg Academy founded
1540	Johannes Magnus, *Historia Gothorum*
1543	Copernicus, *De revolutionibus*
1543	Ramus, *Aristotelicae animadversiones*
1543	Vesalius, *De corporis humani fabrica*
1545–63	Council of Trent
1547	Goujon, Fontaine des Innocents begun
1549	Du Bellay, *Défense et illustration de la langue française*
1550	Beza, *Abraham sacrifiant*
1550	Držić, *Dundo Maroje*
1550–9	Ramusio, *Navigationi*
1550	Vasari, *Vite de' più eccellenti pittori*
1552	Ronsard, *Amours*
1555	Lassus, *Il primo libro de madrigali*
1555	Labé, *Oeuvres*
1556	Jesuit college founded in Prague
1558	Johannes Magnus, *Historia de gentis septentrionalibus*
*c.*1559	Montemayor, *Diana*
1561–7	Guicciardini, *Storia d'Italia*, posthumous
1563	Orta, *Coloquios dos simples*
1564	Gil Polo, *Diana enamorada*
1565	Heere, *Den Hof en Boomgaerd*
1565	Jesuit college founded at Braniewo (Braunsberg)
1565–74	Monardes, *Dos Libros*
1569	Ercilla, *La Araucana*, part 1
1569	Jesuit college founded at Vilnius (Wilno)
1570	Baïf founded Académie de Poésie et de Musique

1570	Noot, *Het Bosken*
1570	Ortelius, *Theatrum Orbis Terrarum*
1570	Palladio, *Quattro Libri*
1572	Camões, *Os Lusíadas*
1572	Jean de la Taille, *Saül le furieux*
1573	Tasso, *Aminta*
1575	Huarte, *Examen de Ingenios*
1576	Bodin, *Six Livres de la Politique*
1578	Kochanowski, *Odprawa poslow greckich*
1580	Montaigne, *Essais 1–2*
1580	Tasso, *Gerusalemme Liberata*
1581	Beaujoyeux, *Ballet comique de la reine*
1581	Vincenzo Galilei, *Dialogo della musica antica et della moderna*
1583	León, *Nombres de Cristo*
1584	Lipsius, *De constantia*
1585	Teatro Olimpico, Vicenza, opened
1585	Cervantes, *Galatea*
1589	*Intermedi* for wedding of Ferdinando de'Medici
1589	Botero, *Ragion di Stato*
1589	Busbecq, *Legatio Turcica*
1589	Guarini, *Pastor Fido*
1589	Hakluyt, *Navigations*
1590	Arcimboldo, Rudolf II as Vertumnus
1590–	Bry, *America*
1590	Stevin, *Burgerlick Leven*
1590	Lomazzo, *Idea*
1590	Spenser, *Faerie Queene* Books 1–3
1591	Marinella, *La nobiltà et l'eccellenza delle donne*
1594	Shakespeare, *Rape of Lucrece*
1598	Peri, *Dafne*, performed
1600	Giordano Bruno burned in Rome
1600	Peri, *Euridice*, performed
1600	Shakespeare, *Hamlet*, performed
1600	Pozzo, *Il merito delle donne*
1601	Sęp-Szarzyński, *Rytmy*
1604	Mander, *Het Schilderboek*
1605	Cervantes, *Don Quixote*, part 1
1607–27	D' Urfé, *Astrée*
1607	*Monteverdi*, Orfeo, performed

1608	Monteverdi, *Arianna*, performed
1609	Bacon, *De sapientia veterum*
1609	Lope de Vega, *Arte Nuevo de hacer comedias*
1611	Hooft, *Emblemata amatoria*
1614	Szymonowicz, *Sielanki*
1614	Webster, *Duchess of Malfi*
1616	Heinsius, *Nederduytsche Poemata*
1616	Jonson, *Works*
1616	Jones, Queen's House, Greenwich, begun
1617	Bredero, *Spanse Brabander*
1617	Maier, *Atalanta Fugiens*
1617	Opitz, *Aristarchus*
1619	Jones, Banqueting House, Whitehall, begun
1619	Kepler, *Harmonice Mundi*
1620	Bacon, *New Organon*
1621	Barclay, *Argenis*
1621	Burton, *Anatomy of Melancholy*
1623	Shakespeare, *Works*, first folio
1624	Opitz, *Buch von der deutschen Poeterei*
1627	Schütz, *Daphne*

References

1   Burckhardt (1860).
2   Lyotard (1979); Bouwsma (1979).
3   Farago (1995).
4   Bonfil (1984, 1990).
5   Scholem (1941); Yates (1964), 49–57, 92–4; Rosenthal (1975).
6   Quadflieg (1985).
7   Morison (1955); Hobson (1989).
8   Hale (1993).
9   Burke (1996).
10   Braudel (1974), 2142–8.
11   Geldner (1968–70); Białostocki (1976b).
12   Sorelius and Srigley (1994).
13   Campbell (1995a).
14   Bauch (1903).
15   Jauss (1974); Certeau (1980).
16   Friedman (1989b).
17   Warburg (1932); cf. Gombrich (1970).
18   Febvre (1925), 584.
19   Braudel (1989); cf. Białostocki (1988).
20   Sydow (1948); Pálsson (1993).
21   Mariás (1989); Farago (1995).
22   Pollock (1986).
23   Loewenberg (1995), 46–89.
24   Foucault (1963); Ophir and Shapin (1991).
25   Stinger (1977), 6; Collett (1985).
26   Brann (1981).
27   Torbarina (1931); Kadić (1962).
28   Cherniavsky (1968); Bradshaw (1979).
29   Gruffyd (1990).
30   Białostocki (1965).

31   Cf. Cochrane (1970); Lafond and Stegmann (1981).
32   Mariás (1989).
33   Cf. Sahlins (1985).
34   Fernandez (1977); Lakoff and Johnson (1980).
35   Bartlett (1993), 269–91; cf. Southern (1995).
36   Benevolo (1993), 42.
37   Holmes (1986), 159–60.
38   Grendler (1988).
39   Holmes (1986), 129–58.
40   Southern (1995).
41   Curtius (1947); Bolgar (1954).
42   Hyde (1973); Skinner (1995).
43   Setton (1956); Geanokoplos (1976); Kristeller (1979), 137–50.
44   Branca (1956).
45   Meiss (1951).
46   Ullman (1963), 99ff.
47   Witt (1983).
48   Garin (1961).
49   Sabbadini (1905).
50   Baron (1955).
51   Hyde (1973), 157–64.
52   Trinkaus (1970), 555–62.
53   Garin (1961, 1975), 5–38.
54   Gombrich (1967).
55   Burns (1971); Smith (1992).
56   Onians (1988), 130–46.
57   Paoletti and Radke (1997), 176–90.
58   Garin (1947); Field (1988); Hankins (1991), vol. 1, 267–359.
59   Yates (1964), 62–83; Walker (1972), 30–59.
60   Garin (1961); Secret (1964), 24–43.
61   Branca (1973); Grafton (1991), 47–75.
62   Dempsey (1992).
63   Warnke (1985), 46–54.
64   Holmes (1986).
65   Weiss (1969).
66   Gaeta (1955); Kelley (1970), 29–50; Camporeale (1972); Bentley (1987), 84–137.
67   Schofield (1992).
68   Woods-Marsden (1988); Paoletti and Radke (1997), 246–50, 281–93.
69   Greenstein (1992).
70   Branca (1973).
71   Morison (1955); Raby (1982); Brown (1988); Paoletti and Radke (1997), 258–80.
72   McAndrew (1969); Howard (1980), 114–27.
73   Warnke (1985).
74   Grafton and Jardine (1986), 29–57: King (1980).
75   Huizinga (1919).
76   Panofsky (1953).

77 Hale (1993).
78 Kipling (1977).
79 Morand (1991).
80 Archambault (1974).
81 Gallet-Guerne (1974).
82 Hyma (1950).
83 Campbell (1995b).
84 Warburg (1932).
85 Setton (1956); Luttrell (1960).
86 Rubió i Lluch (1917–18); Rubió (1964).
87 Guillemain (1962).
88 Coville (1934); Ouy (1973); Saccaro (1975).
89 Simone (1961).
90 Meiss (1967), 36–67, 302.
91 Mann (1970, 1980).
92 Segel (1989), 18–35; Weiss (1941), 97–106.
93 Melczer (1979), 33.
94 Weiss (1941), 103–4.
95 Weiss (1941), 61–5, 115–18; Diego de Burgos, quoted in Schiff (1905), 462.
96 Quoted in Witt (1976), 5.
97 Garets (1946).
98 Babinger (1953); Chastel (1966).
99 Csapodi (1969).
100 Białostocki (1976); Feuer Toth (1990); Kaufmann (1995), 39–46.
101 Geldner (1970).
102 Eisenstein (1979), 163–302.
103 Likhachev (1962); Birnbaum (1969); Milner-Gulland (1974).
104 Gukovski (1967); Kovalevsky (1976); Kaufmann (1995), 30–9.
105 Schaeder (1929); Denissoff (1943).
106 Braudel (1974, 1989).
107 Gilbert (1965), 49–200.
108 Chastel (1983); De Caprio (1991).
109 Gilbert (1949); Albertini (1955).
110 Seymour (1967), 55–63; Wilde (1944).
111 Sebastiano del Piombo (1520), quoted in Pastor (1886), vol. 8, 347.
112 Mace (1969).
113 Javitch (1991); Richardson (1994).
114 Summers (1981); cf. Baxandall (1971).
115 Rubin (1995); Haskell and Penny (1981), 7–23.
116 Onians (1988), 225–62.
117 Alberici (1984).
118 Oberhuber (1984); Landau and Parshall (1994), 103–68.
119 Dacos (1969), 5–41; Chastel (1983).
120 Borsellino (1973).
121 Chastel (1983), 169–78.
122 Rico (1978).
123 Spitz (1957).

124   Gunn and Lindley (1991).
125   Knecht (1982), 425–61; Cox-Rearick (1995).
126   Rosenthal (1985).
127   Strelka (1957); Eichberger and Beaven (1995); Boogert and Kerkhoff (1993).
128   Lewalski (1967); Białostocki (1976), 35.
129   Haskell and Penny (1981), 1–6.
130   Lach (1977), 57–64; Dias (1988).
131   Panofsky (1943); Białostocki (1986–7).
132   Spitz (1957); Brann (1981).
133   Renaudet (1916); Rice (1970).
134   Rueda (1973); Bentley (1987), 70–111.
135   Fumaroli (1988).
136   Lopez Rueda (1973); Wilson (1992).
137   Scholem (1941).
138   O'Malley (1968); Wittkower (1949), 102–7; Foscari and Tafuri (1983).
139   Secret (1964), 44–72; Béhar (1996), 13–62.
140   Lauvergnat-Ganière (1988), 197–234.
141   Bataillon (1937), 419–38.
142   Maffei (1956); Kelley (1970); La Garanderie (1976).
143   Fumaroli (1980), 101–15.
144   Pine (1986), 124–234.
145   Overfield (1984), 247–97.
146   Rosenthal (1961).
147   Buck (1988).
148   Pigman (1979).
149   Bataillon (1937); Menchi (1987).
150   Haydn (1950); Hauser (1951), vol. 2, 88–95; Battisti (1962).
151   Shearman (1967); Gombrich (1982).
152   Lafond and Stegmann (1981); Tomlinson (1985), 247.
153   Maravall (1966).
154   Trovato (1991), 219–28; Richardson (1994), 92–126.
155   Melion (1991), 24, 96–7.
156   Puppi (1973); Tavernor (1990).
157   Croll (1966); cf. Fumaroli (1980), 170–9.
158   Hahr (1907–10), vol. 2; Białostocki (1976b).
159   Beach (1992), 53–5; Cahill (1982), 176–83.
160   Spence (1984), 131–2, 141–2, 159.
161   Zavala (1937, 1955).
162   Fraser (1986, 1990).
163   Zamora (1988); Brading (1991), 255–72; MacCormack (1991), 332–82.
164   Telle (1974); Fumaroli (1980), 110–15.
165   Croll (1966); Fumaroli (1980), 152–61.
166   Mortier (1974), 46–59.
167   Dacos (1969), 141.
168   Warnke (1985), 137.

169 Thoren (1985).
170 Guillaume (1983); Kaufmann (1995), 223.
171 Bevers (1985), 22–30, 79–81.
172 Quoted in Marnef (1996), 14.
173 Borsay (1989); Tittler (1991).
174 Puppi (1973); Tavernor (1991).
175 Kaufmann (1995), 143–51.
176 Bardon (1963), 50–73.
177 Summerson (1953), 54; Airs (1988), 49.
178 Białostocki (1965).
179 Hitchcock (1981), 133–4.
180 Białostocki (1965).
181 Girouard (1966).
182 Summerson (1953).
183 Avery (1987), 161; cf. Warnke (1985), 90.
184 Cantimori (1939).
185 Dannenfeldt (1955).
186 Iversen (1961), 59–82; Aufrère (1990).
187 Dubois (1972).
188 Nordström (1944–72); Johannesson (1982).
189 Palisca (1985), 1–22; Owens (1995).
190 Yates (1947), 19–36.
191 Walker (1985); Palisca (1985), 280–332.
192 Rose (1975), 90–117.
193 Rose (1975), 111, 133.
194 Grafton (1991), 178–203.
195 Panofsky (1954).
196 Hannaway (1975).
197 Schmidt (1938).
198 Eisenstein (1979), 575–635.
199 Kuhn (1957); Blumenberg (1965); Rose (1975), 118–42.
200 O'Malley (1965); Carlino (1994).
201 Bakhtin (1975).
202 Villey (1908).
203 Quoted in Balsamo (1992), 75.
204 Quoted in Kelley (1970), 279–80.
205 Quoted in Helgerson (1992), 1.
206 Balsamo (1992), 150–1.
207 Burke (1998a).
208 Weinberg (1986).
209 Quoted in Jones (1953), 71.
210 Forster (1970).
211 Nolhac (1921), 205–35; Maugain (1926).
212 Phillips (1977).
213 Thompson (1988).
214 Jones-Davies (1984); Ferreras (1985); Burke (1989); Cox (1992).
215 Schon (1954).
216 Klaniczay (1977), 47–78.

217   Pastor (1983), 207–75.
218   Quint (1993).
219   Burke (1978).
220   Rico (1970).
221   Kadić (1959).
222   Boughner (1954); Lazard (1978), 211–43.
223   Tedeschi (1974).
224   Dainville (1978); Mészaros (1981).
225   Dainville (1978), 168–70, 186–9.
226   Checa (1992).
227   Evans (1973); Kaufmann (1985); Fuciková (1988).
228   Skovgaard (1973); Christensen (1988); Heiberg (1988).
229   Simon (1966); Schindling (1977); Huppert (1984).
230   Bièvre (1988).
231   Antal (1948); Yates (1957), 108.
232   Weber (1956), 63–106.
233   Walde (1932); Steinmetz (1991).
234   Evans (1973), 140–3, 212–15.
235   González Palencia and Mele (1943).
236   Rosenberg (1955).
237   Riebesell (1989); Robertson (1992).
238   Picquard (1947–8, 1951); Durme (1953), 337–57.
239   Summerson (1953) 46f.; Summerson (1959).
240   Dionisotti (1967), 237–9; Piéjus (1982).
241   Keating (1941), 49–69.
242   Friedman (1989a), 103.
243   Waller (1979); Lamb (1982, 1990).
244   Burke (1995a), 148–50.
245   Grafton and Jardine (1986), 38, 51.
246   Lamb (1985); Warnicke (1988).
247   Steinmetz (1991), 134.
248   Lemaire (1996).
249   Quoted Meiss (1967), 362.
250   Feldman (1995), 104–8.
251   Jordan (1990), 173–7; Rosenthal (1992).
252   Cohen and Cohen (1993), 243–77.
253   Huizinga (1915).
254   Backvis (1958–60); Barycz (1967); Boucher (1986), 97–125.
255   Torbarina (1931), 52.
256   Sozzi (1972).
257   Stone (1965), 549–55; cf. Girouard (1966).
258   Girouard (1978).
259   Henderson (1995).
260   Quoted in Mercer (1962), 99.
261   Goldthwaite (1987, 1993), 226–7; Thornton (1991).
262   Esdaile (1946); Mercer (1962), 217–52; Llewellyn (1996).
263   Mercer (1962), 60–98; Thornton (1991).
264   Welch (1997), part 4.

265 Schubring (1915); Riccardi-Cubitt (1992).
266 Roberts (1995).
267 Hayward (1976).
268 Marquand (1922), 2, 64, and nos 122–42, 157–67, 302–9, 312–20.
269 Rackham (1952).
270 Mercer (1962), 115–20.
271 Brown and Lorenzoni (1993), 29; Schmitt (1989), 215–58.
272 Santore (1988); cf. Liebenwein (1977), Thornton (1998).
273 Philip Hainhofer, quoted in Mercer (1969), 118.
274 Riccardi-Cubitt (1992).
275 Schlosser (1908); Lugli (1983); Impey and MacGregor (1985); Findlen (1989).
276 Zimmermann (1995), 159–62, 187–9.
277 Kaufmann (1994).
278 Lazzaro (1990).
279 Clunas (1996).
280 Warnke (1985), 187; Fleischer (1979).
281 Benevolo (1993), 85–104, 112–23.
282 Lotz (1977).
283 Benevolo (1993), 119.
284 Schindling (1977). Cf. Simon (1966) and Huppert (1984).
285 Fumaroli (1980); Murphy (1983); Skinner (1996), 19–211.
286 Moss (1996).
287 Morford (1991); Burke (1996).
288 Lach (1977), 10–45; Pomian (1987), 35; Morán and Checa (1985).
289 Wardrop (1963); Petrucci (1986).
290 Wüttke (1977).
291 Forster (1969), 1–83.
292 Mączak (1978).
293 Mączak (1978), 272–3.
294 Saulnier (1948), 38–44.
295 Stagl (1980); Rubiès (1995).
296 Oestreich (1969, 1982); Reinhard (1986).
297 Elias (1939); Klaniczay (1990), 83.
298 Céard (1977).
299 Blumenberg (1966), part 3; cf. Blumenberg (1988), Daston (1995).
300 Lugli (1983); Olmi (1992).
301 Albertini (1955); Gilbert (1965), 105–52.
302 Burke (1969); Kelley (1970), 29–50.
303 Curtius (1948); Moss (1996).
304 Bataillon (1960); Rosenthal (1973).
305 Saunders (1989).
306 Panofsky (1939), 146.
307 Panofsky (1924).
308 Fumaroli (1980), 498–519.
309 Oestreich (1982), 267–71; Morford (1987).
310 Jehasse (1976), 636–9; MacDonald and Murphy (1990), 86–95.
311 Gurevich (1995); cf. Batkin (1989).

312 Lach (1965), 204–9; Broc (1980); Lestringant (1991); Grafton (1992).
313 Zimmermann (1995), 121–2, 140.
314 Helgerson (1992), 163–91.
315 Boxer (1948).
316 Burke (1985).
317 Lach (1977), 742–94.
318 Zhiri (1991).
319 Impey and Macgregor (1985); Olmi (1992), 211–52.
320 Broc (1980).
321 Lach (1977), 235–52.
322 Honour (1975); Lestringant (1990, 1991, 1994).
323 Gliozzi (1977), 286–306; Pagden (1982), 109–18.
324 Hay (1957); Chabod (1964).
325 Strauss (1959); Broc (1980), 99–119.
326 Rowse (1950), 31–65; cf. Helgerson (1992), 107–47.
327 Raby (1982); Brown (1988).
328 Lach (1977), 131–72; cf. Lazzaro (1995).
329 Olmi (1992), 21ff.
330 Febvre (1942), 437.
331 Burckhardt (1860), ch. 4; cf. Stierle (1979).
332 Curtius (1948), 183–202; Turner (1966).
333 Wilson (1961).
334 Koerner (1993).
335 Buck (1988), Spadaccini and Talens (1988).
336 Wu (1990), 196.
337 Guglielminetti (1977) Burke (1992).
338 Greenblatt (1980).
339 Jardine (1993).
340 Burke (1998b).
341 Mayer and Woolf (1995).
342 Burke (1995).
343 Zappella (1988).
344 Quoted in Checa (1992), 451.
345 Esdaile (1946), 47–8.
346 Yates (1957): Ferguson (1960); Mercer (1962), 85–90; Girouard (1966).
347 Starobinski (1982).
348 Rousset (1953); Backvis (1963–5).
349 Thorndike (1951).
350 Grant (1978); Schmitt (1983).
351 Shapin (1996).
352 Nicolson (1950); Foucault (1966).
353 Butterfield (1949), viii.
354 Tomlinson (1987).
355 Stechow (1968); Jaffé (1977).
356 Cochrane (1970); Lafond and Stegmann (1981); Tomlinson (1987), 243–60.
357 Borsay (1989), 104–6.

358 Wortman (1995), 42–6.
359 Panofsky (1954); Cochrane (1976), 1057.
360 Fumaroli (1980), 202–26.
361 Kaegi (1936); Flitner (1952), 120–9; Mansfield (1979), 236–58.
362 Fussell (1965).
363 Pocock (1975), 423–552.
364 Spranger (1909); Knoll (1982); Sorkin (1983).
365 Rüegg (1944).
366 Levenson (1958), xx.
367 Tinkler (1992); Crinkley (1970).
368 Toynbee (1954), 557.
369 Tavernor (1990), 151–209.
370 Levey (1960); Bullen (1994), 80–90.
371 Quoted in Gombrich (1961a).
372 Brandt (1992).
373 Milde (1981); Pavoni (1997).
374 Ferguson (1948), 179–252; Bullen (1994).
375 Yashiro (1925), 82–3, 89, 99–101, 148.

Bibliography

The study of the Renaissance is as international an enterprise as the Renaissance itself was. Any manageable bibliography is inevitably brutally selective, but ought at the very least to be both international and interdisciplinary. For recent studies on specific topics, specialist journals such as *Bibliothèque d'Humanisme et Renaissance, Renaissance Quarterly*, and *Renaissance Studies* will offer guidance.

The following list includes only secondary works cited in the preceding chapters, references to primary sources having been given in the text itself. Titles are first cited in the original language of publication.

Airs, Malcolm (1988). 'Architecture', in *16th Century Britain: The Cambridge cultural history*, ed. Boris Ford, 2nd edn, Cambridge, 46–97.

Alberici, Clelia (ed.,) (1984). *Leonardo e l'incisione*, Milan.

Albertini, Rudolf von (1955). *Das Florentinisch Staatsbewusstsein*, Bern.

Antal, Frederick (1948). 'The Social Background of Mannerism', reprinted in his *Classicism and Romanticism*, London, 1966, 158–61.

Archambault, Paul (1974) *Seven French Chroniclers*, Syracuse, NY.

Aufrère, Sydney H. (1990) *La Momie et la tempête: Nicolas-Claude Fabri de Peiresc et la curiosité égyptienne en Provence au début du 17e siècle*, Avignon.

Avery, Charles (1987) *Giambologna: The complete sculpture*, Oxford.

Babinger, Franz (1953) *Mehmed der Eroberer und seine Zeit*, Munich; *Mehmed the Conqueror and His Time*. trans. R. Manheim, Princeton, NJ, 1978.

Backvis, Claude (1958–60). 'Comment les polonais du 16e siècle voyaient l'Italie et les italiens', *AIPHOS*, 15, 195–288.

—— (1963–5). 'Maniérisme ou baroque à la fin du 16e siècle: le cas de Mikolay Sęp-Szarzyński', *AIPHOS*, 16–17, 149–220.

Bakhtin, Mikhail M. (1965). *Rabelais*, trans. H. Iswolsky, Cambridge, MA, 1968.

—— (1975). *The Dialogic Imagination*, trans. C.Emerson and M. Holquist, Austin, TX, 1981.

Balsamo, Jean (1992). *Les rencontres des muses: italianisme et anti-italianisme dans les lettres françaises de la fin du xvie siècle*, Geneva.

Bardon, Françoise (1963). *Diane de Poitiers et le mythe de Diane*, Paris.

Baron, Hans (1955). *The Crisis of the Early Italian Renaissance*, Princeton, NJ.

Bartlett, Robert (1993). *The Making of Europe: Conquest, colonization and cultural change, 950–1350*, 2nd edn, Harmondsworth, 1994.

Barycz, Henryk (1967). 'Italophilia e italofobia nella Polonia del Cinque e Seicento', in *Italia, Venezia e Polonia tra umanesimo e rinascimento*, ed. M. Brahmer, Wrocław, 142–58.

Bataillon, Marcel (1937). *Erasme en Espagne*, Paris; rev. ed. 3 vols, Geneva, 1991.

—— (1960). 'Plus Oultre: la cour découvre le nouveau monde', in *Fêtes et cérémonies au temps de Charles Quint*, ed. Jean Jacquot, Paris, 13–27.

Batkin, Leonid M. (1989) *L'idea di individualità nel Rinascimento italiano*, Italian trans., Rome 1992.

Battisti, Eugenio (1962) *L'Antirinascimento*, Milan.

Bauch, Gustav (1903) *Die Reception des Humanismus in Wien*, Breslau.

Baxandall, Michael (1971) *Giotto and the Orators*, Oxford.

Beach, Milo (1992) *Mughal and Rajput Painting*, Cambridge.

Béhar, Pierre (1996) *Les langues occultes de la Renaissance*, Paris.

Benevolo, Leonardo (1993) *The European City*, Oxford.

Benson, Pamela J. (1992) *The Invention of the Renaissance Woman*, Philadelphia.

Bentley, Jerry H. (1987) *Humanists and Holy Writ: New Testament scholarship in the Renaissance*, Princeton, NJ.

Bevers, Holm (1985) *Das Rathaus von Antwerpen*, Hildesheim.

Białostocki, Jan (1965) 'Mannerism and Vernacular in Polish Art', in *Walter Friedlaender zum 90. Geburtstag*, Berlin, 47–57.

—— (1976a). *The Art of the Renaissance in Eastern Europe*, London.

—— (1976b). 'The Baltic Area as an Artistic Region in the Sixteenth Century', *Hafnia*, 11–24.

—— (1986–7). 'Dürer and the Humanists', *Bulletin of the Society for Renaissance Studies*, 4, 2, 16–29.

—— (1988) 'Renaissance Sculpture in Poland in its European Context', in *The Polish Renaissance in its European Context*, ed. Samuel Fiszman, Bloomington, IN, 281–90.

Bièvre, Elisabeth de (1988) 'Violence and Virtue: History and Art in the City of Haarlem', *Art History*, 11, 303–34.

Birnbaum, Henrik (1969). 'Some Aspects of the Slavonic Renaissance', *Slavonic and East European Review*, 47, 37–56.

Blumenberg, Hans (1965). *Die kopernikanische Wende*, Frankfurt.

—— (1966). *Die Legitimität der Neuzeit*, English trans., *The Legitimacy of the Modern Age*, Cambridge, MA, 1983.

—— (1988). *Der Prozess der theoretische Neugierde*, Frankfurt.

Bolgar, Robert R. (1954). *The Classical Tradition and its Beneficiaries*, Cambridge.

Bonfil, Robert (1984). 'The Historian's Perception of the Jews in the Italian Renaissance', *Revue des Etudes Juives*, 143, 59–82.

—— (1990). *Rabbis and Jewish Communities in Renaissance Italy*, Oxford.

Boogert, Bob van den, Kerkhoff, Jacqueline, et al (eds) (1993). *Maria van Hongarije*, Zwolle.

Borsay, Peter (1989). *The English Urban Renaissance: Culture and society in the provincial town, 1660–1770*, Oxford.

Borsellino, Niccolo (1973). *Gli anticlassicisti del '500*, Rome and Bari.

Boucher, Jacqueline (1986). *La cour de Henri III*, La Guerche-de-Bretagne.

Boughner, Daniel (1954). *The Braggart in Renaissance Comedy*, Minneapolis.

Bouwsma, William (1979). 'The Renaissance and the Drama of Western History', reprinted in his *A Usable Past: Essays in European Cultural History*, Berkeley, CA, 1990, 348–65.

Boxer, Charles R. (1948). *Three Historians of Portuguese Asia*, Macāo.

—— (1963). *Two Pioneers of Tropical Medicine*, London.

Brading, David (1991). *The First America: The Spanish monarchy, Creole patriots and the liberal state, 1492–1867*, Cambridge.

Bradshaw, Brendan (1979). 'Manus the Magnificent: O'Donnell as a Renaissance Prince', *Studies in Irish History presented to R. Dudley Edwards*, ed. A. Cosgrove and D. McCartney, Dublin, 15–37.

Branca, Vittore (1956). *Boccaccio medievale*, Florence, English trans. *Boccaccio*, New York, 1976.

—— (1973). 'Ermolao Barbaro and Late Quattrocento Venetian Humanism', in *Renaissance Venice*, ed. John R. Hale, London, 218–43.

Brandt, Kathleen (1992). 'Mrs Gardner's Renaissance', *Fenway Court 1990-1*, 10–30.

Brann, Noel L. (1981). *The Abbot Trithemius (1462–1516): The Renaissance of monastic humanism*, Leiden.

Braudel, Fernand (1974), 'L'Italia fuori d'Italia', *Storia d'Italia*, 2, Turin, 2092–2148.

—— (1989) *Le Modèle italien*, Paris.

Broc, Numa (1980) *La géographie de la Renaissance*, Paris.

Brown, Clifford M. and Lorenzoni, Anna Maria (1993). *Our Accustomed Discourse on the Antique: Cesare Gonzaga and Gerolamo Garimberto*, New York.

Brown, Patricia F. (1988) *Venetian Narrative Painting in the Age of Carpaccio*, New Haven.

Buck, August (ed.) (1983). *Biographie und Autobiographie in der Renaissance*, Wiesbaden.

—— (1988) *Erasmus and Europa*, Wiesbaden.

Bullen, J. B. (1994). *The Myth of the Renaissance in Nineteenth-Century Writing*, Oxford.

Burckhardt, Jacob (1860) *Kultur der Renaissance in Italien; The Civilisation of the Renaissance in Italy*, trans. S. G. C. Middlemore (1878), Harmondsworth, 1990.

Burke, Peter (1969) *The Renaissance Sense of the Past*, London.

—— (1978) *Popular Culture in Early Modern Europe*, London.

—— (1985) 'European Views of World History from Giovio to Voltaire', *History of European Ideas*, 6, 237–51.

——(1989) 'The Renaissance Dialogue', *Renaissance Studies*, 3, 1–12.

—— (1992). 'Anthropology of the Renaissance', *Journal of the Institute for Romance Studies*, 1, 207–15.

—— (1995a) *The Fortunes of the Courtier: The European reception of Castiglione's Cortegiano*, Cambridge.

—— (1995b). 'The Renaissance, Individualism and the Portrait', *History of European Ideas*, 21, 393–400.

—— (1996a). 'The Myth of 1453: Notes and Reflections', *Querdenken: Dissens und Toleranz im Wandel der Geschichte: Festschrift Hans Guggisberg*, ed. Michael Erbe et al., Mannheim, 23–30.

—— (1996b). 'Humanism and Friendship in Sixteenth-Century Europe', *Groniek* 134, 90–8; revised version forthcoming in *Medieval Friendship*, ed. Julian Haseldine, London, 1998.

—— (1998a). 'Translations into Latin in Early Modern Europe', in *Il latino nell'età moderna*, ed. Rino Avesani, Rome.

——(1998b). 'Individuality and Biography in the Renaissance', forthcoming in *Kunst und Individualität*, ed. Enno Rudolph, Frankfurt.

Burns, Howard (1971). 'Quattrocento Architecture and the Antique', in *Classical Influences in European Culture*, ed. Robert R. Bolgar, Cambridge, 269–88.

Butterfield, Herbert (1949). *Origins of Modern Science, 1300–1800*, London.

Cahill, James (1982). *The Compelling Image: Nature and Style in Seventeenth-Century Chinese Painting*, Cambridge, MA.

Campbell, Ian (1995a). 'Linlithgow's "Princely Palace" and its Influence in Europe', *Architectural Heritage*, 5, 1–20.

—— (1995b). 'A Romanesque Revival and the Early Renaissance in Scotland', *Journal of the Society of Architectural Historians*, 54, 301–25.

Camporeale, S. (1972) *Lorenzo Valla: umanesimo e teologia*, Florence.

Cantimori, Delio (1939) *Eretici italiani del '500*, Florence.

Carlino, Andrea (1994) *La fabbrica del corpo: libri e dissezione nel Rinascimento*, Turin.

Céard, Jean (1977) *La nature et les prodiges: l'insolite au 16e siècle, en France*, Geneva.

Certeau, Michel de (1980) *L'invention du quotidien*, Paris; *The Practice of Everyday Life*, Berkeley, CA, 1984.

Chabod, Federico (1964). *Storia dell'idea di Europa*, Bari.

Chastel, André (1966). 'La Renaissance italienne et les ottomans', in *Venezia e l'Oriente*, ed. Agostino Pertusi, Florence.

—— (1983) *The Sack of Rome*, Princeton, NJ.

Checa, Fernando (1992) *Felipe II, mecenas de la artes*, Madrid.

Cherniavsky, Michael (1968) 'Ivan the Terrible as a Renaissance Prince', *Slavic Review*, 27, 195–211.

Christensen, Charlotte (1988). 'Christian IVs renæssance', in *Christian IVs Verden*, ed. Svend Ellehøj, Copenhagen, 302–35.

Clunas, Craig (1996). *Fruitful Sites: Garden Culture in Ming Dynasty China*, London.

Cochrane, Eric (1976). 'Science and Humanism in the Italian Renaissance', *American Historical Review*, 81, 1039–57.

—— (1981). *Historians and Historiography in the Italian Renaissance*, Chicago.

Cochrane, Eric (ed.) (1970). *The Late Italian Renaissance, 1525–1630*, London.

Cohen, Elizabeth S. and Cohen, Thomas V. (1993). *Words and Deeds in Renaissance Rome*, Toronto.

Collett, Barry (1985). *Italian Benedictine Scholars and the Reformation*, Oxford.

Coville, Alfred (1934). *Gontier et P. Col et l'humanisme en France au temps de Charles VI*, Paris.

Cox, Virginia (1992). *The Renaissance Dialogue: Literary Dialogue in its Social and Political Contexts, Castiglione to Galileo*, Cambridge.

Cox-Rearick, Janet (1995). *The Collection of François I: Royal Treasures*, Antwerp.

Crinkley, Richmond (1970). *Walter Pater: Humanist*, Lexington, KY.

Croll, Morris W. (1966). *Style, Rhetoric and Rhythm*, Princeton, NY.

Csapodi, Csaba and Csapodi, Klára (eds) (1969). *Biblioteca Corvina*, Shannon.

Curtius, Ernst R. (1948). *Europäisches Literatur und Lateinisches Mittelalter*; *European Literature and the Latin Middle Ages*, trans. W. R. Trask, New York, 1953, new edn, 1963.

Dacos, Nicole (1969). *La découverte de la Domus Aurea et la formation des grotesques à la Renaissance*, Paris.

Dainville, François de (1978). *L'éducation des jésuites (16e–18e siècles)*, Paris.

Dannenfeldt, Karl H. (1955). 'The Renaissance Humanists and the Knowledge of Arabic', *Studies in the Renaissance*, 2, 96–117.

Daston, Lorraine (1995). 'Curiosity in Early Modern Science', *Word and Image*, 11, 391–404.

De Caprio, Vincenzo (1991). *La tradizione e il trauma: idee del rinascimento romano*, Rome.

Dempsey, Charles (1992). *The Portrayal of Love: Botticelli's Primavera and Humanist Culture at the Time of Lorenzo the Magnificent*, Princeton, NJ.

Denissoff, Elie (1943). *Maxime le Grec et l'Occident*, Paris and Leuven.

Dias, Pedro (1988). *A arquitectura manuelina*, Lisbon.

Dionisotti, Carlo (1967). *Geografia e storia della letteratura italiana*, Turin.

Dubois, Claude-Gilbert (1972). *Celtes et Gaulois au 16e siècle: le développement littéraire d'un mythe nationaliste*, Paris.

Durme, Maurice van (1953). *Antoon Perrenot*, Brussels.

Eichberger, Dagmar and Beavers, Lisa (1995). 'The Portrait Collection of Margaret of Austria', *Art Bulletin*, 77, 225–48.

Eisenstein, Elizabeth L. (1979). *The Printing Press as an Agent of Change*, Cambridge.

Elias, Norbert (1939). *Der Prozess der Zivilisation*, 2 vols, Basel; *The Civilizing Process*, trans. E. Jephcott, 2 vols, Oxford, 1981–2.

Esdaile, Katherine A. (1946). *English Church Monuments 1510 to 1840*, London.

Evans, Robert J. W. (1973). *Rudolf II and his World*, Oxford.

Farago, Claire (ed.) (1995). *Reframing the Renaissance*, New Haven.

Febvre, Lucien (1925). 'La première renaissance française', rpr his *Pour une histoire à part entière*, Paris, 1962, 529–603.

—— (1942). *Le problème de l'incroyance au 16 siècle*, Paris; *The Problem of Unbelief in the Sixteenth Century*, trans. B. Gottlieb, Cambridge, MA, 1982.

Feldman, Martha (1995). *City Culture and the Madrigal at Venice*, Berkeley, CA.

Ferguson, Arthur B. (1960). *The Indian Summer of English Chivalry*, Durham, NC.

Ferguson, Wallace K. (1948). *The Renaissance in Historical Thought: Five Centuries of Interpretation*, Cambridge, MA.

Fernandez, James W. (1977). 'The Performance of Ritual Metaphors', in *The Social Use of Metaphor*, ed. J. David Sapir and J. Christopher Crocker, Philadelphia, 100–31.

Ferreras, J. (1985). *Les dialogues espagnols du 16e siècle*, Paris.

Feuer-Tóth, Rózsa (1990). *Art and Humanism in Hungary in the Age of Matthias Corvinus*, Budapest.

Field, Arthur (1988). *The Origins of the Platonic Academy of Florence*, Princeton, NJ.

Findlen, Paula (1989). 'The Museum: its Classical Etymology and Renaissance Genealogy', *Journal of the History of Collections*, 1, 59–78.

Fleischer, Manfred P. (1979). 'The Garden of Laurentius Scholtz: a Cultural Landmark of Late Sixteenth-Century Lutheranism', *Journal of Medieval and Renaissance Studies*, 9, 29–48.

Flitner, Andreas (1952). *Erasmus im Urteil seiner Nachwelt*, Tübingen.

Forster, Leonard W. (1969). *The Icy Fire: Five Studies in European Petrarchism*, Cambridge.

—— (1970). *The Poet's Tongues: Multilingualism in literature*, Cambridge.

Foscari, Antonio, and Tafuri, Manfredo (1983). *L'armonia e i conflitti: la chiesa di San Francesco della Vigna nella Venezia del '500*, Turin.

Foucault, Michel (1963). *Naissance de la clinique*, Paris; *The Birth of the Clinic*, trans. A. M. Sheridan Smith, London, 1973.

—— (1966). *Les Mots et les choses*, Paris; *The Order of Things*, London, 1970.

Fraser, Valerie (1986). 'Architecture and Imperialism in Sixteenth-Century Spanish America', *Art History*, 9, 325–35.

—— (1990). *The Art of Conquest: Building in the Viceroyalty of Peru,* Cambridge.

Friedman, Alice T. (1989a). *House and Household in Elizabethan England: Wollaton Hall and the Willoughby Family,* Chicago.

—— (1989b). 'Did England have a Renaissance? Classical and anti-classical themes in Elizabethan Culture', in *Cultural Differentiation and Cultural Identity in the Visual Arts,* ed. S. Barnes and Walter Melion, Hanover, 95–111.

Fuciková, Eliska (1988) 'Zur Konzeption der rudolfinischen Sammlungen', in *Prag um 1600,* Freren, 59–62.

Fumaroli, Marc (1980). *L'age de l'éloquence,* Geneva.

—— (1988). 'The Republic of Letters', *Diogenes,* 143, 129–52.

Fussell, Paul (1965). *The Rhetorical World of Augustan Humanism,* Oxford.

Gaeta, Franco (1955). *Lorenzo Valla: filologia e storia nell'umanesimo italiano,* Naples.

Gallet-Guerne, Danielle (1974). *Vasque de Lucène et la Cyropédie à la cour de Bourgogne,* Geneva.

Garets, Marie-Louyse des (1946) *Un artisan de la Renaissance française au 15e siècle: le roi René,* Paris.

Garin, Eugenio (1947). *Der italienische Humanismus,* Bern; *Italian Humanism,* trans. P. Munz, Oxford, 1965.

—— (1961). *La cultura filosofica del Rinascimento italiano,* Florence.

—— (1975). *Rinascite e rivolutioni,* Rome and Bari.

Geanakoplos, Deno J. (1976) *Interaction of the Sibling Byzantine and Western Cultures,* New Haven.

Geldner, Ferdinand (1968–70). *Die deutsche Inkunabeldrucker,* 2 vols, Stuttgart.

Gilbert, Felix (1949). 'Bernardo Rucellai and the Orti Oricellari: a Study on the Origin of Modern Political Thought', *Journal of the Warburg and Courtauld Institutes,* 12, 101–31.

—— (1965). *Machiavelli and Guicciardini,* Princeton, NJ.

Girouard, Mark (1966). *Robert Smythson and the Elizabethan Country House,* rev. edn, New Haven and London, 1983.

—— (1978). *Life in the English Country House: A social and architectural history,* New Haven and London.

Gliozzi, Giuliano (1977). *Adamo e il nuovo mondo,* Florence.

Goldthwaite, Richard (1987). 'The Empire of Things: Consumer Demand in Renaissance Italy, in *Patronage, Art and Society in Renaissance Italy,* ed. F. William Kent and Patricia Simons, Canberra and Oxford, 153–75.

—— (1993). *Wealth and the Demand for Art in Italy, 1300–1600,* Baltimore, MD.

Gombrich, Ernst H. (1961). 'Mannerism: the Historiographic Background', reprinted in his *Norm and Form,* London, 1966, 99–106.

—— (1967). 'From the Revival of Letters to the Reform of the Arts: Niccolò Niccoli and Brunelleschi', reprinted in his *The Heritage of Apelles,* Oxford, 1976.

—— (1970). *Aby Warburg,* London.

—— (1982). 'Architecture and Rhetoric in Giulio Romano's Palazzo del Tè', reprinted in his *New Light on Old Masters*, Oxford, 1986, 161–70.

González Palencia, Angel and Mele, Eugenio (1943). *Vida y obras de Don Diego Hurtado de Mendoza*, 3 vols, Madrid.

Grafton, Anthony (1991). *Defenders of the Text: the Traditions of Scholarship in an Age of Science, 1450–1800*, Cambridge, MA.

—— (1992). *New Worlds, Ancient Texts*, London.

Grafton, Anthony and Jardine, Lisa (1986). *From Humanism to the Humanities*, London.

Grant, Edward (1978). 'Aristotelianism and the Longevity of the Medieval World View', *History of Science*, 16, 93–106.

Greenblatt, Stephen J. (1980). *Renaissance Self-Fashioning from More to Shakespeare*, Chicago.

Grendler, Paul (1988). *Schooling in Renaissance Italy: Literacy and Learning, 1300–1600*, Baltimore, MD.

Greenstein, Jack M. (1992). *Mantegna and Painting as Historical Narrative*, Chicago.

Gruffyd, R. Geraint (1990). 'The Renaissance and Welsh literature', in *The Celts and the Renaissance*, ed. Glanmore Williams and Robert O. Jones, Cardiff, 17–39.

Guglielminetti, Marziano (1977). *Memoria e scrittura: l'autobiografia da Dante a Cellini*, Turin.

Guillaume, Jean (ed, 1983). *La maison de ville à la Renaissance*, Paris.

Guillemain, Bernard (1962). *La cour pontificale d'Avignon, 1309–76: étude d'une société*, Paris.

Gukovski, Matteo (1967). 'Il Rinascimento italiano e la Russia', in *Rinascimento europeo e rinascimento venziano*, ed. Vittore Branca, Florence, 121–36.

Gunn, Steven J. and Lindley, Phillip G. (1991). *Cardinal Wolsey: Church, State and art*, Cambridge.

Gurevich, Aaron Y. (1995). *The Origins of European Individualism*, Oxford.

Hahr, August (1907–10). *Studier i Johan III:s Renässans*, 2 vols, Uppsala and Leipzig.

Hale, John R. (1993). *The Civilization of the Renaissance in Europe*, London.

Hankins, James (1990). *Plato in the Italian Renaissance*, 2 vols, Leiden.

Hannaway, Owen (1975). *The Chemists and the Word*, Baltimore.

Haskell, Francis and Penny, Nicholas (1981). *Taste and the Antique*, New Haven and London.

Hauser, Arnold (1951). *A Social History of Art*, 2nd edn, 4 vols, London, 1962.

Hay, Denys (1957). *Europe: The emergence of an idea*, Edinburgh.

Haydn, Hiram (1950). *The Counter-Renaissance*, New York.

Hayward, J. F. (1976). *Virtuoso Goldsmiths and the Triumph of Mannerism, 1540–1620*, London.

Heiberg, Steffen (ed.) (1988). *Christian IV and Europe*, Copenhagen.

Helgerson, Richard (1992). *Forms of Nationhood: The Elizabethan writing of England*, Chicago.

Henderson, Paula (1995). 'The Loggia in Tudor and Early Stuart England: the Adaptation and Function of Classical Form', in *Albion's Classicism: The Visual Arts in Britain, 1550–1660*, ed. Lucy Gent, New Haven, 109–46.

Hitchcock, Henry R. (1981). *German Renaissance Architecture*, Princeton, NJ.

Hobson, Anthony (1989). *Humanists and Bookbinders*, Cambridge.

Holmes, George (1986). *Florence, Rome and the Origins of the Renaissance*, Oxford.

Honour, Hugh (1975). *The New Golden Land: European images of America from the discoveries to the present time*, New York.

Howard, Deborah (1980). *The Architectural History of Venice*, London.

Huizinga, Johan (1915). 'Historical Ideals of Life', trans. J. S. Holmes and H. van Marle, in his *Men and Ideas*, New York, 1959, 77–96.

—— (1919). *Herfstij der Middeleeuwen*; *Autumn of the Middle Ages*, new trans. by R. J. Payton and U. Mammitzsch, Chicago, 1995.

Huppert, George (1984). *Public Schools in Renaissance France*, Chicago.

Hyde, J. Kenneth (1973). *Society and Politics in Renaissance Italy: The evolution of the civil life, 1000–1350*, London.

Hyma, Albert (1950). *The Brethren of the Common Life*, Michigan.

Impey, Oliver and MacGregor, Arthur (eds) (1985). *The Origins of Museums: The cabinet of curiosities in sixteenth- and seventeenth-century Europe*, Oxford.

Iversen, Erik (1961). *The Myth of Egypt and its Hieroglyphs in European Tradition*, Copenhagen.

Jaffé, Michael (1977). *Rubens and Italy*, Oxford.

Jardine, Lisa (1993). *Erasmus, Man of Letters*, Princeton, NJ.

Jauss, Hans-Robert (1974). *Literaturgeschichte als Provokation*; *Toward an Aesthetic of Reception*, trans. T. Bahti, Minneapolis, 1982.

Javitch, Daniel (1991). *Proclaiming a Classic: The Canonization of Orlando Furioso*, Princeton, NJ.

Jehasse, Jean (1976). *La Renaissance de la critique*, St-Etienne.

Johannesson, Kurt (1982). *The Renaissance of the Goths in 16th-century Sweden*, English trans. Berkeley, CA, 1991.

Jones, Richard F. (1953) *The Triumph of the English Language*, Stanford, CA.

Jones-Davies, Marie-Thérèse (ed.) (1984). *Le Dialogue au temps de la Renaissance*, Paris.

Jordan, Constance (1990). *Renaissance Feminism*, Ithaca, NY.

Kadić, Ante (1959). 'Marin Držić, Croatian Playwright', *Comparative Literature*, 11, 347–55.

—— (1962). 'The Croatian Renaissance', *Slavic Review*, 21, 65–88.

Kaegi, Werner (1936). 'Erasmus im achtzehnten Jahrhundert', *Gedenkschrift Erasmus*, Basel, 205–27.

Kaufmann, Thomas da Costa (1985). *L'école de Prague: la peinture à la cour de Rudolphe II*, Paris; *The School of Prague*, Chicago, 1988.

—— (1994). 'From Treasury to Museum: the Collections of the Austrian

Habsburgs', in *Cultures of Collecting*, ed. Jas Elsner and Roger Cardinal, London, 137–54.

—— (1995) *Court, Cloister and City: The Art and Culture of Central Europe, 1450–1800*, London.

Keating, L. Clark (1941). *Studies on the Literary Salon in France, 1550–1615*, Cambridge, MA.

Kelley, Donald R. (1970). *Foundations of Modern Historical Scholarship: Language, law and history in the French Renaissance*, New York.

King, Margaret, L. (1980). 'Book-Lined Cells: Women and Humanism in the Early Italian Renaissance', in *Beyond their Sex: Learned women of the European past*, ed. Patricia Labalme, New York, 66–90.

Kipling, Gordon (1977). *The Triumph of Honour*, Leiden.

Klaniczay, Gábor (1990). 'Daily Life and Elites in the Middle Ages', in *Environment and Society in Hungary*, ed. Ferenc Glatz, Budapest, 75–90.

Klaniczay, Tibor (1977). *Renaissance und Manierismus: Zum Verhältnis von Gesellschaftsstruktur, Poetik und Stil*, Berlin.

Knecht, Robert J. (1982). *Renaissance Warrior and Patron: The reign of Francis I*, 2nd edn, Cambridge, 1994.

Knoll, Samson B. (1982). 'Herder's Concept of Humanität', in *J. G. Herder*, ed. W. Koepke, Bonn, 9–19.

Koerner, Joseph L. (1993). *The Moment of Self-Portraiture in German Renaissance Art*, Chicago.

Kovalevsky, Pierre (1976). 'A qui doit-on l'appel des maîtres italiens à Moscou au 15e siècle?', *Arte Lombarda*, 44/45, 153–6.

Kristeller, Paul O. (1979). *Renaissance Thought and its Sources*, New York.

Kuhn, Thomas S. (1957) *The Copernican Revolution*, 2nd edn, New York, 1959.

La Garanderie, Marie-Madeleine de (1976). *Christianisme et lettres profanes (1515–35)*, Paris.

Lach, Donald (1965). *Asia in the Making of Europe: The century of discovery*, Chicago.

—— (1977). *Asia in the Making of Europe: A century of wonder*, Chicago.

Lafond, Jean and Stegmann, André (eds) (1981). *L'automne de la Renaissance, 1580–1630*, Paris.

Lakoff, George and Johnson, Mark (1980). *Metaphors We Live By*, Chicago.

Lamb, Mary E. (1982). 'The Countess of Pembroke's Patronage', *English Literary Renaissance*, 12, 162–79.

—— (1985). 'The Cooke Sisters: Attitudes toward Learned Women in the Renaissance', in *Silent but for the Word: Tudor Women as Patrons, Translators and Writers of Religious Works*, ed. Margaret P. Hannay, Kent, OH, 107–25.

—— (1990). *Gender and Authorship in the Sidney Circle*, Madison, WI.

Landau, David and Parshall, Peter (1994). *The Renaissance Print 1470–1550*, New Haven.

Lauvergnat-Gagnière, Christiane (1988). *Lucien de Samosate et le lucianisme en France au 16e siècle*, Geneva.

Lazard, Madeleine (1978). *La Comédie humaniste au 16 siècle et ses personnages*, Paris.

Lazzaro, Claudio (1990). *The Italian Renaissance Garden*, New Haven.

Lazzaro, Claudia (1995). 'Animals as Cultural Signs', in *Reframing the Renaissance*, ed. Claire Farago, New Haven, 192–228.

Lemaire, Claudine (1996). 'La bibliothèque de la reine Marie de Hongrie', *Bibliothèque d'Humanisme et Renaissance*, 58, 119–40.

Lestringant, Frank (1990). *Le Huguenot et le sauvage*, Paris.

——— (1991). *L'atelier du cosmographe ou l'image du monde à la Renaissance*, Paris; *Mapping the Renaissance World: The geographical imagination in the age of discovery*, trans. D. Fausett, Cambridge, 1994.

——— (1994). *Le Cannibale: grandeur et décadence*, Paris.

Levenson, Joseph R. (1958). *Confucian China and its Modern Fate*, 2nd edn. as *Modern China and its Confucian Past*, New York, 1964.

Levey, Michael (1960). 'Botticelli in 19th-Century England', *Journal of the Warburg and Courtauld Institutes*, 23, 291–306.

Lewalski, Kenneth F. (1967). 'Sigismund I of Poland: Renaissance King and Patron', *Studies in the Renaissance*, 14, 49–72.

Liebenwein, Wolfgang (1977). *Studiolo. Die Entstehung eines Raumtyps und seine Entwicklung bis um 1600*, Berlin.

Likhachev, Dimitri S. (1962). *Die Kultur Russlands während der osteuropäischer Frührenaissance vom 14. bis zum Beginn des 15. Jht*, Dresden.

Llewellyn, Nigel (1996). 'Honour in Life, Death and the Memory: Funeral Monuments in Early Modern England', *Transactions of the Royal Historical Society*, 6, 179–200.

Loewenberg, Peter (1995). 'The Creation of a Scientific Community', in *Fantasy and Reality in History*, New York, 46–89.

López Rueda, J. (1973). *Helenistas españoles*, Madrid.

Lotz, Wolfgang (1977). *Studies in Italian Renaissance Architecture*, Cambridge, MA.

Lowry, Martin J. C. (1979). *The World of Aldus Manutius*, Oxford.

Lugli, Adalgisa (1983). *Naturalia e Mirabilia. Il collezionismo enciclopedico nelle Wunderkammer d'Europa*, Milan.

Luttrell, Anthony (1960). 'Greek Histories Translated and Compiled for Juan Fernández de Herèdia', *Speculum*, 35, 401–7.

Lyotard, Jean-François (1979). *La condition post-moderne*, Paris; *The Post-Modern Condition*, trans. G. Bennington and B. Massumi, Manchester, 1982.

McAndrew, John (1969). 'Sant-Andrea della Certosa', *Art Bulletin*, 51, 15–28.

MacCormack, Sabine G. (1991). *Religion in the Andes: Vision and imagination in early colonial Peru*, Princeton, NJ.

Macdonald, A. A., Lynch, M. and Cowan, I. B. (eds) (1994). *The Renaissance in Scotland*, Leiden.

MacDonald, Michael and Murphy, Terence R. (1990). *Sleepless Souls: Suicide in Early Modern England*, Oxford.

Mace, Dean T. (1969). 'Pietro Bembo and the Literary Origins of the Italian Madrigal', *Muscial Quarterly*, 55, 65–86.

Mączak, Antoni (1978). *Travel in Early Modern Europe*, trans. U. Phillips, Cambridge, 1995.

Maffei, Domenico (1956). *Gli inizi dell'umanesimo giuridico*, 2nd edn, Milan, 1972.

Mann, Nicholas (1970). 'Petrarch's Role as a Moralist in Fifteenth-Century France', in *Humanism in France*, ed. Anthony H. T. Levi, Manchester, 6–28.

—— (1980). 'Petrarch and Humanism: the Paradox of Posterity', in *Francesco Petrarca Citizen of the World*, Padua, 287–99.

Mansfield, Bruce (1979). *Phoenix of his Age: Interpretations of Erasmus c. 1550–1750*, Toronto.

Maravall, José Antonio (1966). *Antiguos y modernos*, Madrid.

Mariás, Fernando (1989). *El largo siglo xvi: los usos artisticos del Renacimiento español*, Madrid.

Marnef, Guido (1996). *Antwerp in the Age of Reformation*, Baltimore, MD.

Marquand, Allan (1922). *Luca della Robbia and his Atelier*, 2 vols, Princeton, NJ.

Maugain, Gabriel (1926). *Ronsard en Italie*, Strasbourg.

Mayer, Thomas F. and Woolf, Daniel R. (eds) (1995). *The Rhetorics of Life-Writing in Early Modern Europe*, Ann Arbor, MI.

Meiss, Millard (1951). *Painting in Florence and Siena after the Black Death*, Princeton, NJ.

—— (1967). *French Painting in the Time of Jean de Berry*, 2 vols, London.

Melczer, Walter (1979) 'Albrecht von Eyb et les racines italiennes du premier humanisme allemand', in *L'humanisme allemand*, ed. Joël Lefebvre and Jean-Claude Margolin, Paris, 31–44.

Melion, Walter S. (1991). *Shaping the Netherlandish Canon*, Chicago.

Menchi, Silvana Seidel (1987). *Erasmo in Italia, 1520–1580*, Turin.

Mercer, Eric (1962). *English Art, 1553–1625*, Oxford.

—— (1969). *Furniture 700–1700*, London.

Mészáros, István (1981). *Xvi századi városi iskoláink és a studia humanitatis*, Budapest.

Milde, Kurt (1981). *Neorenaissance in der deutschen Architektur des 19. Jhts*, Dresden.

Milner-Gulland, Robin (1974). 'Russia's Lost Renaissance', in *The Old World: Discovery and Rebirth*, ed. David Daiches and Anthony Thorlby, London, 435–68.

Monter, E. William (1969). *Geneva*, New York.

Morán, J. Miguel, and Checa, Fernando (1985). *El coleccionismo en España*, Madrid.

Morand, Kathleen (1991). *Claus Sluter: Artist at the Court of Burgundy*, Austin, TX.

Morford, Mark (1987). 'The Stoic Garden', *Journal of Garden History*, 7, 151–75.

—— (1991). *Stoics and Neostoics: Rubens and the circle of Lipsius,* Princeton, NJ.

Morison, Stanley (1955). *Venice and the Arabesque,* London.

Mortier, Roland (1974). *La Poétique des ruines en France,* Geneva.

Moss, Ann (1996) *Printed Commonplace Books and the Structuring of Renaissance Thought,* Oxford.

Murphy, James J. (ed.) (1983). *Renaissance Eloquence,* Berkeley, CA.

Nicolson, Marjorie H. (1950) *The Breaking of the Circle: Studies in the effect of the new science upon seventeenth-century poetry,* Evanston, IL.

Nolhac, Pierre de (1921). *Ronsard et l'humanisme,* Paris.

Nordström, Johannes (1944–72). 'Goter och Spanjorer', *Lychnos,* 257–80, 171–8.

Oberhuber, Konrad (1984). 'Raffaello e l'incisione', in Fabrizio Mancinelli et al., *Raffaello in Vaticano,* Milan, 333–42.

Oestreich, Gerhard (1969). *Geist und Gestalt des frühmodernen Staates,* Berlin.

—— (1982). *Neostoicism and the Early Modern State,* Cambridge.

Olmi, Giuseppe (1992). *L'inventario del mondo: catalogazione della natura e luoghi del sapere nella prima età moderna,* Bologna.

O'Malley, Charles (1965). *Andreas Vesalius of Brussels,* Berkeley, CA.

O'Malley, John W. (1968). *Giles of Viterbo on Church and Reform,* Leiden.

Onians, John (1988). *Bearers of Meaning: The classical orders in Antiquity, the Middle Ages and the Renaissance,* Cambridge.

Ophir, Adi and Shapin, Steven (1991). 'The Place of Knowledge', *Science in Context,* 4, 3–21.

Ouy, Gilbert (1973). 'L'humanisme et les mutations politiques et sociales en France au 14e et 15e siècles', *L'humanisme français au début de la Renaissance,* ed. Jean Stegmann, Paris, 27–44.

Overfield, James H. (1984) *Humanism and Scholasticism in Late Medieval Germany,* Princeton, NJ.

Owens, Jessie A. (1995). 'Was there a Renaissance in Music?', in *Language and Images of Renaissance Italy,* ed. Alison Brown, Oxford, 111–26.

Pagden, Anthony (1982). *The Fall of Natural Man,* Cambridge.

Palisca, Claude (1985). *Humanism in Italian Renaissance Musical Thought,* New Haven.

Pálsson, Gisli (ed.) (1993). *Beyond Boundaries: Understanding, translation and anthropological discourse,* Oxford.

Panofsky, Erwin (1924). *Idea: ein Beitrag zur Begriffsgeschichte der älteren Kunsttheorie,* Leipzig, 2nd edn, Berlin, 1960; *Idea: A Concept in Art Theory,* trans. J. J. S. Deake, Columbia, SC, 1968.

—— (1939). *Studies in Iconology: Humanistic themes in the art of the Renaissance,* 2nd edition, New York, 1962.

—— (1943). *The Life and Art of Albrecht Dürer,* Princeton, NJ.

—— (1953). *Early Netherlandish Painting, its Origins and Character,* 2 vols, Cambridge, MA.

—— (1954). *Galileo as a Critic of the Arts,* The Hague.

Paoletti, John T. and Radtke, Gary M. (1997). *Art in Renaissance Italy*, London.

Pastor, Ludwig von (1886–) *Geschichte der Päpste*, Freiburg; *History of the Popes*, trans. F. I. Antrobus et al., London, 1891–

Pastor Bodmer, Beatriz (1983). *El discurso narrativo de la conquista de América*, Havana; trans. *The Armature of Conquest*, Stanford, CA, 1992.

Pavoni, Rosanna (ed.) (1997). *Reviving the Renaissance*, Cambridge.

Petrucci, Armando (1986). *La scrittura: ideologia e rappresentazione*, Turin.

Phillips, Mark (1977). *Francesco Guicciardini: The historian's craft*, Manchester.

Piéjus, Marie-Françoise (1982). 'La première anthologie de poèmes féminins', *Centre de Recherches sur la Renaissance Italienne*, 10, 193–214.

Pigman, G. W. III (1979). 'Imitation and the Renaissance Sense of the Past: the Reception of Erasmus's Ciceronianus', *Journal of Medieval and Renaissance Studies*, 9, 155–78.

Pine, Martin L. (1986). *Pietro Pomponazzi, Radical Philosopher of the Renaissance*, Padua.

Picquard, Maurice (1947–8). 'Le cardinal de Granvelle, les artistes et les écrivains', *Revue Belge d'Archéologie*, 17, 133–9.

—— (1951). 'Les livres du cardinal de Granvelle à la bibliothèque de Besançon', *Libri*, 1, 301–23.

Pocock, John G. A. (1975). *The Machiavellian Moment*, Princeton, NJ.

Pomian, Krzysztof (1987). *Collectionneurs, amateurs et curieux*, Paris; trans. Elizabeth Wiles-Portier, *Collectors and Curiosities*, Cambridge, 1990.

Puppi, Lionello (1973). *Andrea Palladio*, 2 vols, Milan.

Quadflieg, Ralph (1985). 'Zur Rezeption islamischer Krankenhaus-architektur in der italienischen Frührenaissance', in *Europa und die Kunst des Islam*, ed. E. Liskar, Vienna, 73–81.

Quint, David (1993). *Epic and Empire: Politics and generic form from Virgil to Milton*, Princeton, NJ.

Raby, Julian (1982). *Venice, Dürer and the Oriental Mode*, London.

Rackham, Bernard (1952). *Italian Maiolica*, 2nd edition, London, 1963.

Reinhard, Wolfgang (1986). 'Humanismus und Militarismus', in *Krieg und Frieden im Horizont des Renaissance-Humanismus*, ed. F. J. Worstbrok, Bonn, 185–204.

Renaudet, Augustin (1916). *Preréforme et humanisme à Paris pendant les premières guerres d' Italie, 1494–1517*, Paris.

Riccardi-Cubitt, Monique (1992). *The Art of the Cabinet*, London.

Rice, Eugene F. jr (1970). 'Humanist Aristotelianism in France: Jacques Lefevre d'Etaples and his Circle', in *Humanism in France*, ed. Anthony H. T. Levi, Manchester, 132–49.

Richardson, Brian (1994). *Print Culture in Renaissance Italy: The editor and the vernacular text, 1470–1600*, Cambridge.

Rico, Francisco (1970). *La novela picaresca y el punto de vista*, Barcelona; *The Spanish Picaresque Novel and the Point of View*, trans. C. Davis and H. Sieber, Cambridge, 1984.

—— (1978). *Nebrija frente a los barbaros*, Salamanca.

Riebesell, Christine (1989). *Die Sammlung des Kardinal Farnese*, Weinheim.

Roberts, Sasha (1995). 'Lying among the Classics: Ritual and Motif in Elite Elizabethan and Jacobean Beds', in *Albion's Classicism*, ed. Lucy Gent, New Haven, 325–58.

Robertson, Clare (1992) *'Il Gran' Cardinale'*: *Alessandro Farnese Patron of the Arts*, New Haven.

Rose, Paul L. (1975). *The Italian Renaissance of Mathematics*, Geneva.

Rosenberg, Eleanor (1955). *Leicester: Patron of Letters*, New York.

Rosenthal, Earl J. (1961). *The Cathedral of Granada: A study in the Spanish Renaissance*, Princeton, NJ.

—— (1973). 'The Invention of the Columnar Device of the Emperor Charles V', *Journal of the Warburg and Courtauld Institutes*, 36, 198–230.

—— (1985). *the Palace of Charles V at Granada*, Princeton, NJ.

Rosenthal, Fritz (1975). *The Classical Heritage in Islam*, London.

Rosenthal, Margaret F. (1992). *The Honest Courtesan: Veronica Franco*, Chicago.

Rousset, Jean (1953). *La Littérature de l'âge baroque en France*, Paris.

Rowse, A. Leslie (1950). *The England of Elizabeth: The structure of society*, London.

Rubiès, Joan-Pau (1995). 'Instructions for Travellers', *History and Anthropology*, 1, 1–51.

Rubin, Patricia L. (1995). *Giorgio Vasari: Art and History*, New Haven.

Rubió, J. (1964). *Cultura catalana del Renaixement*, Barcelona.

Rubió i Lluch, Antoni (1917–18). 'Joan I humanista', *Estudis Universaitaris Catalans*, 10, 1–107.

Rueda, José Lopez (1973). *Helenistas españoles del siglo xvi*, Madrid.

Rüegg, Walter (1944). 'Der Begriff "Humanismus"', reprinted in his *Anstösse: Aufsätze und Vorträge zur dialogischen Lebensform*, Frankfurt.

Sabbadini, Remigio (1905). *Le scoperte dei codici latini e greci ne'secoli xiv e xv*, Florence.

Saccaro, Alexander P. (1975). *Französischer Humanismus des 14. und 15. Jhts*, Munich.

Sahlins, Marshall (1985). *Islands of History*, Chicago.

Santore, Cathy (1988). 'Julia Lombarda "Somtuosa Meretrice": a Portrait by property', *Renaissance Quarterly*, 41, 44–83.

Saulnier, Verdun-Louis (1948). *Maurice Scève*, Paris.

Saunders, Alison (1989). *the Sixteenth-Century French Emblem Book*, Geneva.

Schaeder, Hildegard (1929). *Moskau das dritte Rom*, reprint, Darmstadt, 1957.

Schiff, Mario (1905). *La bibliothèque du marquis de Santillane*, Paris.

Schindling, Anton (1977). *Humanistische Hochschule und freie Reichstadt*, Wiesbaden.

Schlosser, Julius von (1908). *Die Kunst- und Wunderkammer der Spätrenaissance*, Leipzig.

Schmidt, Albert-Marie (1938). *La poésie scientifique en France au 16e siècle*, Paris.

Schmitt, Annegrit (1989). 'Der Einfluss des Humanismus auf die Bild-programme fürstlicher Residenzen', in *Höfischer Humanismus*, ed August Buck, Bonn, 215–58.

Schmitt, Charles B. (1983). *Aristotle and the Renaissance*, Cambridge, MA.

Schofield, Richard (1992). 'Avoiding Rome: an Introduction to Lombard Sculptors and the Antique', *Arte Lombarda*, 100, 29–44.

Scholem, Gershom G. (1941). *Major Trends in Jewish Mysticism*, New York.

Schon, Peter M. (1954). *Vorformen des Essays in Antike und Humanismus*, Wiesbaden.

Schubring, Paul (1915). *Cassoni*, Leipzig.

Secret, François (1964). *Les Cabbalistes chrétiens de la Renaissance*, Paris.

Segel, Harold B. (1989). *Renaissance Culture in Poland: The rise of humanism, 1470–1543*, Ithaca, NY.

Setton, Kenneth M. (1956). 'The Byzantine Background to the Italian Renaissance', *Proceedings of the American Philosophical Society*, 199, 1–76.

Seymour, Charles, jr (1967). *Michelangelo's David: A search for identity*, 2nd edn, New York, 1974.

Seznec, Jean (1940). *La survivance des dieux antiques; The Survival of the Pagan Gods*, trans. B. F. Sessions, New York, 1953.

Shapin, Steven (1996). *The Scientific Revolution*, Chicago.

Shearman, John (1967). *Mannerism*, Harmondsworth.

Simon, Joan (1966). *Education and Society in Tudor England*, Cambridge.

Simone, Franco (1961). *Il rinascimento francese; The French Renaissance*, trans. H. G. Hall, London, 1969.

Skinner, Quentin (1995). 'The Vocabulary of Renaissance Republicanism: a Cultural Longue Durée?', in *Language and Images of Renaissance Italy*, ed. Alison Brown, Oxford, 87–110.

—— (1996). *Reason and Rhetoric in the Philosophy of Hobbes*, Cambridge.

Skovgaard, Joakim A. (1973). *A King's Architecture: Christian IV and his buildings*, London.

Smith, Christine (1992). *Architecture in the Culture of Early Humanism*, New York.

Sorelius, Gunnar and Srigley, Michael (eds) (1994). *Cultural Exchange between European Nations during the Renaissance*, Uppsala.

Sorkin, David (1983). 'Wilhelm von Humboldt: the Theory and Practice of Self-Formation (*Bildung*)', *Journal of the History of Ideas*, 44, 55–73.

Southern, Richard W. (1995). *Scholastic Humanism and the Unification of Europe*, Oxford.

Sozzi, Lionello (1972). 'La polémique anti-italienne en France au 16e siècle', *Atti della Accademia delle Scienze di Torino*, 106, ii, 99–190.

Spadaccini, Nicholas and Talens, Jenaro (eds) (1988). *Autobiography in Early Modern Spain*, Minneapolis.

Spence, Jonathan D. (1984). *The Memory Palace of Matteo Ricci*, New York.

Spitz, Lewis W. (1957). *Conrad Celtis: The German arch-humanist*, Cambridge, MA.

Spranger, Eduard (1909). *Wilhelm von Humboldt und die Humanitätsidee*, Berlin.

Stagl, Justin (1980). 'Die Apodemik oder "Reisenkunst" als Methodik der Sozialforschung vom Humanismus bus zur Aufklärung', in *Statistik und Staatsbeschreibung in der Neuzeit*, ed. Mohammed Rassem and Justin Stagl, Paderborn, 131–202.

Starobinski, Jean (1982). *Montaigne en mouvement*, Paris; trans. *Montaigne in Motion*, Chicago, 1985.

Stechow, Wolfgang (1968). *Rubens and the Classical Tradition*, Cambridge, MA.

Stegmann, André (ed.) (1973). *L'humanisme français au début de la Renaissance*, Paris.

Steinmetz, Wiebke (1991). *Heinrich Rantzau: ein Vertreter des Humanismus in Nordeuropa und seine Wirkungen als Förderer der Künste*, 2 vols, Frankfurt.

Stierle, Karlheinz (1979). *Petrarcas Landschaften: Zur Geschichte ästhetische Landschaftserfahrung*, Krefeld.

Stinger, Charles L. (1977). *Humanism and the Church Fathers: Ambrogio Traversari and Christian Antiquity in the Italian Renaissance*, Albany, NY.

Stone, Lawrence (1965). *The Crisis of the Aristocracy, 1558–1641*, Oxford.

Strauss, Gerald (1959). *Sixteenth-Century Germany: Its topography and topographers*, Madison, WI.

Strelka, Josef (1957). *Der Burgundische Renaissancehof Margarethes von Österreich*, Vienna.

Summers, David (1981). *Michelangelo and the Language of Art*, Princeton, NJ.

Summerson, John (1953). *Architecture in Britain 1530 to 1830*, 5th edn, Harmondsworth, 1969.

—— (1959). 'The Building of Theobalds, 1564–85', *Archaeologia*, 97, 107–26.

Sydow, Carl W. von (1948). 'Geography and Folk-Tale Oicotypes', in *Selected Papers on Folklore*, Copenhagen, 44–69.

Tavernor, Richard (1990). *Palladio and palladianism*, London.

Tedeschi, John (1974). 'Italian Reformers and the Diffusion of Renaissance Culture', *Sixteenth-Century Journal*, 5, 79–94.

Thompson, Colin (1988). *The Strife of Tongues: Fray Luis de León and the Golden Age of Spain*, Cambridge.

Thoren, Victor E. (1985). 'Tycho Brahe as the Dean of a Renaissance Research Institute', in *Religion, Science and Worldview: Essays in Honor of Richard S. Westfall*, Cambridge, 275–96.

Thorndike, Lynn K. (1951). 'Newness and Novelty in Seventeenth-Century Science', *Journal of the History of Ideas*, 12, 584–98.

Thornton, Dora (1998). *The Scholar in his Study*, New Haven and London.

Thornton, Peter (1991). *The Italian Renaissance Interior*, London.

Tinkler, John F. (1992). 'J. S. Mill as a Nineteenth-Century Humanist', *Rhetorica*, 10, 165–91.

Tittler, Robert (1991). *Architecture and Power: the Town Hall and the English Urban Community c.1500–1640*, Oxford.

Tomlinson, Gary (1987). *Monteverdi and the End of the Renaissance*, Berkeley, CA.

Torbarina, Josip (1931). *Italian Influence on the Poets of the Ragusan Republic*, London.

Toynbee, Arnold J. (1954). *A Study of History*, vol. XII: *The Inspirations of Historians*, London.

Trinkaus, Charles (1970). *In Our Image and Likeness: Humanity and divinity in Italian humanist thought*, London.

Trovato, Paolo (1991). *Con ogni diligenza corretto: la stampa e le revisioni editoriali dei testi letterari italiani, 1470–1570*, Bologna.

Turner, A. Richard (1966). *The Vision of Landscape in Renaissance Italy*, Princeton, NJ.

Ullman, Bernhard L. (1963). *The Humanism of Coluccio Salutati*, Padua.

Villey, Pierre (1908). *Les sources italiennes de la Défense et Illustration de la langue française*, Paris.

Walde, Otto (1932). 'Studier i Äldre Dansk Biblioteks-Historia', *Nordisk Tidskrift för Bok- och Biblioteksväsen*, 19, 21–51.

Walker, Daniel P. (1972). *The Ancient Theology: Studies in Christian Platonism*, London.

—— (1985). *Music, Spirit and Language in the Renaissance*, ed. Penelope Gouk, London.

Waller, Gary F. (1979). *Mary, Countess of Pembroke*, Salzburg.

Warburg, Aby (1932). *Die Erneuerung der Heidnische Antike: Gesammelte Schriften*, 2 vols, Leipzig and Berlin; Italian trans. *La Rinascita del paganesimo antico*, Florence, 1966.

Wardrop, James (1963). *The Script of Humanism*, Oxford.

Warnicke, Retha M. (1988). 'Women and Humanism in the Renaissance', in *Renaissance Humanism*, ed. Albert Rabil jr, Philadelphia, vol. 2, 39–54.

Warnke, Martin (1985). *Hofkünstler*, Cologne; *The Court Artist*, trans. D. McLintock, Cambridge, 1993.

Weber, Henri (1956). *La Création poétique au 16e siècle en France*, 2 vols, Paris.

Weinberg, Florence M. (1986). *Gargantua in a Convex Mirror: Fischart's view of Rabelais*, New York.

Weiss, Roberto (1941). *Humanism in England*, 2nd edn, Oxford, 1957.

—— (1969). *The Renaissance Discovery of Classical Antiquity*, Oxford.

Welch, Evelyn S. (1997). *Art and Society in Italy, 1350–1500*, Oxford.

Wilde, Johannes (1944). 'The Hall of the Great Council of Florence', reprinted in *Renaissance Art*, ed. Creighton Gilbert, New York, 1970, 92–132.

Wilson, Donald B. (1961). *Ronsard, Poet of Nature*, Manchester.

Wilson, N. G. (1992). *From Byzantium to Italy: Greek studies in the Italian Renaissance*, London.

Witt, Ronald G. (1983). *Hercules at the Cross-Roads: The life, work and thought of Coluccio Salutati*, Durham, NC.

Wittkower, Rudolf (1949). *Architectural Principles in the Age of Humanism*, London.

Woods-Marsden, Joanna (1988). *The Gonzaga of Mantua and Pisanello's Arthurian Frescoes*, Princeton, NJ.

Wortman, Richard S. (1995). *Scenarios of Power: Myth and ceremony in Russian monarchy*, Princeton, NJ.

Wu, Pei-Yi (1990). *The Confucian's Progress: autobiographical writings in Traditional China*, Princeton, NJ.

Wüttke, Dieter (1977). *Aby M. Warburgs Methode als Anregung und Aufgabe*, Göttingen.

Yashiro, Yukio (1925). *Sandro Botticelli*, 3 vols, London.

Yates, Frances A. (1947). *French Academies of the Sixteenth Century*, London.

—— (1957). 'Elizabethan Chivalry: the Romance of the Accession Day Tilts', reprinted in *Astraea: The imperial theme in the sixteenth century*, London, 1975, 88–111.

—— (1964). *Giordano Bruno and the Hermetic Tradition*. London.

Zamora, Margarita (1988). *Language, Authority and Indigenous History in the Comentarios Reales de los Incas*, Cambridge.

Zapella, Giuseppina (1988). *Il ritratto nel libro italiano del '500*, 2 vols, Milan.

Zavala, Silvio (1937). *La Utopia de Tomás Moro en la nueva España*, Mexico.

—— (1955). *St Thomas More in New Spain*, London.

Zhiri, Oumelbanine (1991). *L'Afrique au miroir de l'Europe: Fortunes de Jean Léon l'Africain à la Renaissance*. Geneva.

Zimmermann, T. C. Price (1995). *Paolo Giovio: The historian and the crisis of sixteenth-century Italy*, Princeton, NJ.

Index